Social Structure and Self-Direction

To Wlodzimierz Wesolowski,
whose idea it was.

Social Structure and Self-Direction

A Comparative Analysis of the United States and Poland

MELVIN L. KOHN AND
KAZIMIERZ M. SLOMCZYNSKI

with the collaboration of Carrie Schoenbach

Basil Blackwell

Copyright © Melvin L. Kohn and Kazimierz M. Slomczynski 1990

First published 1990

Basil Blackwell, Inc.
3 Cambridge Center
Cambridge, Massachusetts 02142, USA

Basil Blackwell Ltd
108 Cowley Road, Oxford, OX4 1JF, UK

Library of Congress Cataloging in Publication Data
Kohn, Melvin L., 1928–
    Social structure and self-direction: a comparative
analysis of the United States and Poland / Melvin L. Kohn, Kazimierz M.
Slomczynski.
        p. cm.
    Includes bibliographical references.
    ISBN 1–55786–018–1
    1. Social classes–United States–Cross-cultural studies.
2. Social classes–Poland–Cross-cultural studies.   3. Social
structure–United States–Cross-cultural studies.   4. Social
structure–Poland–Cross-cultural studies.   5. Personality–Social
aspects–United States–Cross-cultural studies.   6. Personality–
Social aspects–Poland–Cross-cultural studies.   I. Slomczynski,
Kazimierz M.   II. Title.
HN90.S6K64   1990
305.5'0973–dc20   90–118

British Library Cataloguing in Publication Data
A CIP catalogue record for this book is available from the British Library.

Typeset in 10 on 12pt Sabon
by Hope Services (Abingdon) Ltd.
Printed in Great Britain by T.J. Press (Padstow) Ltd, Padstow, Cornwall.

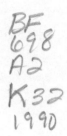

Contents

List of Figures and Tables

Preface

In this book, we propose a thoroughgoing interpretation of the relationship of social structure and personality. Since ours is a general interpretation, meant to be applicable to all industrialized societies, we test this interpretation by doing parallel analyses of data from a capitalist and a socialist society – the United States and Poland. We attempt to test our interpretation rigorously, using analytic methods that we believe are particularly well suited to comparative analysis.

The book is both the third installment of a trilogy and a decidedly new intellectual enterprise. It is the third part of a trilogy in that it represents the culmination and definitive statement of an interpretation of social structure and personality first enunciated and partially tested in Kohn's *Class and Conformity* (1969) and summarized in Kohn and Schooler's (1969) article, "Class, occupation, and orientation," later extensively elaborated and more rigorously tested in Kohn and Schooler's *Work and Personality* (1983), and now further refined and tested cross-nationally. This book is decidedly new, however, in that it takes a thesis originally developed and tested for the United States, reformulates this thesis to apply more generally to industrialized societies, and tests this more general thesis cross-nationally. This book also extends the thesis conceptually, from its early focus on the relationship of social stratification and personality, to an enlarged focus that systematically considers both social class and social stratification.

The inspiration for the cross-national analysis – and hence, for this book – came from Wlodzimierz Wesolowski, a leading figure in Polish sociology and an internationally renowned student of social stratification. Wesolowski (1975) saw *Class and Conformity* as providing a vehicle for the comparative analysis of the social psychology of social stratification in capitalist and socialist society. That book had concluded that the relationships of social stratification with values and orientations could be explained largely in terms of the close relationship between social stratification and conditions of work that facilitate or restrict the exercise of occupational self-direction.

The empirical support for such an interpretation had been provided by extensive analyses of US data, buttressed by more limited analyses of Italian data. Wesolowski asked whether the relationships of social stratification to job conditions, and of job conditions to values and orientations, that had been found in these capitalist societies are similar in socialist society. To find out, he proposed, then sponsored, a Polish replication of the principal US survey on which the analyses of *Class and Conformity* had been based.

Slomczynski planned that study, with the collaboration of Krystyna Janicka and Jadwiga Koralewicz-Zebik, worked intensively with Kohn in the development of the interview schedule, then spent the better part of several years analyzing those data in collaboration with Kohn and, at decisive times, also with Joanne Miller and Carrie Schoenbach.

The first major analysis focused on the key issue that had inspired the Polish replication: whether the relationship of social stratification to job conditions, and of job conditions to values and orientation, is similar in socialist Poland and in the capitalist United States. In attempting to answer this question, Slomczynski, Joanne Miller, and Kohn (1981) attempted also to develop a rationale and methods for systematic comparative cross-national analysis. Rather than simply replicating the earlier US analyses with Polish data, they re-analyzed the US and analyzed the Polish data in tandem, using methods that had not even been invented at the time when *Class and Conformity* was written. In the process, they also by necessity worked out a rationale for explicitly comparative cross-national research.

If that were all we had to report, there would be no need for this book, since the results were published in the United States in an article in the *American Sociological Review* (Slomczynski, Miller, and Kohn, 1981) and later in Poland in an extended version of that same paper in *Sisyphus* (Slomczynski et al., 1987). But, as new data from wives and children were collected in both countries, we could deal with issues that went far beyond the formulations of *Class and Conformity*, particularly with respect to social stratification and the transmission of values in the family (Kohn, Slomczynski, and Schoenbach, 1986). Moreover, as Kohn enlarged the scope of his original formulation to include not only social stratification but also social class (Kohn and Schoenbach, 1983), the exciting question of whether or not one could conceptualize and index social class for a socialist society came to the forefront. This we addressed, in preliminary fashion, in a Polish-language book (Slomczynski and Kohn, 1988), that also incorporated all our previously published papers. We subsequently carried the comparative analysis of position in the class structure and psychological functioning much further, in collaboration with Atsushi Naoi, Carmi Schooler, and Carrie Schoenbach (Kohn et al., 1990), in a three-nation comparison of the United States, Poland, and Japan. We had long since gone beyond simply replicating or even improving on the analyses of *Class and Conformity*, greatly enlarging the formulation to address questions far beyond the scope of that original inquiry.

Even the accumulation of a formidable set of papers would hardly require this book. What did, in our judgement, require this book was the combination of three things. First, the body of analysis and interpretation had by now grown so large as to require an integrated treatment of the entire corpus of research and an overall interpretation that took account of the several diverse strands. Kohn (1987) attempted such an integrated treatment in his presidential address to the American Sociological Association, but the full development of the interpretation could not be achieved in such brief compass. Nor had we, even then, examined all pertinent empirical issues, particularly those involved in explaining the cross-national differences that we uncovered. Second, social class had come to center stage in our thinking: we wanted in this book to do a thoroughgoing assessment of the psychological impact of *both* class and stratification. Third, we had a growing sense that our earlier analyses had been unduly limited in scope and less powerful than we now were capable of doing, and – far and away the most important consideration – that our earlier interpretations had been partial and incomplete. Kohn decided to do a comprehensive re-analysis of the Polish data, much as he and Schoenbach (1983) had done of the US data, greatly enlarging the scope of analysis, using methods of analysis that we have now more completely mastered, and addressing a much broader range of interpretive issues.

We have thereby made a deliberate change of strategy in how we do comparative research. In the original analyses, we strove, insofar as possible, for exact comparability in our US and Polish analyses. As a consequence, we limited many of our analyses of the US data to the cross-sectional data of the original survey, foregoing the use of the longitudinal data of a ten-year follow-up survey because we had nothing comparable for Poland (Slomczynski et al., 1981). Having established the equivalence of the US and Polish concepts and indices, we now felt justified in making full use of the US longitudinal data, to do the best analyses of each country that the data allow, even if this means that the analyses of cross-sectional Polish data can only approximate those of the longitudinal US data. In our re-analyses of the Polish data, we have even made assumptions – based in part on the longitudinal US data – that have made possible the quasi-longitudinal analysis of the cross-sectional Polish data. Later, of course, we systematically tested those assumptions. Our re-analyses revealed nothing inconsistent with what we had previously reported, but our new models are considerably more powerful and the scope of analysis is broader and much more complete. Thus, this book represents not only an extension of the interpretations presented in our earlier publications, but also a comparative analysis that supersedes and goes considerably beyond any that we had previously reported.

From the beginning, we had always to keep in the forefront of our minds the logic of cross-national inquiry, inventing a methodology wherever no established methodology existed, modifying our methodology as we learned more. In our published reports, the larger questions of the logic and methodology of cross-national research hover in the background, journal editors never allowing enough space for the discussion of such issues, at least not in substantive articles. (Joanne Miller, Slomczynski, and Ronald Schoenberg did, however, publish in 1981 one methodological paper specifically addressed to the comparability of measurement in cross-national research.) In this book, we want to make the logic of comparative inquiry a decided, even if secondary, theme. The reader will be much better able to evaluate our analyses and interpretations if these issues and our way of dealing with them are made explicit. Perhaps more important, we think we have learned some lessons about the logic of cross-national research that will be of use, not only to students of social structure and personality, but also to students of other substantive problems.

There is, then, a dual purpose to this book: primarily, to present our substantive analyses and our reflections on their implications for understanding the relationship of social structure and personality; secondarily, to use these analyses as a basis for more extended reflection on the logic of cross-national comparative inquiry. Thus, for example, we shall not only develop indices of our central concepts that we believe to be comparable for Poland and the United States, but shall also discuss more generally the issues that are involved in developing indices that are both valid for a particular national culture and social system and are none the less appropriate for comparative analysis with other cultures and social systems. We shall even provide heuristic descriptions of the logic of the principal methods on which we rely, namely confirmatory factor analysis and reciprocal-effects causal modelling. We have no intent of writing a general methodological treatise; but we do not see how it is possible to present the actual indices we developed, nor the actual causal models that we employed, without some broader discussion of the issues that we were trying to address and the logic that we employed in developing these indices and models.

Acknowledgements

In the course of conducting this long-term, cross-national inquiry, we have accumulated an astonishing degree of debt to an astonishingly large number of collaborators and colleagues, which we happily and gratefully acknowledge.

Wlodzimierz Wesolowski, initiator, sponsor, and godfather to our inquiry, gave us thoughtful advice and encouragement throughout. We are delighted to be able to show our appreciation by dedicating this book to him.

Carmi Schooler, partner in the design, analysis, and interpretation of the US inquiries on which we so heavily depend, and collaborator with Kohn in developing the central ideas that guided our inquiry, gave invaluable advice throughout and collaborated actively in the three-nation comparative analyses of social class, on which we draw.

Krystyna Janicka and Jadwiga Koralewicz-Zebik collaborated with Slomczynski in the design of the Polish inquiry, with Krystyna Janicka subsequently taking major responsibility for administering the survey of men. Andrzej Wejland and Pawel Danilowicz conducted the pilot studies. Andrzej Mokrzyszewski, Anna Sianko, and Stanislawa Walkowska took responsibility for fieldwork, coding, and preparation of the data. Anna Zawadzka played a key role in the preparation of the survey instrument for interviewing Polish mothers and children and in supervising those interviews.

Joanne Miller was our collaborator in the early comparative analyses of social stratification and psychological functioning. She thereby played a major part in developing a strategy of comparative analysis and in developing cross-nationally valid indices of some of our central concepts. She also collaborated in the finer-grained analyses of older, middle-aged, and younger cohorts of US and Polish workers that we describe in the final chapter.

Carrie Schoenbach was Kohn's collaborator in refining the US analyses of class, stratification, and psychological functioning, on which we draw in several chapters. She was also our joint collaborator in the comparative analyses of the transmission of values in the family, which forms the basis of chapter 7. She collaborated as well in the three-nation comparative analysis of social class. Moreover, she has contributed her technical skills to almost every analysis that we have done and has contributed her editorial skills to our writing. From start to finish, she has been indispensable.

Karen A. Miller was Kohn and Schooler's collaborator in developing the concept of educational self-direction, and in the analyses of educational self-direction and psychological functioning that we have incorporated into our analyses of the transmission of values.

Ronald Schoenberg has been our expert advisor on matters of causal modelling, as well as the creator of the MILS computer program on which most of our analyses rely.

Our Japanese collaborators, Ken'ichi Tominaga and Atsushi Naoi, provided encouragement and a valuable "third-country" perspective, which has greatly enlarged our understanding, most notably of cross-national similarities and differences. Naoi was also our collaborator (along with Carmi Schooler and Carrie Schoenbach) in the three-nation comparative analyses of position in the class structure and psychological functioning. We do not in this book present a detailed analysis of the Japanese data, but those analyses inform our interpretation at every step.

In the early analyses of the US and Polish data, we benefited from the help of several capable research assistants – Cheryl Keller, Diane Mueller, Margaret Renfors, and Bruce Roberts. Later, Carrie Schoenbach provided immensely valuable technical advice and assistance to Kohn in his re-analyses of the Polish data. Pam Skalski accurately and uncomplainingly typed all the tables.

Many colleagues have given us valuable advice or have critiqued earlier drafts of one or more of the chapters in this book. Our gratitude to each is much greater than including them in an alphabetical list can possibly connote, but that is all that space allows. For their critical advice, we wish to thank: Wladyslaw Adamski, Karl Alexander, Stephen Bunker, Christopher Chase-Dunn, Andrew Cherlin, John A. Clausen, Henryk Domanski, Glen H. Elder, Bernard Finifter, William Form, David R. Heise, James S. House, Krystyna Janicka, Grazyna Kacprowicz, Janet G. Kohn, Bogdan Mach, Alejandro Portes, Zbigniew Sawinski, Carmi Schooler, Jerzyna Slomczynska, William H. Sewell, Ken'ichi Tominaga, Wlodzimierz Wesolowski, Erik Olin Wright, and the graduate students in Kohn's seminar on Cross-national Research on Social Structure and Personality. Our friends, colleagues, and students may not recognize their contributions to this book, and they may very well not want to take responsibility for the outcome, but their contributions, individually and collectively, were very great indeed.

Finally, we gratefully acknowledge institutional support: from the Polish

Academy of Sciences, which sponsored and provided the financial support for the Polish surveys, and which conducted the actual surveys; from the (US) National Institute of Mental Health, which provided financial support for the US surveys and for the analysis of both the US and Polish data; from the National Opinion Research Center, which conducted the US surveys; and from the John Simon Guggenheim Memorial Foundation, whose provision of a Fellowship to Kohn made this book possible.

The University of Chicago Press has granted permission to use materials from Kohn, 1963, from Kohn, 1977 and from Kohn et al., 1990. The Ablex Publishing Corporation has similarly permitted our use of materials from Kohn and Schoenbach, 1983, as have: the Eastern Sociological Society for materials from Kohn et al., 1986; the American Sociological Association for materials from Slomczynski et al., 1981, and from Kohn, 1987, and for the quotations from House, 1981, in chapter 1; the University of North Carolina Press for materials from Kohn, 1989; the Yale University Press for materials from Kohn, 1990; and Lawrence Erlbaum Associates for the quotations from Spenner, 1988b, in chapter 9.

1

Introduction: a Rationale for Cross-national Inquiry into the Relationship of Social Structure and Personality

In this introductory chapter, we describe our approach to the study of social structure and personality – an approach that we have been developing for many years – and then explain the rationale for what makes this book distinct: its determinedly cross-national approach.

INTERPRETING THE RELATIONSHIPS BETWEEN SOCIAL STRUCTURE AND PERSONALITY

Definitions of key terms

Social structure[1] Our definition of "social structure" is borrowed from House's historical and analytic review (1981) of the field of social structure and personality. House thinks of "social structure" as "persisting patterns of behavior and interaction between people or social positions" (p. 525). This depiction is so general as to encompass everything from the patterns of behavior and interaction of a nuclear family or even of an informally organized small group to the overall social structure of an entire society. Later (pp. 526–7), adopting "an eclectic and catholic approach to conceptualization of social structure, personality, and the relationship

[1] For an analytic history of the definitions and usages of the concept "social structure" in sociology, anthropology, and related fields, see Smelser, 1988. Smelser comments that "the idea of social structure is at the very heart of sociology as a scientific enterprise. The component 'social' connotes the distinctive subject matter and analytic level of the field, and the component 'structure' connotes preoccupation with regularities characteristic of any scientific enterprise" (p. 103).

between them," he says that "social structure commonly refers to any and all aspects of social systems, especially more macro-social phenomena." This comes close to Williams's classic definition of social structure as patterned, predictable regularities in behavior (1960, pp. 20–2).

House (p. 542) makes his definition of social structure more precise by differentiating "social structure" from the closely related concept, "culture." "A *culture* is a set of cognitive and evaluative beliefs – beliefs about what is or what ought to be – that are shared by the members of a social system and transmitted to new members. A *social structure* is a *persisting* and bounded *pattern* of social relationships (or pattern of behavioral interaction) among the units (that is, persons or positions) in a social system." This definition, particularly when applied to larger social systems, will adequately serve our purposes. Our interest is focused on the structure of the society as a whole, particularly the fundamental lines of organization and cleavage characteristic of that society: class, stratification, race, gender, ethnicity, age, and the like. Our analyses will focus on two principal facets of social structure – class and stratification.

Class and stratification Since the terms "social class" and "social stratification" are often used interchangeably, we shall in subsequent chapters devote considerable attention to defining them precisely, developing cross-nationally valid indices of both, examining their empirical relationship, and assessing whether class and stratification independently affect personality. For now, we trust that it will suffice for us simply to offer general definitions. By social classes, we refer to groups defined in terms of their relationship to ownership and control over the means of production, and of their control over the labor power of others. By social stratification, we mean the hierarchical ordering of society in terms of power, privilege, and prestige.

We might as well admit from the beginning that we shall give short shrift to other major facets of social structure, bringing them into play mainly as statistical controls. We focus on class and stratification to such an extent that it may at times seem that we fail to recognize the importance or even the existence of such other dimensions of social structure as race and gender. This is not the case. We focus on class and stratification not because they are the only important facets of social structure, but because they offer a prototype for a thoroughgoing interpretation of the relationship between social structure and personality, an interpretation that we mean to test as thoroughly as we can.

Personality In that same analytic review from which we draw our definition of "social structure," House defines "personality," implicitly, as "individual psychology and behavior" (p. 525), later (p. 527) saying that "personality" is generally used as a "generic label for relatively stable and enduring individual psychological attributes (values, attitudes, motives, needs, beliefs, and so forth)." He thereby sidesteps the need for a more formal definition of personality as a theoretical entity, asserting instead that the study of social structure and personality has moved away from the global characterization of societies and cultures and the global characterization of modal personality types to more differentiated analyses of the relationships between dimensions of social structure and dimensions of personality. We agree; and this book is very much part of that development. We see the very looseness of House's definition of personality, not as a failing, but as an advantage. We even use the terms, "personality" and "psychological functioning," interchangeably. For better or worse, we offer no systematic theory of personality, only an attempt to characterize (and to index) some principal dimensions of personality, such as intellectual flexibility and self-directedness of orientation. We do not even claim that these are necessarily the principal dimensions of personality, but only that these dimensions of personality are of critical importance for understanding the *relationship* between social structure and personality. To our great regret, we have no measures of "behavior," other than behavior in the interview situation itself.

In this book, then, we examine the relationships of two principal dimensions of social structure – class and stratification – with several important dimensions of subjective experience, which we collectively characterize as personality or as psychological functioning. The task before us is to describe these relationships, to interpret them, and to test this interpretation cross-nationally.

Position in the social structure, proximate conditions of life, and psychological functioning

The fundamental premise of our approach to social structure and personality is that people's social class positions and their place in the stratification order affect their psychological functioning mainly by their decisive influence on proximate conditions of life. It is these proximate conditions of life that influence personality.

As Kohn put it a quarter of a century ago in his initial efforts to conceptualize the relationship between social stratification (which he then called social class) and parent–child relationships:

The present analysis . . . starts with the assumption that social class has proved to be so useful a concept because it refers to more than simply educational level, or occupation, or any of the large number of correlated variables. It is so useful because it captures the reality that the intricate interplay of all these variables creates different basic conditions of life at different levels of the social order. Members of different social classes, by virtue of enjoying (or suffering) different conditions of life, come to see the world differently – to develop different conceptions of social reality, different aspirations and hopes and fears, different conceptions of the desirable. (Kohn, 1963, p. 471)

The thesis is stated even more forcefully in the concluding chapter of *Class and Conformity* (1969):

Our thesis – the central conclusion of our studies – is that social class is significant for human behavior because it embodies systematically differentiated conditions of life that profoundly affect men's views of social reality. (p. 189)

Suitably expanded – to apply more generally to social structure – our thesis remains the same: the key to interpreting the relationships between social structure and personality lies in discovering "the systematically differentiated conditions of life" attendant on social-structural position. "It is chiefly by shaping the everyday realities people must face that social structure exerts its psychological impact" (Kohn, 1977, p. xlviii).

House (1981) put the matter more formally – and quite usefully – in commenting that Blumer's (1956) famous critique of "variable" analysis was right for the wrong reasons. House argues that it is not because sociologists have analyzed "variables" (in our terms: dimensions of social structure, occupation, and personality) that our results have been so meager. Rather, it is because so many of the analyses have been merely mechanical examinations of the relationships between a standard set of social-demographic variables and individual personality and behavior. "Consequently, we know a great deal about the extent of differences in individual personality or behavior by age, race, sex, and so forth; yet we know very little about how and why these differences occur. . . . [This lack stems] from a failure to formulate an even minimally adequate conceptual and empirical analysis of how and why a social structure, position, or system, could or should affect the individual" (p. 540).

House then proposed three "key principles" for any such analysis:

The components principle. First, we must adequately understand the nature of the social structure, position, or system in question. Such social phenomena almost always have multiple aspects, dimensions, or components and we must be clear about what they are. . . .
The proximity principle. Second, we must recognize that the effects of social structures, positions, or systems are transmitted to individuals through stimuli that

impinge directly on the individual. Therefore, the effects on the individual of large complex structures, systems, or positions generally must be understood in terms of how they affect the smaller structures and patterns of intimate interpersonal interaction or communication that constitute the *proximate* social experiences and stimuli in a person's life. . . . Thus, a major theoretical task in the study of social structure and personality is to trace how macro-social structures and processes affect increasingly smaller structures (for example, formal organizations) and ultimately those micro-social phenomena that directly impinge on the individual.

The psychological principle. Finally, we must understand individual psychology adequately so that we can specify and test when, how, and to what extent macro-social phenomena and the proximal micro-social phenomena and stimuli they produce (or influence) affect individual personality or behavior. . . . Sociologists . . . have resisted use of psychological theories despite eloquent arguments. . . . Without such psychological theories, however, we cannot adequately understand the relationship between social structure and personality. (pp. 540–1).

We shall address House's first principle, the components principle, in chapter 3, where we deal in detail with the conceptualization and indexing of social class and social stratification. On another level, we address the components issue anew in chapter 5, in our analysis of the "components" of occupational self-direction.

House's second principle, the proximity principle, is a more formal restatement of Kohn's earlier formulation about the central importance of the conditions of life attendant on social-structural position for understanding how social structure affects individual psychological functioning. We see this as *primus inter pares* of the three principles, an issue of quintessential importance for understanding the relationship of social structure to personality. Interpreting how and why social-structural position affects personality is more than anything else a matter of discovering *which* are the critical proximate conditions of life that mediate between position in the larger social structure and individual personality and *how* those experiences actually do affect personality.

We shall not "test" the premise that the key to understanding the effects of social-structural position on individual psychological functioning lies in discovering the key experiences attendant on that position; the premise is too fundamental to our analysis to be tested. Rather, this premise provides the framework within which we shall test a much more limited formulation, namely, that *job conditions* are a crucial explanatory link between positions in the class and stratification structures and psychological functioning. This more limited formulation is quite large enough to challenge us.

As our analysis unfolds, we shall argue not only that job conditions are a principal mediating mechanism by which social class and social stratification affect individual psychological functioning, but that a small set of job conditions – those determinative of how much self-direction a worker can exercise in his work – are of particularly great importance. We see three job conditions as particularly crucial: the substantive complexity of the work itself, how closely it is supervised, and how routinized it is. The exercise of occupational self-direction is greatly facilitated by doing substantively complex work; it is seriously restricted by close supervision and by routinized conditions of work. To state our principal hypothesis forcefully, even if a bit too simply, position in the class structure of a society, and position in the stratification order of that society, matter for personality primarily because they greatly affect one's opportunities to be self-directed in one's work. Occupational self-direction, in turn, decidedly affects values, cognitive functioning, and orientation to self and society.

Our way of dealing with House's third principle, the psychological principle, is to rely on the most straightforward psychological model: learning-generalization.[2] Our hypothesis is that job conditions affect adult personality mainly through a *direct* process of learning from the job and generalizing what has been learned to other realms of life. Although such indirect processes as compensation and reaction-formation may also contribute to the effects of work on adult personality (K. Miller and Kohn, 1983; Kohn, 1980; Staines, 1980), there is accumulating evidence that job conditions affect adult personality mainly through this direct learning-generalization process (Kohn and Schooler, 1983; Kohn, 1990; but see House, 1981). Thus, people who do intellectually demanding work come to exercise their intellectual prowess not only on the job but also in their non-occupational lives (Kohn and Schooler, 1978, 1981; J. Miller et al., 1979); they even seek out intellectually demanding activities in their leisure-time pursuits (K. Miller and Kohn, 1983). More generally, people who do self-directed work come to value self-direction more highly, both for themselves and for their children, and to have self-conceptions and social orientations consonant with such values (Kohn, 1969; Kohn and Schooler, 1969; Coburn and Edwards, 1976; Hoff and Grüneisen, 1978; J. Miller et al., 1979; Mortimer and Lorence, 1979a, b; Grabb, 1981b; Naoi and Schooler, 1985; Kohn and Schooler, 1983; Bertram, 1983; Mortimer et al., 1986). In short, the lessons of work are directly carried over to non-occupational realms.

[2] Here we part company from House. He dismisses learning-generalization rather cavalierly, on the grounds that we do not know much about the actual processes involved either in learning or in generalizing what has been learned to non-work spheres of life. He then inventories alternative psychological theories. In so doing, he becomes preoccupied with assessing alternative psychological theories qua theories, losing sight of whether these theories help explain the relationship of social structure to personality. In reaching for too-abstract a formulation of his third principle, he abandons his crucially important second principle. The remedy is not to dismiss learning-generalization but to investigate it.

All these findings are consistent with the fundamental sociological premise that experience in so central a domain of life as work must affect orientations to and behavior in other domains as well (Marx, 1964, 1971). The findings are also consistent with the theoretical expectation that "transfer of learning" extends to a wide spectrum of psychological functioning (Schooler, 1989; Gagne, 1968; see also Breer and Locke 1965). Learning-generalization, which we think of as equivalent to "transfer of learning," is integral to a number of psychological theories. Such concepts as the "generalized response" of reinforcement theory (e.g., Skinner, 1953), "generalized imitation" of social-learning theory (e.g., Gewirtz, 1969) and "generalized psychological pattern" of cognitive dissonance theory (e.g., Festinger, 1957), posit that knowledge and orientations acquired in one situation are generalized or transferred to other situations. According to the theory of social action, "generalization is perhaps the most important of the learning mechanisms" (Parsons et al., 1951, p. 12).

Admittedly, "learning-generalization" is a bit of a black box: we do not know very much about the actual processes by which either learning or generalization occur. But, all evidence points to its being the *right* black box. The analytic task for the future is to specify these processes rather than posit some more complex psychological process, or some indirect process, for which there is no theoretical need nor, as yet, any compelling evidence.

It should be emphasized that our interpretation asserts more than simply that occupational self-direction affects psychological functioning, and more than that the process by which occupational self-direction affects psychological functioning is primarily one of learning from the job and generalizing these lessons to non-occupational realms of life. Our interpretation asserts also that the class structure and the stratification order are important determinants of the crucial job conditions. Ours is a study not just of work and personality, but more fundamentally of social structure and personality. We wish to assess, not only the effects of occupational self-direction but also – and crucially – whether occupational self-direction helps explain the psychological effects of social class and of social stratification.

Presuppositions of our analyses of work and personality[3]

Our thesis – that the conditions of work determinative of occupational self-direction provide a crucial explanatory link between social structure and personality – is based on several presuppositions about the relationship between work and personality.

First, we take it as an underlying premise that, in attempting to

---

[3] These presuppositions are discussed more fully in Kohn, 1990.

disentangle the complex interrelationships between work and personality, it is fruitful to base one's analyses on dimensions of work – job conditions such as job complexity, closeness of supervision, and routinization. This may seem so obvious as not to be worthy of notice. Yet, if one looks back at the history of research on work and personality, one soon discovers that there have been two predominant approaches, neither of which provides a method for distinguishing *which* dimensions of work are pertinent to *which* dimensions of personality.

One approach has been case studies of named occupations – railway men, teachers, taxi drivers, or whatever. These studies have been invaluable for sensitizing us to the multidimensionality of occupations, and thus have been very useful for generating hypotheses; but since any given occupation represents a package of interlocked job conditions, case studies of named occupations do not provide a way to examine the psychological impact of any particular dimension of work apart from all the other aspects of work with which it is interlocked.

The other approach has been to reduce the multidimensionality of occupation to a single dimension, the prime example (in sociological usage) being occupational status. In terms of impact on personality, though, occupational status serves mainly as a gross indicator of a job's location in the hierarchial organization of the economic and social system. The status of the job is closely linked to such structural conditions of work as how substantively complex it is, how closely it is supervised, and what sorts of pressures it entails. It is these structural realities, not status as such, that affect personality.[4]

Our second presupposition is that – insofar as it is possible to do so – analyses of the relationship between work and personality should begin with objective conditions of work – what workers do, who determines how they do it, in what physical and social circumstances they work, to what risks and rewards they are subject – rather than with workers' subjective appraisals of those job conditions. Granted, it is difficult to measure job conditions objectively, especially when relying on survey data. However, we think it imperative that one define job conditions objectively and attempt to measure them as objectively as possible, recognizing it to be a limitation of

---

[4] A particularly unfortunate result of equating *occupation* with *occupational status* is that sociologists often attempt to assess the relative effects of "occupation" and of "education" on personality by using indices of occupational *status* and educational *attainment* as independent variables *vis-à-vis* one or another aspect of personality in multiple-regression or similar analyses, often concluding that "education" has stronger effects than does "occupation." But, as we shall see later in this book, much of education's psychological impact is indirect, through job conditions. Occupational status is a poor surrogate for job conditions; education may actually be a better surrogate.

the research when, and in the degree to which, we fall short of this ideal.[5]

Our third presupposition is that any analysis of the relationships between work and personality should allow for the possibility of reciprocal effects – that work may both affect and be affected by personality – a perspective for which we cannot claim originality, since Weber came to the same conclusion in 1908 (see Eldridge, 1971, p. 104). Although it will not be evident until chapter 6, the research reported in this book has been premised on the assumption of reciprocity.

Finally, we hold it an article of faith that it is possible to establish reasonably firm evidence as to whether job conditions affect personality (and vice versa) without having to do controlled experiments – which means, crucially, without having to assign workers randomly to specified job conditions. Granted, controlled experiments are the ultimate in scientific proof; but realistic experiments are exceedingly difficult to conduct in this field, and experiments that only partially simulate the reality of actual job conditions impacting on people's actual lives over a substantial length of time fall too far short to be definitive. Statistical analyses (preferably based on longitudinal data) provide a much better basis for drawing inferences about work and personality.

These, then, are the principal presuppositions that will underlie our efforts to assess the role of occupational self-direction in explaining the psychological effects of social structure: that analyses of the work–personality relationship should be based on dimensions of work; that it is desirable to define and measure job conditions as objectively as possible; that any assessment of the relationships between work and personality should allow for the possibility of reciprocal effects; and that one can draw reasonably firm conclusions about the work–personality relationship on the basis of non-experimental data. Our analyses will fall short of the demands imposed by these presuppositions in several respects – for example, in failing to provide indices of job conditions that are as objective as we should like – but these are the ideals against which our efforts should be judged.

---

[5] Not all students of work and personality agree with us on this issue (see, for example, Hackman and Lawler 1971). An alternative approach employed by many investigators deliberately begins with subjective appraisals of job conditions, on the rationale that job conditions become important for psychological functioning only as they enter into the perceptions of workers. Investigators using this approach measure boredom rather than routinization, interest in the work rather than its substantive complexity, and "alienation in work" rather than actual working conditions. We believe that this approach ignores the possibility that there may be a gap between the conditions to which workers are subject and their awareness of those conditions. The presence or absence of such a gap is itself problematic and may be structurally determined. Moreover, conditions felt by workers to be benign may have deleterious consequences, while conditions felt to be onerous may have beneficial consequences.

THE REASONS FOR STUDYING THE PSYCHOLOGICAL
EFFECTS OF SOCIAL STRUCTURE IN THE UNITED STATES
AND POLAND

Why a cross-national comparison?

There is nothing nation-specific about our thesis that job conditions, particularly those determinative of men's opportunities to be self-directed in their work, provide a key to our understanding of the effects of social structure on psychological functioning. The thesis is clearly meant to apply, not just to the United States, nor to any other specific country, but to all industrialized societies.[6] To test this thesis requires cross-national inquiry.[7]

We are convinced that cross-national research is valuable, even indispensable, for establishing the generality of findings and the validity of interpretations derived from single-nation studies. In no other way can we be certain that what we believe to be social-structural regularities are not merely particularities, the product of some limited set of historical or cultural or political circumstances. We also believe that cross-national research is equally valuable, perhaps even more valuable, for forcing us to revise our interpretations to take account of cross-national differences and inconsistencies that could never be uncovered in single-nation research. In either case, cross-national research provides an especially useful method for generating, testing, and further developing sociological theory. As with any research strategy, cross-national research comes at a price: it is costly in time and money; it is difficult to do; it often seems to raise more interpretive problems than it solves (see Kohn, 1987; Hill, 1962; Sarapata, 1985; Kuechler, 1987). Yet it is potentially invaluable and, in our judgment, grossly under-utilized.

Many of the US analyses that we shall discuss here have already been presented in Kohn and Schooler's book, *Work and Personality* (1983). What is new is the systematically comparative nature of the analyses presented here. In the absence of appropriate cross-national evidence, there would be no way of knowing whether the findings and interpretations of the US studies apply outside the particular historical, cultural, and political contexts of the United States at the times our surveys were conducted. No analyses based solely on US data could tell us whether the relationships

[6] It might be that the thesis applies to non-industrialized societies as well, but on that we make no claim: we know too little about the relationship of job conditions to the larger social and economic structures of such societies to be confident that our interpretation applies.

[7] To be more precise, testing this thesis requires a particular type of cross-national inquiry, what Kohn (1987) has termed "nation as context of analysis."

between social stratification and personality are an integral part of the social-stratification system typical of industrial societies, or are to be found only in the United States, or only in countries that have capitalist economies. Comparative analyses of other countries are essential to test the generality of the US findings and the validity of the interpretation.

The choice of countries in cross-national comparative analysis

The original research was conducted in the United States. The choice of Poland for the comparative inquiry was initially made by Wlodzimierz Wesolowski (1975, p. 98), who proposed and then sponsored the Polish–US comparative study. He did so for precisely the reason Kohn found the prospect so attractive when Wesolowski suggested it to him: to see whether the US findings and the interpretation of those findings would apply as well to a socialist society. The study was funded and carried out by the Polish Academy of Sciences, who thought the issues important for Polish sociology and Polish society.

From one perspective, then, the choice of the United States and Poland was dictated by the nationality of the original investigator and the nationality of the man who decided to sponsor a replication of that study. Still, choice was involved: all of the principals were convinced that a comparative analysis of these two countries would be a worthwhile enterprise. And even though their choices were limited to doing or not doing this particular comparative study, it is always useful to examine any comparative inquiry in perspective, not only of what countries actually were studied, but more broadly in terms of what other choices might rationally have been made.

Our preferred strategy for analyzing the relationship between social structure and personality is the deliberate choice of a small number of nations that provide maximum leverage for testing theoretical issues.[8] One may begin with a study in one country, with subsequent extensions of the inquiry to other countries, as we do here in using Poland to learn whether US findings are applicable to a socialist society. Alternatively, one can select pivotal countries that provide maximum opportunity to test some general hypothesis, as Skocpol (1979) did (in quite another type of inquiry) in selecting France, Russia, and China for her study of the causes and consequences of social revolutions, or as Walton (1984) did in selecting the Philippines, Colombia, and Kenya for his comparative analysis of national revolts in underdeveloped societies. Whether one starts with one country

[8] An alternative strategy, most often used in secondary analyses, is to do less intensive studies of a larger number of countries – as when analysts use data from all countries for which pertinent information is available. For a discussion of this strategy, see Kohn, 1987.

and then extends the inquiry to others, or begins with a small set of countries, does not seem to us to be crucial. Either way, the deliberate choice of a small number of countries for systematic, intensive study offers maximum leverage for testing general propositions about social process.

How, then, does one decide which countries to compare? The only rule of thumb we know is that cross-national research is maximally useful when it can resolve a disputed question of interpretation. A strategic comparison at one stage of knowledge, though, may be overly cautious or overly audacious at another.

At an early stage of Kohn's research, for example, when he had established little more than that white middle-class parents in Washington, DC, valued self-direction for their children more highly than did white working-class parents in that same city at that one time, the focal issue was Washington's atypicality. Was the Washington finding peculiar to the times and circumstances of that relatively affluent, economically secure, mainly non-industrial city, with its relatively conservative working class, in the late 1950's, or did the finding reflect a more general relationship between social stratification and parental values?

Leonard Pearlin (1971; Pearlin and Kohn, 1966) resolved the question by demonstrating a similar relationship of social stratification to parental values in Turin, Italy – an industrial city, less affluent and less economically secure than Washington, and with a more radical working-class tradition. A more cautious choice of locale would have been an industrial city in the United States or perhaps in English-speaking Canada or in Australia. A more audacious choice would have been an industrial city in a non-Western country or in a socialist country. The choice of Turin, in retrospect, was neither too cautious nor too audacious: different enough from Washington that if the findings proved to be similar, the increment to our knowledge would be considerable; but not so different from Washington that if the findings had proved to be dissimilar, we would have been at a complete loss to know why. Turin was not the only city that could have served the purpose; several other Western European cities might have served as well. At that state of our knowledge, though, Warsaw or Tokyo would probably not have been optimal choices, because it would have been too difficult to interpret dissimilar findings.

The choice of countries should always be determined by asking whether comparing these particular countries will shed enough light on important theoretical issues to be worth the investment of time and resources that cross-national research will certainly require (Galtung, 1967, p. 440). One must always ask, If I find cross-national consistencies, will this particular cross-national comparison extend the scope of my interpretation enough to have made the venture worthwhile? And if I find differences, will this particular cross-national comparison shed light on crucial interpretive problems? Cross-national research is always a gamble; one might as well gamble where the payoff is commensurate with the risk.

The question for us now is whether a comparison of the United States and Poland is strategic. Obviously, the study is done and it is too late to reconsider the investment of time and resources; it is not too late, though, to consider whether the United States and Poland were a wise choice in terms of the theoretical utility of comparing them.

The United States and Poland as exemplars of actually existing capitalist and socialist societies

Our thesis – only partially explicated to this point – is that class and stratification are fundamental features of industrialized societies; that class and stratification are largely determinative of job conditions; and that job conditions are among the principal proximate conditions of life that affect individual psychological functioning. There is nothing in this thesis that is specific to the United States or to capitalist societies or even to Western societies. Thus, any cross-national comparison, even of Canada or Australia to the United States, would have been informative, in telling us whether or not the findings and interpretations of the original US inquiry had generality beyond the United States.

Still, some comparisons are more strategic than others. To test the generality of our interpretation beyond Western culture, for example, one would not want to compare Canada, Australia, or any European country to the United States. Instead one would do what our close collaborators Carmi Schooler and Atsushi Naoi have done, a comparison of Japan to the United States (Naoi and Schooler, 1985; Schooler and Naoi, 1988). This comparison is invaluable for telling us whether the original US findings apply as well to a non-Western capitalist society.

Our intent in this book is of another sort: we deal here not with the generality of findings and interpretations in different cultures, but in different economic and political systems. It seems to us that, a priori, the greatest challenge to our interpretation would be if we were to learn that the relationship of class and stratification to job conditions, and of job conditions to personality, is not necessarily built into the structure of industrialized societies, but only into the structure of *capitalist* industrialized societies. This, indeed, would be a fundamental challenge to our interpretation. Assessing the possibility that this might be true is fully worth the considerable cost of doing a comparative cross-national analysis.

Nothing makes a US–Polish comparison uniquely valuable for our purposes. Other countries might have served as well: perhaps West Germany or Great Britain instead of the United States; perhaps Hungary instead of Poland or, if it had been possible to do such research there at that time, the Soviet Union. It is often the case that no one country is uniquely appropriate for cross-national comparison. Other considerations – research feasibility, the availability of potential collaborators, funding, happenstance – may then legitimately enter in.

We believe, though, that the United States and Poland are not merely adequate choices for our purposes, but that this comparison is particularly well suited to our theoretical purpose of testing the hypothesis that position in the social structure has generally similar psychological effects in capitalist and socialist society. We do not mean to imply that the United States is exemplary of some ideal type of capitalist society, nor Poland of some ideal type of socialist society (Wesolowski, 1988). We do mean that, at the time we carried out our research, the United States was an excellent prototype of "actually existing" capitalist society; Poland was an excellent prototype of "actually existing" socialist society. Neither society met the standards of its ideological proponents nor of its ideological opponents. For our purposes, that is not necessary. We simply want to compare two societies that exemplify the major contrast in political and economic organization represented by actually existing capitalism and actually existing socialism, to see whether our interpretation applies equally to both. Whether the United States of the 1960s and 1970s really was capitalist or was some hybrid of capitalism and welfare statism, or whether Poland really was socialist or was state capitalist or was some hybrid of socialism and capitalism, is beside the point.[9] The two countries were at that time different from each other in the crucial respect of how their economies were organized – one an economy in which market forces predominated, the other a centrally planned and administered economy, the two as different from one another in this respect as any two societies that might have been studied. Poland was certainly a better exemplar of "actually existing socialism" at the time of our study, in 1978, than it is today, with the dramatic changes that are now taking place, or than was any other country open to study at that time.

If we should find cross-national *similarity* in the effects of class and stratification on psychological functioning in the United States and Poland and in the reasons why class and stratification have such effects, we would not thereby have conclusive evidence that these processes are the same in all socialist and all capitalist societies. This would, though, provide solid

[9] Admittedly, the agricultural sector of the Polish economy was even at the time of our survey predominantly in private hands. But, as will be seen in the next chapter, our inquiry is limited to the urbanized regions of Poland, where the economy was predominantly nationalized.

evidence that the interpretive model developed for the United States applies not only to a capitalist country but to at least one socialist society. Moreover, since the United States and Poland are such diverse societies, cross-nationally consistent findings would provide prima facie evidence that the psychological impact of social stratification is much the same, and for much the same reasons, in *all* industrialized societies.

Admittedly, inconsistent findings from research in *any* industrialized society would require a modification of this interpretation or a restriction of its generality. Admittedly, too, the interpretation speaks only to existing societies. We could say nothing from a US–Polish comparison, or even from a much broader comparison, as to whether it is hypothetically possible for there to be an industrialized society in which one or another link in the explanatory chain is broken – a society with a less pronounced system of social stratification; a society in which class and stratification are not so intimately linked with opportunities for occupational self-direction; even a society where occupational self-direction has less effect on personality. Nevertheless, cross-nationally consistent findings for the United States and Poland would tell us that in decidedly diverse societies – arguably, in all industrialized societies – social class and social stratification are associated with values, social orientations, and cognitive functioning, in large part because people of more advantaged position have greater opportunity to be self-directed in their work.

Cross-nationally *dissimilar* findings would lead us, instead, to search for explanations that do not purport to be the same for all industrialized societies, but specific to the histories, cultures, and political and economic systems of particular societies or particular types of societies.

Since cross-national consistencies and cross-national inconsistencies have fundamentally different implications for our interpretations, it is well for us to think about them in advance of the actual analyses.

Cross-national consistencies and inconsistencies

Many discussions of cross-national research (Ragin and Zaret, 1983, is a thoughtful example) contrast two research strategies – one that looks for statistical regularities, another that searches for cultural or historical differences. We prefer to pose the distinction, not in terms of research strategies, nor of methodological preferences, nor even of theoretical proclivities toward "transhistorical" generalizations or "historically con-textualized knowledge," but in terms of interpreting the two basic types of research findings – similarities and differences. Granted, what can be treated as a similarity at one level of analysis can be thought of as a myriad of differences at more detailed levels of analysis. Still, the critical issue is how to interpret similarities, and how to interpret differences, when one finds them.

Finding cross-national similarities greatly extends the scope of sociological knowledge. Moreover, cross-national similarities lend themselves readily to sociological interpretation; cross-national differences are much more difficult to interpret. As we argued (albeit a little too categorically) in our first published analysis of our comparative data about the United States and Poland,

Insofar as cross-national analyses of social structure and personality yield similar findings in the countries studied, our interpretation can ignore whatever differences there may be in the cultures, political and economic systems, and historical circumstances of the particular countries, to deal instead with social-structural universals. But when the relationships between social structure and personality differ from country to country, then we must look to what is idiosyncratic about the particular countries for our interpretation. (Slomczynski et al., 1981, p. 740)

The first half of this formulation asserts that when the relationship between social structure and personality is the *same* in two or more countries, then the unique historical experiences of each country, their distinctive cultures, and their particular political systems are not of focal importance for interpreting the relationship. The formulation does *not* assert that history, culture, and political context have been irrelevant in shaping social structures, but that the resultant social structures have cross-nationally consistent psychological effects. The explanation of these effects should be sought in terms of how people experience the resultant social structures, rather than in terms of the historical or cultural processes that shaped those structures.

This may not always be the best interpretive strategy. Apparent similarities may mask profound differences; what seems to call for a unitary interpretation may actually require entirely different explanations. Nevertheless, we believe that where we find cross-national similarities *in the relationship between social structure and personality*, the most efficient strategy in searching for an explanation is to focus on what is structurally similar in the countries being compared, not on the often divergent historical processes that produced these social-structural similarities. The basic point is that social-structural similarities may have been brought about by very different historical processes and yet have essentially similar psychological consequences.

The second half of the formulation directs us to interpret cross-national *differences* in terms of historical, cultural, political, or economic idiosyncrasies. Przeworski and Teune (1970) argued that what appear to be cross-national differences may really be instances of lawful regularities, if thought of in terms of some larger, more encompassing interpretation. We agree, but we also believe that developing such interpretations is an immensely difficult task. A necessary first step is to try to discover which of the many differences in history, culture, and political or economic systems that distinguish any two countries are pertinent to explaining the differences we find in their social structures or in how these social structures affect people's lives. We do not contend that cross-national differences cannot be lawfully explained – quite the contrary – but only that explanations of cross-national differences require more explicit consideration of historical, cultural, and political-economic particularities than do explanations of cross-national similarities.

Ultimately, the distinction between cross-national similarities and differences breaks down; the issues cannot be simply and neatly dichotomized. None the less, it is a useful way to think about these issues. In chapters 3–7, we shall emphasize the cross-national similarities, our primary objective in these chapters being to develop and test a general interpretation of the relationships of social class and social stratification with men's values, intellectual flexibility, and self-directedness of orientation. As we go along, though, we shall carefully note any and all cross-national differences. In chapter 8, we shall review and attempt to interpret these differences, regarding them not only as important in their own right, suggesting an interplay of history and social structure, but also as potentially important in that they may require us to modify, limit, or even enlarge our interpretation of the relationship between social structure and personality.

2
The Methodology of the Research

This chapter lays the groundwork for the analyses to come. We begin with a general discussion of a methodological issue that will pervade the entire book: assuring comparability of meaning in cross-national research. This issue is no less important at the collecting stage than at the stage of analyzing the data. Our overriding concern with issues of comparability of meaning provides the context for our description of the methods employed in collecting and coding the data from both the US and Polish surveys. We particularly emphasize the methods employed in the Polish surveys, because these were designed to be replications of a survey that had already been carried out in the United States. Thus, all efforts to assure comparability in methods of data-collection were necessarily made in the Polish, not the US, surveys. Our efforts to achieve comparability at the data-collection and data-processing stage of the inquiry is of crucial importance for our analyses, for no matter how relentlessly we pursue issues of comparability of meaning and measurement in our analyses of the data, it is of no avail unless equal attention has been paid to such issues in the collection and coding of those data.

THE CRITICAL IMPORTANCE OF COMPARABILITY OF
MEANING IN CROSS-NATIONAL RESEARCH

The most fundamental methodological issue in cross-national research is whether our comparisons are meaningful. Stefan Nowak (1976, p. 105) posed the issue with characteristic clarity:

How do we know we are studying 'the same phenomena' in different contexts; how do we know that our observations and conclusions do not actually refer to 'quite different things', which we unjustifiably include into the same conceptual categories? Or if they seem to be different, are they really different with respect to the same (qualitatively or quantitatively understood) variable, or is our conclusion about the difference between them scientifically meaningless?[1]

The issue is so complex that a thorough treatment would require quite another book. Here, instead, we deal with issues of equivalence of concepts and indices in a more practical manner, trying only to assure that the particular concepts we use are appropriate for both the United States and Poland, and that the methods we employ and the indices we develop are appropriate to each country and comparable for the two countries.

In principle, methodological differences between studies could produce either cross-nationally consistent or inconsistent findings (Finifter, 1977). Still, when one finds cross-national similarities despite differences in research design, even despite defects in some of the studies, it is unlikely that the similar findings were actually produced by the methodological differences. Substantive similarity in the face of methodological dissimilarity might even argue for the robustness of the findings. But when one finds cross-national *differences*, then dissimilarities and defects in research design make for an interpretive quagmire – there is no way to be certain whether the apparent differences in findings are real or artifactual. The best that one can hope to do is to marshall available evidence that methodological incomparability is insufficient to explain the differences in findings.[2]

To obviate the possibility that any differences we may find between the United States and Poland are merely artifacts of differences in method, we have tried to design the studies to be as comparable as possible, to establish both linguistic and conceptual equivalence in questions and in coding answers, and to establish truly equivalent indices of the underlying concepts. With that intent, we shall in this chapter describe our efforts to make the design of the two studies as comparable as possible; to ascertain, insofar as possible, linguistic equivalence in the questions asked; and to code the data in ways that minimize the possibilities of artifactual differences. In later chapters we shall be concerned with similar questions about the analysis of the data, questions pertaining to the meaningfulness and cross-national comparability of indices and of causal models.

---

[1] For other instructive discussions of this fundamental issue, see Almond and Verba, 1963, pp. 57–72; Scheuch, 1967, 1968; Smelser, 1968; Nowak, 1977, 1989a. Marsh, 1967; Armer, 1973.

[2] For pertinent extended discussions of issues in cross-national comparability of research design and of measurement, see especially Scheuch, 1968; see also Przeworski and Teune, 1970; Armer, 1973; J. Elder, 1976; and Kuechler, 1987.

SAMPLES, METHODS OF DATA-COLLECTION, AND PROCESSING OF THE DATA

The US surveys

The two US surveys were designed by Kohn and his close collaborator, Carmi Schooler, with the fieldwork carried out by the National Opinion Research Center (NORC) of the University of Chicago.[3] The first survey, conducted in 1964, was based on a representative sample of 3,101 men employed in civilian occupations throughout the country. The second survey, conducted ten years later, was a follow-up of a representative subsample of those men – 687 men still under 66 years of age.

Every man in the original sample who was the father of one or more children between the ages of 3 and 15 and living at home was asked about his values *vis-à-vis* one of those children, randomly selected. When, ten years later, NORC re-interviewed the subsample of men selected for the follow-up survey, they also interviewed the wives of married respondents and the "child" about whom the values questions had been asked ten years before, these "children" now being 13–25 years old. We shall discuss these data further in chapter 7, when we deal with the transmission of values in the family.

Sample selection   The sample employed in the 1964 survey is an area probability sample of 3,101 men.[4] These men are representative of all men in the United States, 16 years of age or older, who were at that time employed in civilian occupations at least twenty-five hours a week. Because a major focus of the inquiry is job conditions, and because the experiences of unemployment might overshadow the experiences of past employment (see Bakke, 1940), Kohn and Schooler excluded men not currently employed. They also excluded men in the military, since the problems both of sampling and of inquiry seemed too formidable to make their inclusion worthwhile. They excluded women, because they thought that their inclusion would have required a much larger sample. They did not exclude any men on grounds of race, language (a few men were interviewed in languages other than English), or any other basis.

In interviewing fathers, they wanted to direct the questions about values and parent–child relationships to one specific child, so chosen as to ensure

[3] The logic that Kohn and Schooler followed, and the procedures that they used in developing the interview schedule, are discussed in Kohn, 1969 (particularly appendix C) and in Kohn and Schooler, 1983 (particularly appendix A).

[4] For information about the sampling method used, see Sudman and Feldman, 1965.

an unbiased selection and an even distribution of ages. To make that selection, the interviewer asked for the names and ages of all children aged 3 through 15 who were living at home and then applied a random-sampling procedure (described in Kohn, 1969, p. 238) to select a particular child.

Pretesting the interview schedule   Kohn, Schooler, and their associates carried out the early rounds of unstructured and, later, structured pretest interviews in the Washington–Baltimore area. The final pretests were conducted by NORC, which carried out 100 interviews – six in each of ten widely separated places, with an emphasis on small towns and rural areas, plus twenty in Chicago and twenty in New York City, with an emphasis in these cities on less educated respondents. (The intent in concentrating on small town, rural, and less educated urban respondents was to subject the interview schedule to the most demanding tests.) Kohn and Schooler assessed the detailed reports of the interviews and met with the interviewers from Chicago and New York to discuss each question in the interview schedule. The batteries of items designed to measure the several aspects of orientation to self and society were statistically assessed for their scale characteristics, other items for their clarity of meaning and distributional characteristics. The schedule was revised and shortened once again, and was then thought ready for use in the survey proper.

Administration of the 1964 survey   The survey was carried out by the field staff of NORC during the spring and summer of 1964. Overall, 76 percent of the men selected for the sample gave reasonably complete interviews. Considering that it is more difficult to get employed men than most other people to participate in a survey, and that the interviewers were asking the respondents to undertake an especially long interview (the median interview took two and a half hours), we think this rate is acceptable.

From the point of view of generalizing to the population at large, though, it is necessary to examine the characteristics of the nonrespondents. Loss of respondents assumes particular importance if it occurs disproportionately in delimited segments of the population. For our research, it is especially important that nonrespondents not be concentrated in a particular social stratum. A complete analysis of this issue is not possible, for we lack data on the socioeconomic status of many of the nonrespondents. One important source of information, however, is available: most medium-sized cities have city directories that contain tolerably accurate occupational data. For such cities, it was possible to determine whether or not the nonrespondents differ in occupational level from the men who granted interviews. Kohn and Schooler found little difference overall. The one exception is that the nonresponse rate for small business owners is somewhat higher than that for other men, but this difference is probably an artifact of city directories having more complete coverage of small business owners than of other segments of the population. We conclude that, for cities where data are available, nonresponse rates do not seem to vary appreciably by occupational level.

Furthermore, for those cases where data about occupational level are available, there is no relationship between the occupational levels of nonrespondents and the reasons they gave for not granting an interview. Nor is there any relationship between nonrespondents' occupational levels and the interviewers' characterizations of their apparent attitudes. Rates and types of nonresponse do not seem to be appreciably related to social-stratification position.

There is, however, one social characteristic that made a notable difference in the rate of nonresponse – the size of the community in which men live. Nonresponse rates are directly proportional to size of community. Nothing in the data explains this phenomenon. The simple fact is that the larger the community, the more difficult it was to get employed men to grant long interviews. These analyses suggest that the final sample is reasonably representative of the population to which we generalize, except insofar as it underrepresents larger cities and overrepresents smaller communities.

Further comparisons of the characteristics of the 3,101 men actually interviewed in the 1964 survey with the characteristics of employed males enumerated in the 1960 decennial Census indicate that the sample is closely comparable to the population of employed men. There are only two types of discrepancy between the characteristics of the sample and those of employed males generally: (1) as was shown by the analysis of non-respondents, the sample underrepresents men in the largest metropolitan areas; (2) the selection criteria imposed certain limitations, i.e., that the respondents be at least 16 years old, be currently employed, and be employed at least 25 hours per week. Differences between these criteria and the Census definition of "employed males" are reflected in the findings that the sample is somewhat older and better educated than are employed males generally, with a larger proportion married and a smaller proportion at the very bottom of the income range. Aside from differences in criteria and the sample bias against metropolitan areas, though, the sample matches the 1960 Census data quite closely. The sample can thus be taken to be adequately representative of the population to which we generalize.

Coding and quality control The completed interview schedules were turned over to Kohn and Schooler for coding and analysis. The coding operation was a closely coordinated effort on the part of a small group of people. We think the gains in accuracy repaid the effort of more than two years of painstaking work that went into coding and quality control.

Kohn and Schooler employed three tests of coding reliability. First, the coding of 400 randomly selected interviews was appraised by the coding supervisor. She agreed with the original coder's classification of each question at least 95 percent of the time. Second was a blind experiment based on a random sample of fifty interviews. Five people independently coded all items on which there was any possibility that knowledge of how another person had coded the material might affect one's judgment. A majority of the five agreed, absolutely, at least 90 percent of the time, on all but two of the classifications made. Since this level of agreement was reached under the special circumstances of everyone knowing that this was a reliability study, a third test was employed. This test compared the consensus of the five coders with the original classification that had been made under altogether routine conditions. Except for two classifications, which are of only minor import for the analyses of this book, there was at least 80 percent absolute agreement on each.

Subsequently, a detailed check was done of all possible inconsistencies in respondents' answers – for example, self-employed men telling us about their supervisors. These were individually checked against the original interviews and corrected. There followed a search for "implausibilities" – things that might be true, but were unlikely to happen often, for example, men being married to considerably older women, or men whose first full-time job started at an improbably early age. These too were checked against the original interview and corrected when necessary. Only then was data-analysis begun.

The 1974 follow-up survey   The men chosen for the follow-up study were a representative subsample of the 2,553 men in the original sample who were less than 56 years old at the time of the initial study and thus would be less than 66 years old when re-interviewed. The primary reason for the age restriction was that a large proportion of the older men would be retired, making them inappropriate for the main thrust of the inquiry – assessing the reciprocal effects of ongoing occupational experience and psychological functioning. Excluding the older men also had the desirable consequence of increasing the proportion of men who had children of the appropriate age-range for the inquiries about parental values.

Wherever a selected man was married at the time of the follow-up interview, NORC attempted to interview his wife. The interviewers also attempted to interview the child about whom the parental-values and child-rearing questions had been asked in the 1964 survey. The intent was to try to interview these "children" – now aged 13 through 25 – wherever they lived, wherever they were in their educational, occupational, and family careers.

Pretest procedures were much the same as for the original study, as were the procedures followed in fieldwork. The only major difference in procedures between the original and follow-up studies was that, for the follow-up study, NORC coded the data. But Kohn and Schooler used much the same procedures for assuring quality control as they had used in processing the baseline data.

Generalizability of the subsample NORC succeeded in interviewing 78 percent of the men who had been randomly selected for the follow-up study, 687 men in all. Kohn and Schooler assessed the generalizability of this subsample by two types of analysis.

The first involved systematic comparison of the social and psychological characteristics of the men who were re-interviewed to the characteristics of the men who were randomly excluded from the follow-up study, who constitute a representative subsample of the overall sample and thus are an appropriate comparison group. The differences between the two subsamples are few and small in magnitude: judging from the original interviews, the men who were re-interviewed were a little more intellectually flexible, somewhat more trustful, slightly lower in self-confidence, and they had been reared in somewhat more "liberal" religious denominations than the men in the comparison group. But the two groups do not differ significantly in the social characteristics most important to our analyses – education, social-stratification position, major occupational characteristics, and age – nor even in urbanness.

The second method of assessing the representativeness of the follow-up sample was to repeat the major substantive analyses that had previously been done with the cross-sectional 1964 data, this time limiting the analyses to those men who had been re-interviewed in 1974. Kohn and Schooler repeated all their principal analyses of the relationships among social stratification, occupational conditions, and psychological functioning. The smaller size of the subsample meant that several secondary avenues could not be explored and that some of the earlier findings were no longer statistically significant. But the main findings held up uniformly well. Thus, we can proceed to analyze the longitudinal data with confidence that whatever we find can be generalized to the larger population of employed men in the United States at that time.

The Polish surveys

The Polish surveys were conducted under the auspices and with the financial support of the Polish Academy of Sciences. The initial Polish survey was planned by Slomczynski, Krystyna Janicka, and Jadwiga Koralewicz-Zebik; the survey of mothers and children was planned by Slomczynski and Anna Zawadzka.

Sample selection The initial Polish survey, conducted in 1978, was designed to represent men, aged 19–65, living in urban areas and employed full-time in civilian occupations. The size of this population was approximately 6.2 million in 1978, out of a total Polish population of approximately 35 million. Although the rural peasantry (for whom there is no counterpart in the United States) is not represented, farmers living in proximity to urban centers are included, making the Polish sample more comparable to the US sample than a sample fully representative of Poland would be.

A three-stage probability sampling scheme was devised. In the first stage, all urban centers were listed and given weights proportional to the population size of these units. Twenty-six urban centers, representing 30 percent of the urban male population of Poland, were selected. In the second stage, all electoral districts of the selected urban centers were pooled and a sample of forty-eight districts was randomly selected. In the third stage, the official register of voters was screened for sex and age to provide a final list of potential respondents. From each district, two samples of males, aged 19–65, were randomly selected: a basic sample and an auxiliary sample. The basic sample was the target sample of the approximate size intended for the final sample. It was known, however, that the basic sample would contain cases that would not satisfy the criterion of full-time employment in a civilian occupation. Replacements for such persons, as well as for those who could not be interviewed for other reasons, were obtained from the auxiliary sample.

Interviewers from the survey research staff of the Polish Academy of Sciences secured interviews with 875 of the men in the basic sample. Another 442 of the men in that sample did not satisfy the sampling criteria; 114 could not be reached; and 28 refused to be interviewed. The auxiliary sample provided an additional 682 interviews, for a total of 1,557.

Two random subsamples were selected from among those interviewed. The first (N = 400) was for purposes of psychological testing, to be explained below. The second (N = 752) was selected for a verificational study and reliability assessment of some of the measures of social stratification and of psychological functioning, which will also be explained below.

As in the US baseline survey, each father who had at least one child aged 3–15 living at home was asked about his values *vis-à-vis* a randomly selected child. In 1979–80, interviews were conducted with those children who were then 13–17 years old (N = 177) and with their mothers. We shall discuss these data further in chapter 7.

Design of the interview schedule   The interview schedule used in the study of Polish men was designed to be an exact replication of the main parts of the US interview schedule, including all pertinent questions about class, stratification, occupational self-direction, and psychological functioning. Unfortunately, the Polish interview schedule does not contain information about job conditions other than those directly involved in occupational self-direction – an omission that will haunt us throughout the analyses that follow. The interview schedule does, however, include additional questions specifically pertinent to Poland. One that will be of particular interest for our analyses is whether or not the respondent was a member of the Polish United Workers (Communist) Party.

The interview schedule used for wives was essentially an abridgement of that used for the men, including basic data about social stratification, but little about actual job conditions. The lack of detailed information about the wives' job conditions precludes our doing analyses about the role of occupational self-direction in explaining the psychological effects of class and stratification parallel to those we shall do for men. The data are appropriate, though, for analyses of the transmission of values in the family. The interview schedule for the offspring focuses on values, thus providing the remaining information crucial for our analyses of the transmission of values in the family.

Questions pertaining to values, cognitive functioning, and orientations to self and society, as well as questions about occupational self-direction, were directly adopted from the US interview schedules. The measures of primary dimensions of social stratification – formal education, job income, and occupational status (prestige) – came from previous Polish studies (see Danilowicz and Sztabinski, 1977; Slomczynski and Kacprowicz, 1979), where they had been intensively tested.

Assuring cross-national comparability of meaning   The initial translation of each of the questions adopted from the US surveys was prepared by Slomczynski during a six-week stay in 1976 at the Laboratory of Socio-Environmental Studies of the (US) National Institute of Mental Health. In preparing that translation, Slomczynski discussed each of the questions thoroughly with Kohn and his colleagues, to be certain that the translation captured the intended meaning of the questions. Those discussions were especially valuable for translating questions that use colloquial expressions, such as "going to pieces," "end up causing trouble," and "feel upset," which have several equivalents in Polish.

Another difficulty was finding equivalents for situations that do not arise in Poland. For example, American respondents were asked: "Suppose you wanted to open a hamburger stand and there were two locations available. What questions would you consider, in deciding which of the two locations offers a better business opportunity?" In Poland there are no hamburger stands, but certain types of news-stands (kiosks) are widespread. Slomczynski changed the question to: "Suppose for a moment that you have to decide where a news-stand (kiosk) should be located in a new apartment development. There are two possible locations and you can choose one of them. What questions would you consider in deciding which of the two locations is better?" As we shall see, the Polish version of the question served quite well as an indicator of intellectual flexibility.

In further work, several versions of each translated question were prepared by graduate students of the English Philology Department at the University of Warsaw. The method used for constructing those alternate versions was to substitute single words or entire phrases in appropriate places in the question. The alternative versions of the question were then judged collectively by a group of linguistic experts, who evaluated the semantic and syntactic equivalence of the Polish and English versions.

The resulting interview schedule was subjected to a pilot study, based on interviews with fifty persons selected from the upper and lower ends of the educational and occupational distributions.[5] The interviewers were experienced research workers with graduate training in sociology. They were further trained to conduct the interviews and, simultaneously, to take notes on the respondent's reactions to each question.

The questions were then assessed by two criteria: what proportion of the respondents needed to have a question repeated or explained; and what proportion of the respondents gave answers that did not fit the coding scheme. For example, the agree–disagree question, "Young people should not be allowed to read books that are likely to confuse them," is based on the assumption that such books exist. A respondent may not share this assumption. Or a respondent might answer within a different conceptual framework from the one intended by the question. For example, the question "How often do you feel depressed?" requires one of the following responses: always, frequently, sometimes, rarely, or never. Instead of using these categories, a respondent might answer, "I feel depressed whenever something tragic happens in my life." Formally incorrect answers might also

[5] For a full analysis of the pilot study, see Wejland and Danilowicz, 1978.

result from a lack of knowledge on the part of the respondent, as evidenced by such responses as "I do not know how to answer;" "It is difficult for me to decide," "I have no opinion," and similar responses. Any question that 20 percent of the respondents seemed to find unclear was modified. Any question to which 5 percent of the respondents did not give a formally correct answer was modified. About 10 percent of the questions that had been translated from English were modified at this stage.

The version of the interview schedule containing these modifications was twice tested on university students, discussed by experienced interviewers, and modified.

Training of interviewers and administration of the survey   The Institute of Philosophy and Sociology of the Polish Academy of Sciences had a pool of 300 trained interviewers distributed around the country in proportion to the population size of each region and district. From this pool, 159 interviewers were selected, primarily from locations included in the sample. Interviewers were divided into fifteen groups of ten or eleven persons. An interviewing instructor conducted an intensive training session with each group. After the session, interviewers were examined to assess their familiarity with the questionnaire. The instructor also evaluated trial interviews conducted by each interviewer with two persons who were not members of the actual sample.

The actual interviews were conducted at the respondents' homes, with interviewers conducting no more than two interviews a day. Completed interview schedules were submitted to the supervisor, who checked them for completeness and for formal correctness of answers to the questions. Where there were omissions or evident errors, the interviewer was asked to make another visit. This day-by-day quality control resulted in there being only a small amount of missing data.

The Academy's regular interviewers asked the respondents all the questions except those employing semi-projective tests, two of which – the Embedded Figures test and the Draw-a-Person test – are used in our index of intellectual flexibility. The Polish Psychological Association advised that administration of these tests be done by specially trained interviewers. Since there were only forty such interviewers available, the two tests were given to only a subsample of the respondents, a representative 400 of the 1,557 respondents. Although we feared that having this information for only a subsample of the respondents might seriously hamper the analyses, it turned out to pose only minor difficulties.

The interview record includes information about the interviewer's sex, age, education, and field experience. These data were used to investigate "interviewer effects," which proved to be insubstantial (see, in Polish, Slomczynski and Kohn, 1988, pp. 220–2).

Coding of the data and quality control All interview responses were transcribed onto coding sheets. Ten percent of the coding of "closed" questions was checked by independent coding. The "open" questions were coded independently by two experienced groups. The results were checked by a third group for accuracy of coding and inter-coder consistency. Generally, the inter-coder consistency was relatively high; in cases of discrepancy, the final decision was made by the coding supervisor, who was in frequent contact with the principal investigators.

The coding of occupational position was done by a highly trained group of coders. They used the "Social Classification of Occupations" (Pohoski and Slomczynski, 1978), which consists of 340 occupational categories. This classification system requires detailed information about the respondent's occupation, position in the employing organization, and type of enterprise in which he is employed. Where interview schedules did not provide sufficiently detailed information, the coders had to make inferences about respondents' occupational categories on the basis of additional material such as dictionaries of occupations. Coders recorded whether the coding of occupation was made solely on the basis of information provided by the respondent or required additional inference. Analysis of these data shows that, with respondent's age, education, and occupational position statistically controlled, the average socioeconomic status of those respondents for whom such inferences had to be made does not differ from that of respondents for whom it was not necessary to make such inferences.

Coded data were transcribed onto computer tape and tested for "logical consistency." Among these tests were: making certain that respondents were not classified as having answered questions that it would have been inappropriate for them to have been asked; evaluating pairs of responses that are unlikely to occur together; examining the sequence of dates of various life events, such as leaving school, starting one's first job, joining certain organizations, and age at birth of first child. Suspect data were checked against original interview schedules and corrected when found actually to be in error. Where there was obvious and non-arguable error (whether by respondent or interviewer), the data were recoded as "missing." Less than 0.3 percent of all information had to be corrected.

Verification study Three months after the completion of data-gathering, a verification study was conducted by mail. A sample of 752 respondents, randomly selected from among those respondents who had at least some high school education, were sent a letter and a questionnaire by the Institute of Philosophy and Sociology of the Polish Academy of Sciences. The letter explained the purpose of the second inquiry and asked the respondent to fill out and return the brief questionnaire. The questionnaire contained four questions about the interviewer's performance and eleven substantive questions repeated from the interview schedule.

The results confirm the high quality of the data. All respondents indicated that the interviewer consistently took notes during the interview; no information was obtained that suggested that the behavior of any of the interviewers was in any way inappropriate or improper. The questionnaire contained questions about the respondent's education, occupation, and income – the components for our indices of social-stratification position. It also included four of the questions used in indexing one of our principal dimensions of psychological functioning, authoritarian-conservatism. We shall use this information in subsequent chapters as part of our assessment of the reliability of measurement.

CONCLUSION

We began this chapter with a discussion of the pivotal importance of comparability of meaning in cross-national research. This issue will be with us throughout this book, particularly as we develop indices of social structure and of psychological functioning. In this chapter, our concern has been the quality of the data. For any analysis of social structure and personality, it is essential that the quality of the data be high. For valid cross-national analysis, the requirements are even more stringent: it is not only essential that the data for both countries be of high quality; it is also essential that the procedures used for collecting and processing those data be similar; and, perhaps most important of all, it is essential that considerable care be given to all the nuances of language and culture that can make similar-seeming questions actually have quite different meaning.

We believe that the data of the US and Polish studies provide materials of unusually high quality for our intended analyses. Moreover, we enter into the cross-national analyses of these data with confidence that the extraordinary efforts taken by the Polish Academy of Sciences have done as much to assure true comparability of meaning as is possible with survey methods. In succeeding chapters, we shall endeavor to do as well in our development of indices and of causal models.

3

Social Class and Social Stratification in Capitalist and Socialist Societies

Throughout this book, we deal with two basic facets of social structure: social class and social stratification. In this chapter, we define and index these concepts and examine their interrelationship.

By "social classes," we mean groups defined in terms of their relationship to ownership and control over the means of production, and of their control over the labor power of others. By "social stratification," we mean the hierarchical ordering of society in terms of power, privilege, and prestige. We think of class and stratification as alternative conceptualizations of social structure, both conceptualizations being theoretically useful, albeit not necessarily for answering the same questions. Class is the more fundamental concept, for it addresses the political and economic organization of the society. Yet, classes are internally heterogeneous, each one encompassing a wide spectrum of occupations. In terms of the relationship of social structure to psychological functioning, class produces the basic map, but stratification affords a more fine-grained basis of differentiation. In this sense, the conceptualizations are not so much alternatives as they are complementary.

The distinction between the two concepts will become sharper as we discuss the conceptualization of both, develop indices for both, and examine their interrelationship. For now, we emphasize that *class* is relational: social classes are defined and indexed in terms of their relations to other social classes; moreover, classes are distinct groups ("nominal" categories), not a continuum, not even a set of categories that can be ranked as higher or lower along some *single* underlying dimension. Social stratification, by contrast, is conceived as a single continuum, an ordinal ranking from highest to lowest stratification position. (For statistical purposes, we treat this ordinal ranking as if it were an interval scale – i.e., as if all adjoining positions along this continuum differed from one another by equal intervals.)

Since social classes are conceived of as distinct entities, the question of just what constitutes a particular social class is of fundamental importance for empirical study; hence the voluminous literature about theoretically appropriate "class boundaries." Any divisions of the stratification continuum into named categories, however, are merely heuristic, for the essential presupposition of social stratification is that there are no sharp dividing lines, only higher or lower rankings along a single underlying dimension.

CONCEPTUALIZATION AND MEASUREMENT OF SOCIAL CLASS IN THE CAPITALIST UNITED STATES AND SOCIALIST POLAND

Is it possible to conceptualize and to index social class not only for a capitalist society, but also for a socialist society? Furthermore, can we develop indices of social class that not only are valid for each country, each with its own distinctive history, culture, and political-economic system, but also are comparable from country to country?

Our intent is to *conceptualize* social class on the same theoretical basis for both countries, but to *index* social class in ways specifically appropriate to the particular historical, cultural, economic, and political circumstances of each of the countries. In this way, we hope to achieve meaningful rather than merely mechanical comparability.

It is convenient to deal with the theoretical and practical issues in conceptualizing and indexing social class by first discussing them in the context of an advanced capitalist nation (the United States), then in the context of a socialist nation (Poland).

Social classes in the United States

The classic bourgeoisie–proletariat distinction is generally recognized to be insufficient as a depiction of the class structure of a modern capitalist society. The question is, what further distinctions should be drawn? In postulating a petty bourgeoisie, which like the true bourgeoisie owns the means of production, but which like the proletariat performs labor rather than controlling the labor power of others, Marx proposed both an important distinction and a rationale for making further distinctions. Nearly all subsequent theorists have followed Marx's example, making distinctions that attempt to "disaggregate" the two large composites, owners and workers, into a greater number of more homogeneous categories. We do the same, borrowing from Erik Wright (1976, 1978), Robinson and Kelley (1979), Gagliani (1981), and Mach and Wesolowski (1986).

In his provocative analyses of the class structure of American society, Wright argued that there exist in the United States and other advanced capitalist societies three basic class locations – a bourgeoisie, whose members control investments and the accumulation process, the physical means of production, and the labor power of others; a petty bourgeoisie, whose members control investments and the means of production, but not the labor power of others; and a proletariat, whose members control none of these essential elements of production.

Wright argued that there are, in addition, groups who occupy "contradictory locations." The contradictory location between the proletariat and the bourgeoisie is management, which does not *own* the means of production, but certainly *controls* both the means of production and the labor power of others. He subdivided managers into top managers, middle managers and technocrats, and foremen and line supervisors – the last of these caught between management and the workers they supervise. In practice, though, he – and we – differentiate only two classes of management: management proper, and first-line supervisors, who have no real control over the means of production and only severely limited control over the labor power of others.

Between the proletariat and the petty bourgeoisie is a group Wright termed "semi-autonomous employees," mainly nonmanual technical employees and certain highly skilled craftsmen, who have control over how they do their work and have at least some control over what they produce, but who do not enjoy the degree of autonomy of the self-employed.

The contradictory location between the petty bourgeoisie and the bourgeoisie is composed of small employers, a group of considerable importance to our analyses, since almost all employers interviewed in any representative survey of the population have only a small number of employees.

The evidence is considerable that this conceptualization is empirically potent (Wright and Perrone, 1977; Kalleberg and Griffin, 1980; Robinson and Kelley, 1979). For our purposes, however, Wright's scheme requires some modification. We find problematic his use of "autonomy" (which is similar to our "occupational self-direction") as the criterion for distinguishing semi-autonomous employees from the proletariat. In our view, autonomy, although closely linked to the job's location in the class structure, is not itself definitional of class. The *fact* of being subject to the supervisory authority of an employer or his agent may be determined by one's class position, but the *degree of autonomy* allowed by the supervisory authorities depends on a particular job situation rather than being an invariant concomitant of class.[1] (In later work, Wright [1985, pp. 53–5] comes to a similar conclusion.) We therefore do not employ Wright's distinction between the proletariat and semi-autonomous workers.

We do, however, accept Wright's argument that control over the work of others is a valid criterion of class. Here we follow also the logic of Robinson and Kelley (1979), who would "merge Marx and Dahrendorf" to define classes in terms both of control over the means of production and of control over subordinates. The major import of their argument for our purposes is that the principal distinction among employees would be in terms of their control over other persons. We find this argument compelling; moreover, there is no logical contradiction between using authority over *others* as a criterion of class and then asking whether the psychological effects of class are attributable, at least in substantial part, to control over *one's own* work activities.

Unless we employ some substitute for Wright's distinction between the proletariat and semi-autonomous workers, we may treat as a single class category a large and heterogeneous segment of the work force: all non-supervisory employees. We therefore follow Gagliani (1981), Vanneman and Pampel (1977), Carchedi (1975a, b), and Poulantzas (1975), in treating the distinction between manual and nonmanual work as a further criterion of class. This distinction is certainly time-honored, going back to Marx's discussion of the "mental production" of intellectuals and the "physical production" of workers. Gagliani argues that, even in modern capitalist economies, nonmanual workers have conditions of employment sufficiently distinct from those of manual workers as to make their class situation more akin to that of management than to that of manual workers.

It might be an exaggeration to term the situation of nonmanual workers a "contradictory location" between that of management and that of manual workers, yet it is no exaggeration to say that the basic situation of nonmanual workers – in terms of job security, employment in an office or commercial setting, payment in the form of salary rather than hourly or piece-work wages, and fringe benefits, as well as the rather low incidence of trade-union membership among nonmanual workers – is more like that of management, particularly the lower ranks of management, than is the basic situation of manual workers. As Lockwood (1958, p. 208) concluded from his study of British clerks, "As soon as the term 'class situation' is understood to cover not only market situation but also work situation, it is

---

[1] It should also be noted that, if we were to use autonomy as a criterion for indexing social class, it would be logically inconsistent to then ask (as we shall in chapter 5) whether the psychological effects of social class are attributable to occupational self-direction.

clear that clerk and manual worker do not, in most cases, share the same class situation at all."

With increasing mechanization, standardization, and computerization in offices, and with many service industries blurring the line between manual and nonmanual work, the traditional difference between the work situations of manual and nonmanual workers may be diminishing, but the difference still exists, particularly for male workers, and still provides a valid basis for a class distinction. We therefore take as a working hypothesis that nonmanual workers play a role in the productive process sufficiently distinct from that of manual workers that they occupy a separate class position. If nonmanual workers do not constitute a "basic class," then certainly within the Marxist framework they at least constitute a "non-basic class" (Mach and Wesolowski, 1986, p. 61) and thus should be separately examined (see also Marshall, 1988). In any case, we tentatively employ the manual/nonmanual distinction as a secondary criterion of class. We shall repeatedly check to be certain that the conclusions we draw from our analyses do not result solely, or even primarily, from our using the manual/nonmanual distinction as a criterion of class.

It might be thought that a better line of demarcation would be "intellectual" work, as distinguished from both routinized "white-collar" (sales and clerical) work and manual labor. To make the distinction between intellectual and non-intellectual work a desideratum of class, however, would introduce three serious problems: it is very difficult in practice to make such a distinction. It is questionable whether a classification based on such a distinction could be cross-nationally valid. And – most important – such a distinction comes very close to being a proxy for occupational self-direction, for it would separate into two different social classes those nonmanual workers whose work is more intellectually demanding and those whose work is less intellectually demanding. For our analytic purposes, the classic distinction between manual and nonmanual work is far preferable.

On the basis of these considerations, we divide our sample of men employed in civilian occupations into six class categories, distinguished primarily by their differential relationships to ownership and control over the physical resources and the people involved in production, and secondarily by the employment situation. Our use of ownership, control over resources and the labor power of others, and the employment situation to distinguish these six social classes is illustrated in schematic outline in figure 3.1.

These theoretical considerations do not tell us precisely where to draw the class boundaries. There is, for example, no theoretically compelling basis for deciding whether having a 5 or a 15 or a 50 percent investment in a firm

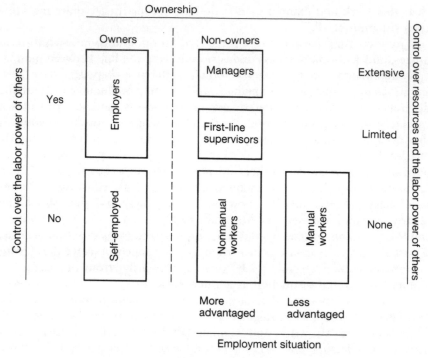

Figure 3.1   *Schematic outline of US class categories.*

constitutes ownership. To resolve such issues, we turn to the rich descriptive data of the interviews.[2] After detailed examination of the interview reports, we draw the line between owners and employees at owning 20 percent of the assets of the firm, which seems to differentiate on-the-job roles that are more like those of owners than like those of employed management or first-line supervisors. More problematic: does having a single employee distinguish a small employer from a petty bourgeois? Two? Three? On the basis of a case-by-case examination of the interview records, we draw the line between three non-family employees and four or more. In the United States, having four non-family employees seems to differentiate firms where the work role of the owner is more that of supervisor than that of primary producer.

[2] The interview schedule used in the 1964 US study is given in full in Kohn, 1969, appendix C, pp. 243–64. The interview schedule used in the 1974 follow-up study was closely modelled (albeit with some significant extensions) on that used in 1964. Most of the pertinent questions in the Polish interview schedule are given in Slomczynski and Kohn, 1988, particularly in appendices C and D, pp. 201–19.

A further problem is that we cannot make all the distinctions we would wish to make, because the sample does not contain sufficient numbers of men in some of the categories. Thus, we have too few men in managerial positions to be able to distinguish between higher and middle management. Furthermore, the category of large employers, however important it may be for social theory, is for us an almost empty cell. We are forced to include the single large employer in our sample in a category that is overwhelmingly comprised of employers of fewer than twenty-five workers. Still, a serviceable classification is possible:

1   Employers: owners who employ four or more non-family workers [N = 18 in 1964, 32 in 1974].
2   Self-employed (petty bourgeoisie): owners who employ no more than three non-family workers [N = 73, 82].
3   Managers: employees who have less than a 20 percent share in the ownership of the enterprise that employs them and who have at least two hierarchical levels beneath them[3] [N = 37, 65].
4   First-line supervisors: employees who have direct supervisory authority over three or more workers and have only non-supervisory workers beneath them[4] [N = 120, 122].
5   Nonmanual workers: non-supervisory employees whose work is predominantly nonmanual in character [N = 138, 106].
6   Manual workers: non-supervisory employees whose work is predominantly manual in character [N = 301, 219].

As is evident from the number of men in each class category, this classification yields a meaningful distribution.

[3] We did not directly ask our respondents how many hierarchical levels are beneath them, but we can infer whether there are at least two such levels from answers to two questions, one asking how many employees are "under you, either because they are directly under you or because they are under people you supervise," the other asking "how many of these are *directly* under you, with nobody in between?" If the total number "under" the respondent is larger than the number who are "directly under" him, we infer that there are at least two levels beneath him. We then systematically checked this inference against the detailed interview record.

[4] The interview records show that employees who supervise one worker are without exception "doers," assisted by a helper, secretary, or trainee. Most employees who have two subordinates are similarly situated, but some actually are first-line supervisors of very small work crews – in most cases, a work crew that is seasonally or situationally smaller than usual. Those men who supervise only two others but who actually function as first-line supervisors have been thus categorized. Those who supervise three others in all instances prove actually to function as first-line supervisors.

Social classes in Poland

Recent conceptualizations of social class in Poland (Wesolowski, 1979; Ladosz, 1977; Widerszpil, 1978; Hryniewicz, 1983, 1984; Drazkiewicz, 1980; Adamski, 1985) share the premise that, at the early stages of the development of socialist society, the class structure is to some extent inherited from the previous formation.[5] From this perspective, the criterion of ownership of the means of production is no longer a valid criterion of social class in a socialist society and classes based on this criterion should be considered as remnants of the previous socioeconomic period, capitalism. A concomitant of this position is the belief that, social classes being relational, in the absence of a *capitalist* class, the *working* class is a "former class" rather than a "class existing at present." Still, class heritage is long-lasting. Even today, many manual workers perceive their class position as that of the traditional working class; many nonmanual workers exhibit internal solidarity in defense of their own interests, and their norms and values resemble those of the traditional intelligentsia. Thus, although socialism eliminated the foundations of the old class structure, some of its characteristics remain (see Wesolowski, 1979, pp. 168–83).[6]

Our approach is rather different. We believe that classes in a socialist society should be distinguished solely on the basis of features characteristic of this type of society: central planning and state control of the economy. We consider the following criteria to be appropriate to class divisions as they existed in Poland at the time of our surveys.

1　*Control over the means of production,* which is a crucial class criterion in the nationalized and centralized economy of Poland. Managers form the most influential and decisive group in the process of economic

---

[5] Detailed and innovative analyses of Marx's theory of social structure in capitalist society (e.g., Hochfeld, 1967; Ossowski, 1963; Wesolowski, 1969a,b, 1979; Jasinska and Nowak, 1973; Kozyr-Kowalski, 1970) have informed the conceptualization of social classes in what was generally seen as a transitional period from capitalism to socialism.

[6] On this rationale, many Polish sociologists have used a class schema based principally on distinguishing the working class from the intelligentsia. In terms of occupational groups, the core of the working class is composed of skilled and unskilled factory workers. The intelligentsia consists of professionals, technicians, and office workers. Three groups, however, are left out of this division: foremen, other employees whose jobs combine nonmanual and manual work, and small commodity producers and artisans who use their own means of production. These three groups are generally treated as an intermediary class, that is, a class between factory workers and the intelligentsia. Past empirical research shows that the division of the urban population into working class, intermediate class, and intelligentsia has considerable utility for the study of social inequality (for reviews, see Wesolowski and Slomczynski, 1977; Tellenback, 1974; see also Lane and Kolankiewicz, 1973).

planning; they are an extension of the state-power apparatus. Managers in socialist countries implement ideological goals and cannot subjugate such goals to a technical or economic rationale. The importance of political goals in administering the economic system affects the class interests of managers and their relation to other classes.

2   *The immediate control over labor*, which separates supervisors not only from their supervisees, but also from higher management. In socialist enterprises, perhaps even more than in capitalist enterprises, the coordination of work is delegated to first-line supervisors, but they are given very limited authority.

3   *Manual versus nonmanual work*, which is a basic distinction even in a nationalized economy. This distinction is deeply rooted in Polish history. Describing the class situation of Poland before the Second World War, a then-prominent sociologist wrote, "Nowhere is the social distance between nonmanual work, be it of the most inferior kind, and manual work, even though it is constructive, so clearly defined as in Poland" (Rychlinski, 1938, p. 180). After the Second World War, the nationalization of industry dramatically changed the position of workers: the capitalist class was eliminated and workers were given new rights, being pronounced the "socialist co-owners" of the means of production. What did not change, however, was the workers' position in the technical system of production, resulting from their relationship to the machine (Szczepanski, 1978). Nor did their place in the division of labor change, for they still remained hired manual workers, subordinate to management. Moreover, the social distance between workers and intelligentsia still remains strong in Poland; in everyday life even today the division between manual and nonmanual work is very pronounced.

4   *Location in the centralized economy*, which divides all manual workers of the nationalized economy into two classes: those who are employed in the large-scale manufacturing and extractive enterprises of the centralized economy – in steel mills, ship-building, auto manufacture, coal mining – and those who are employed in secondary and supportive industries and in service – in transportation, food-processing, and repair. The former, whom we call "production workers," constitute the core of the working class; the latter, whom we call "nonproduction workers," constitute the periphery. In the nationalized economy of Poland in 1978, this distinction was not only descriptive of labor-market segmentation, but constituted a true class distinction. Production workers have been the main force in the immediate bargaining process with the government. Economically, production workers have been pivotal to socialist industrialization; this has been treated by the Government as a factor legitimizing the privileges given to these workers.

   5 *Ownership of the means of production*, which is the basic category
of Marx's theory of social classes in so-called antagonistic formations but
not a major basis of differentiation in the urban, socialized economy of
Poland. The self-employed, or petty bourgeoisie, must nevertheless be
included in the class schema. However, it must be remembered that in
Poland the intervention of the state into small business limits owners'
independence in work-planning and in making other economic decisions.

   The resultant set of class categories (see figure 3.2) is generally similar to
the one we use for the United States, the major differences being that there
was no employer class in Poland at the time of our survey and that we
distinguish two classes of manual workers. Although the class categories are
conceptually similar, however, the precise criteria for defining membership
in each of the classes is tailored to Polish social and economic structures.
Our intent is to assure cross-national comparability in the conceptualization
of social class, while at the same time developing precise criteria of
classification that are true to the realities of class structure in each nation.

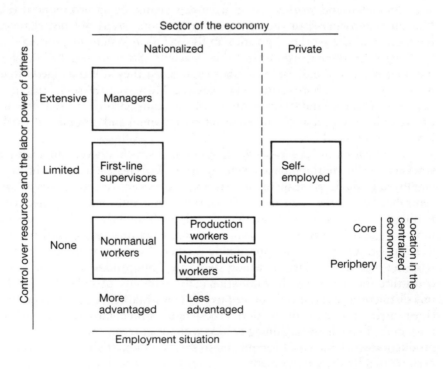

Figure 3.2 *Schematic outline of Polish class categories.*

For Poland, as for the United States, our precise criteria for distinguishing among classes are based on a close analysis of the actual interview data. As a result, for example, we do not use the same criteria for differentiating managers from first-line supervisors in the United States and Poland. Instead, our criteria for what constitutes a "manager" in Poland are tailored to the particulars of the economic structure of Poland; similarly for first-line supervisors. The six classes thus distinguished are:

1 Managers: employees in top decision-making positions in state and cooperative enterprises; employees who have the formal title of supervisor and who have supervisory authority over twenty-five or more people; employees who have supervisory authority over fifty or more subordinates, whether or not they have the formal title of supervisor; and employees who have supervisory authority over two or more levels of subordinates [N = 62].

2 First-line supervisors: employees who have direct supervisory authority over two to twenty-four workers, none of whom is a supervisor [N = 302].

3 Nonmanual workers: non-supervisory employees whose work is predominantly nonmanual in character – the core of the intelligentsia, consisting of professionals, technicians, and office workers [N = 266].

4 Production workers: non-supervisory employees whose work is predominantly manual in character and who are employed in the large-scale manufacturing and extractive enterprises of the centralized economy [N = 526].

5 Nonproduction workers: non-supervisory employees whose work is predominantly manual in character and who are employed in secondary and supportive industries and in service [N = 327].

6 Self-employed: owners of the means of production and members of the owners' families employed in those enterprises [N = 73].

As is evident from the number of men in each class category, this classification yields a meaningful distribution.

We conclude this portion of the analysis, then, with an affirmative answer to the question "Is it possible to conceptualize social class in common terms in such diverse countries as the United States and Poland?" Moreover, we have developed indices of social class that are broadly comparable for the two nations, yet each was developed with due attention to the particular historical, cultural, and political circumstances of the country to which it applies.

CONCEPTUALIZATION AND MEASUREMENT OF SOCIAL STRATIFICATION IN THE CAPITALIST UNITED STATES AND SOCIALIST POLAND

By "social stratification," we mean the hierarchical ordering of society. In this conception, social strata are "aggregates of individuals who occupy broadly similar positions in a hierarchy of power, privilege, and prestige" (Williams, 1960, p. 98; Kohn, 1969, p. 10; Kohn and Schooler, 1983, p. 6).

The issue of whether there can be social stratification in a socialist society had been resolved long before our inquiry began, in a series of studies conducted by Polish sociologists. (For comprehensive reviews of this literature in English, see Tellenback, 1974; Wesolowski and Slomczynski, 1977; and Slomczynski and Krauze, 1978.) Even the question of whether the social-stratification systems of the United States and Poland are essentially similar had been affirmatively resolved before our research began. The problem we faced, then, was simply to develop indices of social-stratification position that meet the two essential criteria that all indices employed in cross-national research must meet: that the indices are valid for each country, yet are sufficiently comparable to provide a basis for systematic comparative analysis.

On the basis of past empirical work by sociologists of both countries, it was from the beginning clear that the major components of social-stratification position in both the United States and Poland would be educational attainment, occupational status, and job income. The issues we faced were not in deciding which components of stratification to measure, but in selecting the best measures of each and in devising the best way to combine these measures into a single index of social-stratification position.

We defer for a moment consideration of the particular measures of educational attainment, occupational status, and job income, since these are best considered in context of the actual measurement model for each country. The more general issue is how to combine measures – any measures – of these three components of social-stratification position into a single composite measure of the overall concept.

The methods used in most previous research have been rather arbitrary. In his early work, for example, Kohn (1969, pp. 12–15) used the Hollingshead Index of Social Position (Hollingshead and Redlich, 1958, pp. 387–97), which weights occupational status seven and education four in an additive score, the weights having been established from an intensive study of a single US city, New Haven, Connecticut. This hardly provides an adequate basis for cross-national inquiry. Other investigators have simply used educational attainment, occupational status, and (sometimes) job income as independent variables in multiple-regression analyses *vis-à-vis* one or another "dependent" variable, e.g. some particular facet of psychological functioning. But such a procedure simply gives educational attainment, occupational status, and (where included in the equations) job income whatever weights maximize their multiple correlation with whichever facet of psychological functioning is the dependent variable in a particular equation. This results in a different linear combination of the three components of social stratification for each facet of psychological functioning and may also exaggerate the magnitudes of the correlations between social stratification and other variables.

It would be much more meaningful to combine the components of social-stratification position by some theoretically appropriate internal criterion than by so atheoretical and inconstant an external criterion. In our analyses, we shall use confirmatory factor analysis, employing the computer program (MILS) developed by Ronald Schoenberg.[7] Since this is the first use made in this book of a method that will be employed repeatedly, but which will not be familiar to some readers, it is worth a digression to explain the rationale of the method and the reasons why it is especially well suited to comparative analysis.[8]

---

[7] MILS is an acronym (the initials standing for Multiple Indicator Linear Structural analysis) for Schoenberg's computer program for latent-variable linear structural equations analysis. The program is a variant of the LISREL program developed by Karl Jöreskog and his associates at the University of Uppsala. MILS has some decided advantages over LISREL and other confirmatory factor-analytic computer programs, one of the most important being that it provides Bartlett-type factor weights, as well as the correlation between factor scores based on these weights and the "true" scores of the underlying concept. With this information, it is possible to correct the attenuation due to unreliability of measurement of all correlations based on these factor scores.

All our confirmatory factor analyses are based on variance-covariance matrices. Since the US and Polish models are not precisely the same, unstandardized coefficients are not directly comparable. For the purpose of assessing cross-national similarity or dissimilarity in the relationships between concepts and indicators, however, standardized coefficients are more appropriate. Therefore, all coefficients shown in the tables and figures have been standardized.

[8] Ours is a heuristic, nonmathematical exposition of confirmatory factor analysis. For more rigorous (and more mathematical) expositions of the method, see Jöreskog, 1969, 1970, 1973a,b; Jöreskog, Gruvaeus, and van Thillo, 1970; Jöreskog and van Thillo, 1972; Jöreskog and Sörbom, 1976a, 1976b; Werts, Jöreskog, and Linn, 1973; and Werts, Linn, and Jöreskog, 1971. Other instructive discussions of methodological issues involved in confirmatory factor analysis are: Alwin, 1973, 1976; Blalock, 1969; Burt, 1973; Hauser and Goldberger, 1971; Heise, 1969, 1970, 1975; Heise and Bohrnstedt, 1970; Lord and Novick, 1968; and Wheaton et al., 1977. Informative applications of the technique are provided in Alwin, 1973; Bielby et al., 1977; Mason et al., 1976; and Otto and Featherman, 1975.

Confirmatory factor analysis

Our twin objectives in developing indices – at the moment, of social stratification; later, of several facets of personality and of occupational self-direction – are to develop measures valid for each country yet comparable from country to country. Confirmatory factor analysis provides an excellent method for accomplishing this difficult task.

The essence of the method lies in the use of multiple indicators for each concept, inferring from the covariation of the indicators the degree to which each reflects the underlying concept that they all are hypothesized to reflect. Each "indicator" of a concept – which is to say, each measured variable – is conceived as if "caused" by the underlying concept that it is believed to reflect, plus idiosyncratic variance, which is considered to be "error" in measurement. Thus, the relationships between an underlying concept and its indicators are portrayed as paths (as in path analysis) from concept to indicators. The computer program actually treats the entire set of relationships between a concept and all of its indicators as a set of simultaneous equations, one equation for each indicator. The test of one's success in differentiating underlying concepts from "errors" in measurement is how well the hypothesized model reproduces the original variance-covariance matrix of the indicators.

Idiosyncratic variance in the indicators – measurement error, as here defined – can be actual error, as one ordinarily uses that term to connote, for example, respondents' misunderstanding a question or coders' misclassifying answers to that question. Of even more critical importance for *cross-national* analysis, though, are other types of idiosyncratic variance that we do not ordinarily think of as error, such as variance resulting from the particular connotation a question may have in a particular cultural or linguistic or political context. There is every reason to believe that particular indicators of any concept will have different connotations in different countries, for reasons having little or nothing to do with the concept we wish to measure. Idiosyncratic variance in indicators is likely to be nation-specific.

If we wish true comparability in our measurement of underlying concepts, it is imperative that we separate such nation-specific idiosyncratic variance from our indices of the underlying concepts we wish to measure. Confirmatory factor analysis is the method of choice for achieving precisely this objective. Ordinary methods of index construction will give us an indecipherable mixture of valid measure of the underlying concept and idiosyncratic variance. Confirmatory factor analysis enables us to separate the two.

This method not only enables one to separate the underlying concept from idiosyncratic variance in each of the indicators taken singly, but also explicitly to model correlations among the residuals of the indicators. This can be valuable when there is any reason to believe that there may be shared variance among some but not all of the indicators – as, for example, when some of the indicators are based on different classifications of the same information or even when some of the indicators are based on the same *mode* of question-asking. In longitudinal analysis, it is especially important to take into account that idiosyncratic variance in any indicator measured at one time may be correlated with idiosyncratic variance in that same indicator measured at another time. For cross-national analysis, there is an even more important advantage to being able to take correlations of residuals into account: there may well be different connotations to *subsets* of the indicators of some concept in different countries, connotations that one would certainly want to separate from our measures of the concepts themselves if we are to measure those concepts comparably from country to country.

Confirmatory factor-analytic models of social-stratification position
Confirmatory factor analysis weights the components of social-stratification position by assessing and building on their shared variance. Thus, the rationale for our measurement models of social stratification is that we conceive of social-stratification position as best inferred from the *covariation* of educational attainment, job income, and occupational status. Our measurement models of social stratification position (see figure 3.3) are second-order models, which is to say, we treat the first-order concepts – educational attainment, job income, and occupational status – as "indicators" of an underlying higher-level concept, social-stratification position. We measure the underlying, second-order concept quite similarly in the two countries. But we measure the *first*-order concepts somewhat differently for the United States and Poland.[9]

To measure educational attainment for the United States, we use the crude but serviceable index that has been employed in most research on educational attainment, the number of years of formal schooling that the respondent has completed. Admittedly, this index fails to capture all the differences embodied in different types and qualities of schooling. It does, however, capture the fundamental fact demonstrated in any number of empirical studies, that years of schooling is a powerful index of educational attainment. For Poland, we use years of schooling as one indicator of educational attainment; but since, in Poland, educational credentials

[9] For the wording of the actual questions used to elicit information about a respondent's educational level, occupational status, and job income, see, for the United States, Kohn, 1969, appendix C; for Poland, Slomczynski and Kohn, 1988, appendix C.

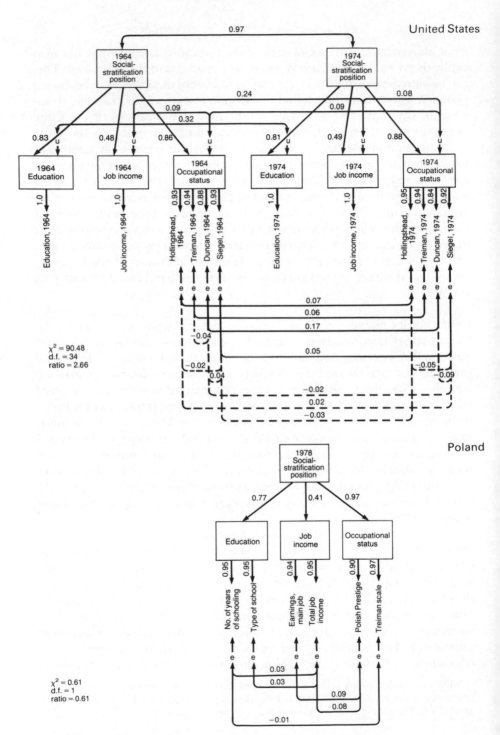

Figure 3.3 *Measurement models of men's social-stratification positions. All parameters shown are statistically significant, $p \leq 0.05$.*

depend not only on the amount but (to a much greater extent than in the United States) also on the type of education, we employ a second indicator as well, namely the type of schooling.[10]

Job income is measured in the United States with a single indicator, income from main job. In Poland, where men are much more likely to earn a substantial portion of their incomes from second jobs, we use two indicators of job income: income from main job and total job income.

In measuring occupational status, we deliberately sidestep the debate between proponents of measures of occupational "prestige" and those of occupational "socioeconomic status," agreeing with Kerckhoff et al. (1989) that the two are alternative, analytically separable yet highly correlated, conceptualizations of the hierarchical ranking of occupations. For our purposes, the differences between the two are unimportant, their commonality of the essence. In our US model, we include both types of measures as indicators of a single underlying dimension, occupational status, relying on confirmatory factor analysis to infer that common dimension from their covariation.

Our measurement models of occupational status attempt to achieve comparability between the two countries by employing as one of their indicators Treiman's (1977) International Prestige Scale, which was developed as the best single index of occupational prestige from a large-scale cross-national inventory. To be certain that our measures of occupational status are not only broadly comparable, but also are precisely appropriate to each country, we also employ measures of occupational status developed for each particular country. Thus, for the United States, we use as indicators of occupational status not only Treiman's International Prestige Scale, but also three indices of occupational status developed specifically for the United States: the Hollingshead occupational classification (Hollingshead and Redlich, 1958, pp. 387–97; for the detailed occupational classification, see Bonjean et al., 1967, pp. 441–8)[11] and later indices

---

[10] The index of type of schooling is a rank-ordering of types of schools in terms of the value of a certificate of completion of that level of schooling as a credential in the job market. The levels are: (1) elementary school; (2) basic vocational school; (3) lyceum (secondary school); (3) technicum (which provides training for semi-professional occupations, mainly for those who do not go on to college); (4) college or university. Slomczynski (1986, pp. 83–4) has also created a four-indicator index of educational attainment, based on years of schooling, type of schooling, cost of education, and age at which education was completed. A construct based on these four measures correlates so highly with the two-indicator model we use here ($r = 0.96$), that we concluded that adding the other two measures would merely add redundancy.

[11] Although not much used in current research, the Hollingshead occupational classification proves to be as reliable a measure of occupational status as is any of the newer classificatory methods, reflecting the underlying concept almost perfectly. Although it is not as well justified as are newer classifications geared to sample surveys of the entire US population, the

developed by Duncan (1961) and by Hodge, Siegel, and Rossi (1964; Siegel, 1971). For Poland, we use as indicators of occupational status, not only Treiman's International Prestige Scale, but also a measure developed specifically for Poland, the Polish Prestige Score (Slomczynski and Kacprowicz, 1979).[12]

The second-order portions of the models treat educational attainment, job income, and occupational status as "indicators" of social-stratification position. In the US model, education and occupational status appear to be equally powerful indicators of social-stratification position, with income of decidedly lesser importance. In the Polish model, occupational status is an even more powerful indicator of social-stratification position, educational attainment is decidedly secondary to occupational status, and job income is again the least powerful indicator.

The difference that we find between the US and Polish models in the relative importance of occupational status and educational attainment is probably an artifact of our having longitudinal data for the United States and only cross-sectional data for Poland: if we were to base the US model on only the cross-sectional data of the 1964 US survey (as in Slomczynski et al., 1981), the parameters would be closer to those of the cross-sectional Polish model – particularly in showing occupational status to have greater importance than educational attainment for social stratification. Either way, we conclude that the models for the US and Poland are markedly similar, reflecting the essential similarity of social stratification systems in the two countries, despite the one being capitalist and the other socialist.

It might be argued that our models exaggerate the importance of occupational status, relative to that of education and of income, since all the classifications of occupational status that we employ as indicators of occupational status either explicitly or implicitly take into account the educational requirements and income levels of occupations. Our models may therefore overestimate the magnitudes of the correlations of occupational status with educational attainment and job income and, as a consequence, may overestimate the magnitude of the path from social-

---

Hollingshead classification does have some advantages over these indices in that it makes distinctions that other indices, which in the main are based on Census classifications of occupations, cannot make (see the discussion in Kohn, 1969, pp. 13–15).

[12] The correlation of Treiman's International Prestige Scale with a prestige scale developed specifically for Poland is lower than are those of the International Prestige Scale with prestige scales developed for some capitalist countries (Treiman, 1977, p. 176). Our model nevertheless suggests that Treiman's Scale is as valid a measure of occupational status for Poland as is the Polish Prestige Scale (Slomczynski and Kacprowicz, 1979). Treiman's scale measures a more universal pattern of occupational prestige than does the Polish scale, which reflects specific changes within Polish society since the Second World War (see Sarapata and Wesolowski, 1961; Pohoski et al., 1976).

stratification position to occupational status. Perhaps so, but the possible redundancy of measurement does not affect the basic rationale of the measurement models nor the comparability of the US and Polish models.

It should also be noted that the models are robust: the main parameters of these models would be little affected if the US model had fewer indicators of occupational status – making it more formally comparable to the Polish model – or if the Polish model used only one indicator of educational attainment and of job income – which would be more formally comparable to the US model. Our strategy of analysis, though, is to develop the best possible model for each country, rather than to use formally identical procedures.

We believe that, despite the possibly greater importance of occupational status and lesser importance of educational attainment for Poland than for the United States, our measurement models of social-stratification position are markedly similar for the two countries and each model provides a valid index of social-stratification position for the particular country.[13] This is precisely what we need to compare the psychological effects of social stratification in the two countries.

THE RELATIONSHIP BETWEEN SOCIAL CLASS AND SOCIAL STRATIFICATION

Are social class and social stratification not only conceptually but also empirically distinct? More precisely, are class and stratification sufficiently distinct empirically that, in actual analysis, there is any utility in differentiating them?

Descriptive statistics demonstrate that, although social class and social stratification have much in common, they are far from identical (see table

[13] We can have greater confidence in the reliability and even the validity of the US measurement model, because the US model is based on truly longitudinal data. Further evidence of the reliability and validity of the Polish model is provided by the follow-up mail questionnaire, described in chapter 2. In that questionnaire, sent three months after the actual interview, respondents were asked questions as similar as possible to those asked in the interview about their educational attainment, job income, and occupational position. For educational attainment and our classification of occupational status, there were fewer than 5 percent discrepancies; for job income (a ten-category classification), discrepancies amounted to 6.8 percent. For all three variables, the correlations between classifications based on the interviews and on the questionnaires was greater than 0.95, indicating very high reliability. Moreover, discrepancies in the information given about one component of social stratification were not greatly correlated with discrepancies in the information given about the other two. Thus, even the small degree of unreliability in our measurement of each of the three components of social stratification constitutes random measurement error, not systematic bias, in our measurement of the second-order construct, social stratification.

Table 3.1 *Relationship of social class to social stratification*

	N	Social stratification	Education	Job income	Occupational status
			Means[a]		
A US men (1964)					
Employers	(18)	0.90	0.70	1.08	0.82
Self-employed	(73)	0.23	0.00	0.30	0.43
Managers	(37)	1.16	0.93	1.15	1.04
First-line supervisors	(120)	0.22	0.09	0.15	0.26
Nonmanual workers	(138)	0.80	0.75	0.07	0.83
Manual workers	(301)	−0.71	−0.54	−0.37	−0.76
Correlation (*eta*)[b]		0.73*	0.55*	0.42*	0.72*
Correlation, combining manual and nonmanual workers		0.41*	0.27*	0.39*	0.39*
B US men (1974)					
Employers	(32)	0.70	0.45	1.27	0.76
Self-employed	(82)	0.14	−0.11	0.22	0.34
Managers	(65)	0.80	0.67	0.81	0.78
First-line supervisors	(122)	0.12	0.03	−0.04	0.18
Nonmanual workers	(106)	0.78	0.71	−0.12	0.72
Manual workers	(219)	−0.83	−0.58	−0.42	−0.92
Correlation (*eta*)[b]		0.72*	0.51*	0.47*	0.71*
Correlation, combining manual and nonmanual workers		0.41*	0.28*	0.39*	0.44*

C *Polish men (1978)*

Managers	(62)	1.89	1.40	1.30	1.88
First-line supervisors	(302)	0.66	0.51	0.42	0.66
Nonmanual supervisors	(266)	0.89	0.94	-0.01	0.85
Production workers	(526)	-0.62	-0.55	-0.16	-0.60
Nonproduction workers	(327)	-0.74	-0.57	-0.50	-0.73
Self-employed	(73)	0.15	-0.16	0.60	0.20
Correlation (*eta*)[b]		0.82*	0.69*	0.43*	0.78*
Correlation, combining manual and nonmanual workers		0.57*	0.41*	0.40*	0.55*

[a] Expressed as standardized differences from grand mean for the particular country at the particular time.
[b] Corrected for unreliability of measurement.
* Statistically significant, $p < 0.05$.

3.1).[14] In particular, the relationships of social class with social stratification and with the components of social stratification are not linear or even ordinal. For example, our data from the United States, both at the time of the baseline interviews in 1964 and again at the time of the follow-up interviews in 1974, show that employers do not rank highest in overall social-stratification position; managers do. Managers rank especially high in education, with nonmanual workers – a class that includes professionals – outdistancing both employers and the self-employed. But employers do rank very high in job income, particularly in the follow-up survey, when the men were ten years further along in their occupational careers. Manual workers rank lowest on all components of social stratification in both countries, but by a wider margin for occupational status than for income and education. In both countries, first-line supervisors rank lower than nonmanual workers in education and in occupational status; but they rank higher in income. In short, these descriptive data justify the contention that social classes are discrete categories, not a socioeconomic continuum. Class is a nominal, not an interval nor even an ordinal, variable.

None the less, the correlations between social class and social stratification – expressed in terms of *eta*, a correlation coefficient appropriate to the non-ordinal classification of social class[15] – are very substantial: 0.73 for the United States in 1964, 0.72 for the United States in 1974, and 0.82 for Poland. All these correlations (and all other correlations reported in this

---

[14] In table 3.1 (and in subsequent tables that show means for the several social classes), the means are expressed as standardized deviations from the grand mean for the particular country at the particular time. The standardized deviation from the grand mean is calculated by subtracting the mean value of a given variable for the entire sample from the mean value of that variable for a particular social class, then dividing that figure by the standard deviation of that variable for the entire sample. This statistic presents most clearly the comparisons we wish to make, that is, comparisons *among* social classes *within* a particular country at a particular time. This procedure makes it less likely that an unwary reader will make the mistake of trying to make methodologically dubious comparisons across countries within social classes.

[15] As calculated from an analysis of variance, *eta* is the square root of the ratio of (a) the "between groups" sum of the squared deviations from the mean, to (b) the total sum of the squared deviations from the mean. *Eta* is directly analogous to the product–moment correlation coefficient, in that it represents the square root of the proportion of the variance in a dependent variable that can be attributed to the independent variable(s). Since the independent variables in an analysis of variance are not linear, though, it is meaningless to think of *eta* as being either positive or negative. One learns from *eta* the magnitude of relationship but nothing about the nature of that relationship. To learn about the nature of the relationship, one must examine the means for the categories of the independent variable, e.g. for the several social classes. In our analyses, all correlations based on *eta* have been corrected for measurement error, to make the statistics presented for social class comparable to those presented for social stratification.

book) are corrected for unreliability of measurement.[16] Although these correlations are a good deal less than unity, there is no gainsaying that social class and social stratification have a very great deal in common. Similarly for the correlations (*etas*) of social class with the components of social stratification, particularly with occupational status: the correlations are substantial, albeit well below unity.

It is worth noting, though, that the correlation (*eta*) between class and stratification is somewhat higher for Poland than for the United States – primarily because the correlation between class and educational attainment is higher in Poland. We shall consider the implications of this, the first cross-national difference of note that we have found, in a later assessment (in chapter 8) of all cross-national differences and their implications for our interpretation.

The sharp differences in the social-stratification positions of manual workers and nonmanual workers, in both countries, suggest that our treating manual and nonmanual workers as distinct social classes contributes to, and might even explain, the correlations between social class and social stratification. This would hardly be surprising, since the manual versus nomanual distinction overlaps, albeit imperfectly, with occupational status, a principal component of social stratification. Indeed, the manual versus nonmanual distinction does contribute to the magnitudes of those correlations; but even if we were to combine all non-supervisory employees into a single social class, the proletariat, the correlations between social class and social stratification would remain substantial for both countries (again, see table 3.1). The relationship between social class and social stratification is not simply a function of the nonmanual versus manual distinction, but results also from the differential occupational statuses, educational attainments, and incomes of men who stand in different positions with respect to ownership and control of the means of production and the labor power of others.

There is an apparent – but only apparent – contradiction between our

---

[16] The MILS computer program provides the correlation between Bartlett-type factor scores based on a measurement model for a particular concept and "true scores" for that concept; this correlation is identical to the reliability of the factor scores. One can therefore correct the unreliability of all correlations between factor scores for any particular concept and other variables by using the standard psychometric procedure of dividing the correlation between factor scores for that concept and some other variable by the reliability of the factor scores. (If the correlation involves two such concepts, one divides that correlation by the product of their reliabilities.) In analyses involving social class, a non-ordinal variable, we have to assume that class itself is perfectly measured. But, in analyzing the relationships between social class and other concepts, we can adjust the correlations for unreliability in the factor scores used to index the other concepts by adjusting the correlations of those concepts with each of the class categories.

showing a very substantial correlation between social stratification – which we consider to represent a single rank-ordering of the population in terms of relative power, privilege, and prestige – and social class, which we treat as a nominal, not an ordinal, variable. The explanation is that there are *several* dimensions of advantage in the class structure: ownership of the means of production, control over the means of production, control over the labor power of others, and a more or less advantaged employment situation. A particular social class can be more advantaged than some other social class in terms of one dimension, less advantaged in terms of another. As a result, the classes do not comprise a single rank-ordering and must be treated as nominal categories.

We have thus found that in both countries social class is highly correlated with, yet distinct from, social stratification. In the analyses of social structure and personality that follow, we shall examine the psychological effects of both class and stratification, differentiating them at every step of the analytic process.

4

Class, Stratification, and Psychological Functioning

In this chapter, we examine the relationships of class and stratification with psychological functioning. If we find similarities in the relationships between social-structural position and psychological functioning in the capitalist United States and socialist Poland, we can have considerable confidence that our findings have generality, not only beyond the boundaries of either nation but also beyond either *type* of society. If we find cross-national differences, our deliberate choice of such diverse types of societies will help us to establish the limits of generality of our findings and perhaps even to understand whatever differences we find.

To learn whether the relationships of class and stratification with psychological functioning are similar or different (or in some respects similar and in other respects different) in the two countries would appear to be a straightforward and even simple task. This apparently simple task requires, however, a considerable amount of tooling up: we need to develop indices of all the dimensions of psychological functioning that we wish to examine in these analyses. Moreover, as we noted in chapter 2, "tooling up" is no mere mechanical process. It requires that we face some of the most complex issues in cross-national research, issues of comparability, not only in the indices themselves, but also in the underlying concepts that these indices are designed to measure.

CONCEPTUALIZATION AND MEASUREMENT OF PSYCHOLOGICAL FUNCTIONING IN THE UNITED STATES AND POLAND

We deal with three broad aspects of psychological functioning – values, cognition, and orientations to self and society. Since these concepts and our indices of these concepts will be employed throughout all the analyses that follow, it is important that we consider carefully our conceptualizations and our indices, asking at every turn whether they meet the twin criteria for comparative analysis: that each is appropriate to the particular country, yet sufficiently comparable as to provide a firm basis for comparative analysis. As will be seen, these questions take a different form, and require different evidence, for each of the three broad aspects of psychological functioning.

Conceptualization and measurement of values

By values, we mean standards of desirability – criteria of preference (see Williams, 1960, pp. 402–3; 1968; 1970, pp. 439–48). By parental values, we mean those standards that parents would most like to see embodied in their children's behavior – the characteristics they consider it most desirable to inculcate in their children (Kohn, 1969, pp. 18–19). There is every reason to believe that parents' values for their children reflect their more general values, not only for children, but also for themselves. A review of pertinent studies (Kohn, 1977), suggests that studying values for children is a particularly strategic way of studying general values.

Our method for measuring values has a long history, only the essentials of which need be summarized here. It began with Kohn's (1959) efforts to measure parental values in a study conducted in Washington, DC, in the late 1950s. His approach to studying values was based on the theoretical premise that a central manifestation of value is to be found in *choice*. It tells us little to know merely that a parent values honesty for his child; the critical question is whether that parent values honesty more or less than self-control, or obedience, or some other valued characteristic. Kohn was also concerned lest any index of values put a premium upon articulateness or imagination, which may be primarily reflective of formal education. These considerations led him to use the device of presenting all parents with a list of characteristics known from open-ended pretest interviews to be generally valued and asking the parents to choose the few that they value most of all for a child of the age and sex of a randomly selected child of their own.

His analyses, using this form of the index of parental values, demonstrated that the index did not simply reflect parents' appraisals of their own child's strengths or weaknesses; nor did socioeconomic differences in parents' values merely reflect differences in the meanings attributed to the characteristics. Rather, he concluded that parents are likely to accord high priority to those characteristics that are not only important, in that failing to achieve them would affect a child's future adversely, but also problematic, in that they are difficult of achievement. This method of indexing values thus measures conceptions of the "important but problematic."

For their 1964 survey of employed men, Kohn and Schooler (1969; Kohn, 1969, chapter 4) used the results of Kohn's analyses of the Washington data and of further extensive pretesting to refine the original list of characteristics to a more comprehensive set, thirteen characteristics in all. These are:

1   That he (she) is considerate of others.
2   That he (she) is interested in how and why things happen.
3   That he (she) is responsible.
4   That he (she) has self-control.
5   That he (she) has good manners.
6   That he (she) is neat and clean.
7   That he (she) is a good student.
8   That he (she) is honest.
9   That he (she) obeys his (her) parents well.
10 That he (she) has good sense and sound judgment.
11 That he (she) acts like a boy (girl) should.
12 That he (she) tries hard to succeed.
13 That he (she) gets along well with other children.

Kohn and Schooler also modified the mode of inquiry: instead of simply asking which characteristics a father valued most highly for a child of the same age and sex of a randomly selected child of his own, they now asked each father to partially rank the set of characteristics by choosing, from among these thirteen, the three he considers to be most desirable, the one that is most desirable of all, the three that are least important (even if desirable), and the one that is least important of all. This procedure makes it possible to place fathers' valuations of each characteristic along a five-point scale:

5 = The most valued of all.
4 = One of the three most valued, but not the most valued.
3 = Neither one of the three most nor one of the three least valued.
1 = One of the three least valued, but not the least valued.
1 = The least valued of all.

Kohn's analyses of parents' values from the Washington study, Kohn and Schooler's analyses of fathers' values from the 1964 study of employed men throughout the United States, and several other studies by other investigators who have borrowed their method of inquiry[1] all attest that the mode of

[1] Campbell (1978) successfully used the method in another study of Washington, DC; Morgan, Alwin, and Griffin (1979), in Louisville, Kentucky; and Alwin and Jackson (1982a), in Detroit, Michigan. Of perhaps greatest relevance, the National Opinion Research Center has successfully employed a modified version of this method of inquiry in several of its General Social Surveys, based on representative samples of the US population (see Kohn 1976b).

inquiry is appropriate to the study of US parents' values for their children. Moreover, the list of thirteen characteristics, brief though it be, is reasonably exhaustive of the characteristics that US parents value most highly for children in the age-range of 3–15 years. Further pretesting and subsequent analyses demonstrate, too, that with some modification of wording, the list of characteristics is equally appropriate for the follow-up inquiry, *vis-à-vis* values for offspring aged 13–25 years.

In using this mode of inquiry for cross-national analysis, though, we must ask whether the list of characteristics, and the mode of inquiry, are equally appropriate for inquiring about parental values in other countries – for our purposes, particularly in Poland. Fortunately, we need not be concerned as to whether the concept, values, is equally important for understanding Polish society as for understanding US society. A long tradition of Polish sociological inquiry demonstrates that it is (see, for example, Nowak, 1981; Marody and Nowak, 1983). The issues are more mundane. Is this rather highly structured mode of inquiry meaningful to Polish parents? Do Polish parents cope with such a means of inquiry in much the same manner as do US parents? And is this particular list of characteristics equally appropriate for Polish as for US parents – might there be other characteristics that should be added to the list or substituted for some of those used in the US study?

We shall try to answer these questions in three ways: by describing the extensive pretest procedures used in the Polish inquiry to ensure that the mode of inquiry and the list of characteristics are truly appropriate to a Polish study; by citing other Polish studies that have successfully borrowed our mode of inquiry and analysis; and by statistical analysis of the Polish data thus secured.

In pretesting questions to be used in survey analyses, particularly questions imported from studies done in other countries, the survey research specialists of the Polish Academy of Sciences do not simply use those questions in preliminary inquiry and then do statistical analyses of the results; they also test those questions intensively by asking their pretest respondents what meaning the questions have to them, by doing linguistic analyses, and by persistently asking whether both the questions and the answers have the meaning for the respondents ascribed to them by the investigators (see the general discussion of these issues in chapter 2). For the inquiry into parental values, both the mode of inquiry and the list of characteristics were intensively scrutinized. They passed muster. Moreover, extensive unstructured inquiry failed to uncover any other characteristics that should be added to the set of thirteen to make the question maximally meaningful for a study of Polish parents' values. By the time this intensive preliminary stage of inquiry had been completed, it was clear that the mode of inquiry and the list of characteristics are as appropriate for the study of Polish parents' values as for the study of US parents' values.[2]

Other Polish investigators – notably Sokolowska, Firkowska-Mankiewicz, Ostrowska, and Czarkowski (1978; see also Firkowska et al., 1978), in a study of Warsaw mothers, and Titkow (1983), in a nation-wide survey of both men and women – have borrowed the method of inquiry and found it fully appropriate to the study of Polish parents' values. Pertinent, too, is the experience of investigators in several other countries: Pearlin used the method successfully in a study conducted in Turin, Italy (Pearlin, 1971; Pearlin and Kohn, 1966); Bertram (1976a), in Düsseldorf, West Germany; Olsen (1971) in Taipei, Taiwan; Hynes (1979) in Dublin, Ireland; Barnas (personal communication) in Tokyo, Japan; Schooler and Smith (1978; or Smith and Schooler, 1978) in Kobe, Japan; Naoi and Schooler (1985; Kohn, Naoi et al., 1990) in a more extensive study of the Tokyo prefecture; and Katase and Umino (personal communication) in a study of the Miyagi prefecture in Japan. The method of inquiry seems to be generally appropriate for the study of parental values in all countries where it has been used, certainly including Poland. The statistical analyses, to be presented below, confirm this conclusion.

So much for the mode of inquiry. The next issue that confronts us is developing *indices* that meet the essential criteria for cross-national analysis: cross-national comparability and intra-national validity.

As we did in developing indices of social-stratification position, we use confirmatory factor analysis as our method of index construction. In developing measurement models of parental values, though, we face three issues that we did not encounter in developing measurement models of social-stratification position – one stemming from our using "choice" as a major desideratum of values; another resulting from our asking parents to make their choices from among a particular set of characteristics; and a third in deciding which dimensions of value are of prime importance for our analysis.

The issue created by our use of choice as a desideratum of values is that having parents rate a set of characteristics results in a linear dependency of their valuation of each of the characteristics on the set of all the others. That is, if one knows how a parent rates all but one of the characteristics, then (except in cases with incomplete answers or errors in coding) one can predict with absolute certainty how that parent rates the remaining characteristic. It follows that, if one knows a parent's ratings of fewer than twelve of the characteristics, one can predict that parent's ratings of the others, while not perfectly, certainly better than if one did not have such

[2] The exact question wording in English is given in Kohn, 1969, appendix C, p. 257. The version in Polish is given in Slomczynski and Kohn, 1988, appendix D, pp. 212–13.

information.[3] (A corollary is that the magnitudes of the correlations among value-choices are necessarily constrained.) We do not propose to deal with the issue of linear dependency in a fundamental way but to sidestep it. Our method for both the US and Polish models is simply to leave some of the characteristics out of the variance–covariance matrix on which the models are based, thus markedly reducing even if not completely eliminating linear dependency among the remaining characteristics.[4]

The second issue, also posed by the forced-choice method of ranking values but having more to do with the particular characteristics included in any one set, is that, since a parent is asked to rate each characteristic in comparison to specified others, his valuation of any particular characteristic will depend on which alternatives are offered. To take a pivotal example: in Kohn's (1959) earliest study of parental values in Washington, DC, and in Pearlin's replication of that study in Turin, Italy (Pearlin and Kohn, 1966), a parent's valuation of self-control seemed to be the quintessence of valuing self- direction. Pearlin and Kohn (1966) concluded from detailed analyses of the relationships between Italian fathers' choice of self-control and of obedience that it is the "self" part of self-control, not the "control" aspect, that is crucially at issue. By implication, self-control would not be so central to self-direction if parents were offered alternatives that are equally indicative of self-direction but are not concerned with control. This is precisely what has been found in subsequent studies where parents were offered the choice of other "self" characteristics that do not emphasize control – characteristics such as independence, an interest in how and why things happen, and (for older children) responsibility and good sense and sound judgment. The importance of self-control as an indicator of self-direction drops markedly.

The moral is that we can never evaluate the importance of any particular value-choice without considering what alternatives are offered. One implication is that we should abandon the method with which Kohn began his studies of parental values – comparing the proportions of parents of various social strata who value one or another characteristic – and rely

---

[3] In an experiment performed with alternative versions of the parental-values question used by the General Social Survey of NORC, Alwin and Krosnick (1985; Krosnick and Alwin, 1988) compared *rankings* of parental values with *ratings* of those same values. Their extensive analyses demonstrate that we were right in our theoretical premise: values necessarily involve choice; ratings of values, in which people do not have to choose some valued characteristics in preference to other valued characteristics, tell us little more than what we already knew – that people regard many of the characteristics in our standard list as desirable. (That, of course, was the very reason we selected those characteristics.) The use of ratings does not provide a way to avoid the methodological problem of linear dependency.

[4] For an alternative method, see Jackson and Alwin, 1980; Alwin and Jackson, 1982a,b.

instead on methods that examine the dimensions underlying parental values.

This brings us directly to the conceptual problem: which dimensions? From early in his analyses, Kohn's interest has focused on one primary underlying dimension of values, valuation of self-direction versus conformity to external authority. The essential difference between the terms, as we use them, is that self-direction focuses on internal standards for behavior; conformity focuses on externally imposed rules. (One important corollary is that the former is concerned with intent, the latter only with consequences.) Self-direction does not imply rigidity, isolation, or insensitivity to others; on the contrary, it implies only that one bases one's actions on internal standards – that one thinks for oneself. Conformity does not imply sensitivity to one's peers, but rather obedience to the dictates of authority.[5]

In thinking of these concepts, it is instructive to note two pairs of apparently similar characteristics that have very different connotations. "Manners," with its emphasis on the proper forms of behavior, is indicative of conformity to external authority; "consideration," with its emphasis on an empathic concern for the other person, is indicative of self-direction. "Being a good student," with its emphasis on how one's performance is judged by others, is indicative of conformity to external authority; an "interest in how and why things happen," with its emphasis on intellectual curiosity, of self-direction. These two pairs of manifestly similar but connotatively opposite characteristics nicely illustrate the differential emphases on internal process and external form that lie at the heart of the distinction we make between valuing self-direction and valuing conformity to external authority.

The most straightforward method for seeing whether there actually is such a dimension to parental values is to do an exploratory factor analysis.[6] Despite the problem of linear dependency in our measures of parental values, we find that exploratory factor analyses of such data consistently give meaningful results. Table 4.1 presents such an analysis for the 1964 US data. We present there only the first dimension, which is unquestionably valuation of self-direction versus conformity to external authority: the

[5] People who value self-direction are not necessarily more (or less) altruistic than are those who value conformity to authority (see Schooler 1972). Certainly, people who value self-direction are just as much products of their life-conditions as are those who value conformity. But, whatever the process that brought them to hold the values they do, and however noble or selfish their goals, people who value self-direction think it desirable to try to act on the basis, not of authority, but of one's own judgment and standards.

[6] In these analyses, the matrix of correlations of the value-choices is subjected to an orthogonal principal components factor analysis, rotated to simple structure through the varimax procedure.

Table 4.1 Exploratory factor analyses of US national data about parental values

| | Kohn–Schooler "occupations" study[b] | NORC General Social Surveys | | | | | | | |
| | Fathers | Fathers | | | | Mothers | | | |
Characteristics valued	1964	1973	1975	1976	Pooled[c]	1973	1975	1976	Pooled[c]
Considerate of others	0.39	0.40	0.33	0.21	0.32	0.16	0.27	0.21	0.21
Interested in how and why things happen	0.56	0.50	0.11	0.51	0.46	0.53	0.63	0.56	0.57
Responsible	0.19	0.42	0.59	0.29	0.42	0.32	0.49	0.62	0.46
Self-control	0.28	0.34	0.14	0.17	0.29	0.28	0.09	0.06	0.14
Good sense and sound judgment	0.24	0.51	0.39	0.59	0.52	0.54	0.55	0.56	0.56
Good manners	−0.55	−0.51	−0.22	−0.54	−0.51	−0.48	−0.48	−0.57	−0.52
Neat and clean	−0.63	−0.36	0.25	−0.57	−0.32	−0.53	−0.52	−0.34	−0.48
Good student	−0.39	−0.25	−0.50	−0.13	−0.28	−0.14	−0.15	−0.27	−0.19
Obedient to parents	−0.30	−0.62	−0.67	−0.48	−0.60	−0.61	−0.55	−0.52	−0.56
Honest	−0.14	−0.21	−0.10	−0.45	−0.24	−0.32	−0.27	−0.33	−0.31
Acts like a boy/girl (should)[d]	0.00	−0.28	−0.45	−0.18	−0.30	−0.19	−0.21	−0.20	−0.16
Tries hard to succeed	0.14	−0.06	0.20	0.36	0.15	0.14	0.08	0.07	0.08
Gets along well with other children	0.23	0.09	−0.03	0.09	0.02	0.18	−0.02	−0.14	0.02
N =	(1,499)	(216)	(208)	(174)	(598)	(304)	(268)	(271)	(843)

[a] For the Kohn–Schooler "occupations" study, the first factor in a two-factor rotated solution; for the NORC studies, a single-factor solution.

[b] These figures are approximately but not exactly the same as those in Kohn, 1969, table 4.3, p. 58, factor 1. (The figures in Kohn, 1969 are correlations with factor scores based on a twelve-item solution.)

[c] The three NORC General Social Survey samples are here combined and treated as a single sample.

[d] In the NORC surveys, "should" was omitted.

characteristics defining the self-direction pole of this dimension are "an interest in how and why things happen" (i.e., curiosity), "consideration," "self-control," "good sense and sound judgment," and "responsibility;" the characteristics defining the conformity end of this dimension are "neatness and cleanliness," "good manners," "being a good student," and "obedience to parents." A second dimension, not shown in table 4.1, is valuation of maturity, reflecting the age of the child.[7]

Exploratory factor analyses of data from other US studies confirm that the self-direction versus conformity dimension of values is to be found in every pertinent study (Kohn and Schoenbach, 1980). Perhaps the most important such evidence – because it is based on representative samples of the US population – comes from the continuing General Social Surveys conducted by the National Opinion Research Center, several of which have included a modified version of our parental-values question.[8] In table 4.1, we present factor analyses of fathers' and mothers' values from each of the three NORC surveys for the years closest in time to our surveys.[9] Because NORC asked about children of unspecified age, there is no reason to expect an age or "maturity" dimension in these values. We therefore hypothesize that a single-factor solution will reflect self-direction versus conformity to external authority for both fathers and mothers. Clearly, in all three

[7] The self-direction versus conformity dimension is essentially the same whether we do a one-factor solution (in which valuation of self-direction versus conformity to external authority is the only factor), a two-factor solution (in which "age" or "maturity" is the second factor), or a three-factor solution (in which age and striving for success are the second and third factors).

[8] NORC modified the question in two ways. (1) Instead of limiting the inquiry to parents having one or more children in a specified age-range, focusing the inquiry on a randomly selected child in that age-range, and asking a parent to appraise the several characteristics as more or less desirable for a child of the same age and sex as that child, NORC asked the question of all adults, parents and non-parents alike, and the referent of the question is "children," not specified as to age and sex. It is possible to limit our analyses to parents who have children in approximately the same age-range as those in Kohn and Schooler's study. But, since Kohn's findings (1969, Table 4.2, pp. 54–5) show that the sex and, even more, the age of the child have an important bearing on parents' values, the indefiniteness of the NORC referent is problematic. (2) NORC changed "acts like a boy should" or, when the selected child was a girl, "acts like a girl should," to "acts like a boy or girl". They thereby changed the sex-specific referent to the indefinite "boy or girl" to fit their mode of inquiry; and the normative connotation of "should" was lost. A question that had been meant to imply that a parent values a child's conforming to his or her proper sex role thereby lost its intended meaning.

[9] In using these data, we have had to treat as "parents" all respondents who say that they have ever had children and who live in households containing children. NORC's categorization of children's age makes it impossible to select a sample for which the age-range of children matches the 3–15 age-range of the Kohn–Schooler study. To avoid including parents of only infants or very young children, we have had to set the lower limit at 6 years. It is also impossible to set the upper limit at 15 years when using the NORC data; the closest we can come is 17 years.

surveys, it does. Since, even in national surveys of 1,500 respondents each, the numbers of mothers and fathers of appropriately aged children are relatively small, we also pool the three samples, treating them as one combined sample, to get more stable estimates. The pooled data confirm the existence of a strong self-direction versus conformity dimension for both fathers and mothers.[10]

There is evidence, too, of the existence of a self-direction versus conformity dimension in bodies of data collected in countries other than the United States, including Italy, Japan, Taiwan, Ireland, the Federal Republic of Germany, Australia, and the Netherlands.[11] The question for the present analysis none the less remains: is this dimension of parental values basic to *Polish* parents' values?

Fortunately, we have not only the data of the nation-wide study of employed Polish men on which to rely, but also the data of two other Polish studies – a study of Warsaw mothers by Sokolowska and her colleagues (1978; see also Firkowska et al., 1978); and a nation-wide survey of both adult men and adult women by the Centre of Public Opinion Poll and Programme Studies of Polish Radio and Television, conducted by Anna Titkow (1983). The three Polish studies differ from one another in several respects: in whether the respondents were fathers, mothers, or all men and women; in the region studied (urban Poland, Warsaw, or the entire country); in the ages of the children who were the referent of the questions; in the mode of inquiry (whether parents were asked to select only the most desirable characteristics or also to select the least important); and in the particular characteristics the parents were asked to evaluate. Even when the three studies do ask about what in English translation seem to be the same characteristics, the Polish-language renditions of some of these characteristics are quite different. One could throw up one's hands and simply conclude, in advance of any analysis, that the three studies are so different as to be non-comparable. We prefer to treat these methodological differences as a

[10] The pattern differs from that of the Kohn–Schooler 1964 survey (column 1 of our table 4.1) only in that characteristics more indicative of self-direction or of conformity in older children load more highly in the NORC data than in the Kohn–Schooler data. This could easily result either from the indefinite referent of the NORC version of the parental-values question or from the NORC coding scheme forcing us to base these analyses on parents of a somewhat older age-range of children than those in the Kohn–Schooler study.

[11] The evidence for Italy is from a study by Pearlin and Kohn (1966); for Japan, from studies by Schooler and Smith (1978; Smith and Schooler, 1978), by Barnas (personal communication), by Naoi and his colleagues (Kohn et al., 1990), and by Katase and Umino (personal communication); for Taiwan by Olsen (1971); for Ireland by Hynes (1979); for the Federal Republic of Germany by Bertram (1976a) and also in the data of the 1982 ALLBUS survey; for Australia by Burns, Homel, and Gudnow (1984); and for the Netherlands by Bosker, van der Velden, and Otten (1989).

potentially great advantage: if we find a self-direction versus conformity dimension in all three bodies of data, despite all these methodological differences, the evidence that such a dimension really is meaningful for analyses of Polish parents' values is all the stronger.

Factor analyses of all three sets of data (table 4.2) give striking confirmation of the existence of a self-direction versus conformity dimension for both fathers and mothers, despite all the differences in method. Such exceptions to this general pattern as we do find seem mainly to reflect connotations in the Polish wording that are masked in English translation: in the study of employed Polish men, for example, "consideration" was translated, essentially, as "taking others into account," while in the study of Warsaw mothers and in the nation-wide survey of men and women, it was rendered as "being sensitive to others' needs and feelings" or as "empathy." Not surprisingly, "consideration" connotes self-direction in the Warsaw study and (for men) in the nation-wide survey, but fails to do so in the study of employed Polish men. In the study of employed Polish men, "good manners" was translated into a colloquial expression connoting a well brought-up child, but in the Warsaw study it was translated as "behaving in an appropriate way." Thus translated, "manners" connotes conformity to external authority in the study of employed Polish men but fails to do so in the study of Warsaw mothers. Still, all three studies yield a primary dimension of valuation that unquestionably connotes self-direction versus conformity to external authority.[12] Moreover, some pivotal characteristics – namely, responsibility, self-control, and independence (or "having independent opinions") – consistently connote self-direction; other pivotal characteristics – particularly obedience to parents and being a good student – consistently connote conformity to external authority.

Using the study of employed Polish men, Koralewicz-Zebik (1982) did separate exploratory factor analyses of the values held by manual and nonmanual workers. Her analyses show that the self-direction versus conformity dimension is clearly present for both. Moreover, similar analyses of men of differing educational attainment show essentially the same results. Self-direction versus conformity to external authority is an underlying dimension of fathers' values in all segments of Polish society.

These analyses confirm the cross-national validity of our belief that self-direction versus conformity to external authority is a meaningful dimension

---

[12] In the study of employed Polish men and in the nation-wide survey, the factor includes also "tries hard to succeed." It is difficult to separate valuation of success from valuation of self-direction versus conformity to external authority in exploratory factor analyses, but we are able to do so in confirmatory factor analyses both of the data for employed Polish men (to be presented shortly) and of the data for both men and women in the nation-wide survey.

Table 4.2 *Exploratory factor analyses of Polish data about parental values*[a]

Year of fieldwork	1978	1975	1979	
Locale	(Urban) Poland	Warsaw	Polish national sample	
Respondents	Fathers	Mothers	Men	Women
			All	All
Age of child	3–15 years	11–13 years		
Characteristics valued				
Considerate of others (sensitive to others' needs and feelings)	0.05	0.33	0.30	−0.12
Interested in how and why things happen (curious)	0.33	0.54	−0.06	0.18
Responsible	0.47	0.57	0.43	0.41
Self-control	0.31	—	0.28	0.35
Good sense and sound judgment	0.51	0.22	−0.05	0.22
Good manners	−0.46	—	−0.20	−0.11
Neat and clean	−0.32	—	−0.29	−0.03
Good student	−0.50	−0.79	−0.61	−0.42
Obedient to parents	−0.47	−0.79	−0.55	−0.52
Honest	0.07	—	−0.03	−0.48
Acts like a boy/girl should	−0.33	—	−0.09	−0.03
Tries hard to succeed	0.27	—	0.43	0.45
Gets along well with other children	0.05	−0.41	−0.22	−0.22
Independent (has independent opinions)	—	0.60	0.44	0.38
Clever (knows how to achieve goals in life)	—	−0.47	0.00	0.24
Diligent	—	0.12	—	—
N =	(660)	(209)	(695)	(734)

[a] The figures are correlations of items with the underlying factor in a one-factor solution, using exploratory factor analysis.

of parental values. They do not, however, provide the best possible *indices* of this dimension. Just as in the development of indices of social stratification, we again face the central issues of separating underlying concept from error in measurement of indicators, of possible cultural differences in the connotations of particular indicators or of subsets of indicators, and (for the US longitudinal data) of the possibility of errors in the measurement of any one indicator being correlated with errors in the measurement of that same indicator at a later time. We again turn to confirmatory factor analysis to solve these problems.

Measurement models of parental values To develop a longitudinal measurement model of parental values for US fathers, we use the data from the subsample of the fathers, 399 in all, who were re-interviewed in 1974, ten years after the original study. To minimize the problem of linear dependency, we deliberately exclude one pair of characteristics that are negatively correlated with each other – self-control and being a good student – the first indicative of self-direction, the second of conformity to external authority. To further reduce the degree of linear dependency, we exclude other characteristics that prove not to be important indicators of the underlying factors. We retain eight characteristics that are particularly appropriate to younger children as indicators in the 1964 part of the model and seven characteristics that are particularly appropriate to older children as indicators in the 1974 part of the model.

Analyses of the data for 1964, when the children were 3–15 years old, indicate that there are three principal underlying dimensions of valuation: self-direction versus conformity to external authority, maturity (age), and striving for success. Similar analyses of the data for 1974, by which time the children were 13–25 years old, indicate that maturity (age) ceases to be an important dimension. One way to deal with this disparity would be to depict parental values as having three principal dimensions when the children are younger and two principal dimensions when they grow older. A comparable but simpler method, which we use here, is to partial child's age out of the variance–covariance matrix on which the confirmatory factor analysis is based and employ a two-factor schema in both parts of the model (see figure 4.1). Nothing is lost thereby, for the maturity dimension is of no substantive interest in this analysis. There is a small gain, in that the 1964 and 1974 parts of the model are fully equivalent.[13]

For each characteristic included in both the 1964 and 1974 parts of the model, correlations of the residuals of its 1964 and 1974 ratings are tested

[13] Partialling child's age out of the matrix affects only variations in values related to the thirteen-year span in children's ages at the time of each interview; it does not distort the reality of the entire sample of children becoming ten years older.

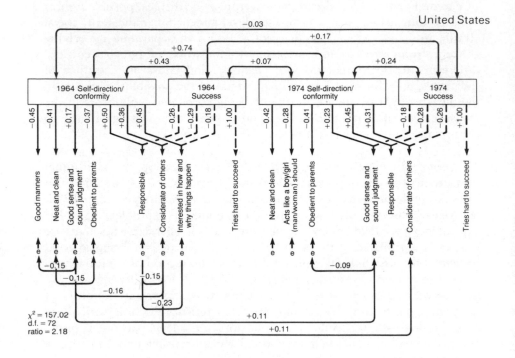

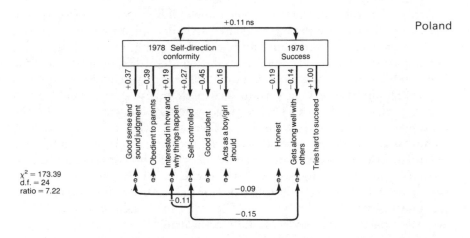

Figure 4.1 *Measurement models of parental values. All parameters shown are statistically significant, $p \leq 0.05$.*

and retained where statistically significant. In addition, as the upper half of figure 4.1 shows, there are several statistically significant intra-time correlations of residuals. This explication of the error structure results in a good fit of model to data.

The Polish model is of course cross-sectional. To avoid linear dependency in this model, we again leave some characteristics out of the variance–covariance matrix on which the model is based, beginning with a pair of characteristics whose components connote the two ends of the self-direction versus conformity factor; for Polish fathers, we drop responsibility and neatness. To reduce the problem of linear dependency even further, we also exclude the two characteristics – manners and consideration – that may suffer in translation. This model fits the data fairly well.

Both the US and the Polish models show a clear underlying factor, one pole of which is valuation of self-direction; the other, valuation of conformity to external authority. The particular characteristics that reflect this underlying factor are somewhat different for Polish and for US fathers – just as they are somewhat different for US fathers of 3–15-year-olds from what they are for these same fathers when the children are aged 13–25. But, clearly, both models depict the same underlying dimension – valuation of self-direction versus valuation of conformity to external authority. Factor scores based on these models provide our indices of this dimension, indices that can be used with assurance for cross-national comparisons of the relationship between social structure and parental values.[14]

Conceptualization and measurement of intellectual flexibility

Our indices of intellectual flexibility are meant to reflect men's actual intellectual performance in the interview situation. We rely on a variety of indicators – including men's answers to seemingly simple but highly revealing cognitive problems, their handling of perceptual and projective

---

[14] Since these are the first measurement models of psychological functioning that we present, this may be the best place to make clear that our objective in developing these models is not to be able to assess cross-national similarities or differences in *personality* but to assess cross-national similarities or differences in the *relationships* between social structure and personality. Thus, our focus of interest will not be whether Polish fathers value self-direction more or less highly than do US fathers (or whether Poles are more or less self-confident or intellectually flexible or anything else than are Americans) or even whether Polish managers value self-direction more or less highly than do US managers. Despite the arguments of Schoenberg (1982), we do not claim that our methods are adequate for making cross-national comparisons of the mean levels of any psychological phenomenon (which would be required for comparing Polish to US men), but only that they provide a sound basis for examining the relationships between social structure and personality, to see whether these relationships are similar or dissimilar in the two countries.

tests, their propensity to "agree" when asked agree–disagree questions, and the impression they made on the interviewer during a long session that required a great deal of thought and reflection. None of these indicators is assumed to be completely valid; but we do assume that all the indicators reflect, to some substantial degree, men's flexibility in attempting to cope with the intellectual demands of complex tasks. We claim neither that this index measures innate intellectual ability nor that intellectual flexibility evidenced in the interview situation is necessarily identical to intellectual flexibility as it might be manifested in other situations; we do not have enough information about the situational variability of intellectual functioning to be certain. We do claim that our index reflects men's actual intellectual functioning in a non-work situation that seemed to elicit considerable intellectual effort from nearly all the respondents. Such an index transcends the criticism made of standard intelligence tests that "the perseverance of a youth- centric . . . measurement of intellectual aging has demonstrated, most conspicuously by its very existence, a serious gap in age- and cohort-fair assessment" (Baltes et al., 1984, p. 36). Ours is most decidedly not a "youth-centric" measure.

That our index is also not artifactual, and that it measures an enduring characteristic, is attested to by the evidence – to be presented shortly – of its remarkably high stability over time. Spaeth's (1976) analysis adds to the credibility of the index by showing that the correlations between an earlier variant of this index and various social phenomena are similar to those for more conventional indices of intellectual functioning.

More concretely and specifically, our measurement models (see figure 4.2) are based on seven indicators of each man's intellectual performance in the interview situation. These are: (1) the Goodenough estimate of his intelligence (see Witkin et al., 1962), based on a detailed evaluation of the Draw-a-Person test; (2) the summary appraisal of Witkin et al. (1962) of the sophistication of body-concept in the Draw-a-Person test; (3) a rating of his performance on a portion of the Embedded Figures test (see Witkin et al., 1962); (4) the interviewer's appraisal of the man's intelligence; (5) the frequency with which he agreed when asked the many agree–disagree questions included in the interview; (6) a rating of the adequacy of his answer to the apparently simple cognitive problem (as asked in the United States), "What are all the arguments you can think of for and against allowing cigarette commercials on TV?;" and (7) a rating of the adequacy of his answer to another relatively simple cognitive problem (as asked in the United States), "Suppose you wanted to open a hamburger stand and there were two locations available. What questions would you consider in deciding which of the two locations offers a better business opportunity?"

In earlier analyses of the 1964 baseline data, Kohn and Schooler performed an exploratory (orthogonal principal components) factor analysis

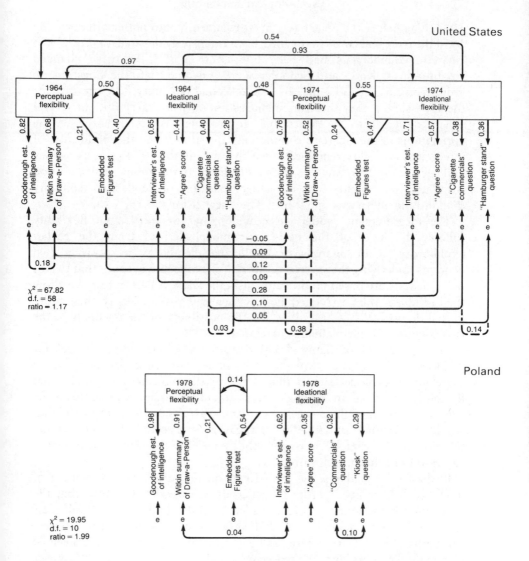

Figure 4.2 *Measurement models of intellectual flexibility. All parameters shown are statistically significant, $p \leq 0.05$.*

of these various manifestations of intellectual flexibility. That analysis yielded two dimensions, one primarily perceptual, the other ideational. In the follow-up study, they secured entirely comparable data, after elaborate pretesting to be certain that the cognitive problems had the same meaning in 1974 as in 1964. They were particularly concerned about the cigarette commercials question. They had been prescient in asking that question in

1964, long before the issue had come prominently into public attention. By 1974 the issue had come to the fore, been extensively debated, and resolved: cigarette commercials had been banned from TV. In these changed circumstances, Kohn and Schooler were concerned lest the question no longer serve as a good indicator of intellectual flexibility. In pretesting for the 1974 survey, they therefore included not only this question, but several others designed to be functional equivalents. To their surprise, the correlations of the cigarette commercials question with other indicators of intellectual flexibility remained much the same in the 1974 pretests as they had been in the 1964 survey; moreover, the cigarette commercials question correlated more highly with the other indicators of intellectual flexibility than did the alternative questions. They kept it for the 1974 survey.

The measurement model we now employ for intellectual flexibility follows the logic of the two-factor model derived from the earlier exploratory factor analysis of intellectual flexibility, in positing two concepts underlying the seven indicators.[15] To take into account that two of the indicators are based on the same task, the Draw-a-Person test, we allow their residuals to be correlated. Following a lead provided by the first-order partial derivatives, we also allow for the possibility of the residuals of the two cognitive problems being correlated.

The upper half of figure 4.2 depicts the US longitudinal model for intellectual flexibility, with the two underlying concepts allowed to correlate. The model shows that some of the indicators of intellectual flexibility reflect the underlying concept to only a modest degree; this is the very reason we thought it necessary to construct a measurement model that would differentiate unreliability of measurement from actual intellectual functioning. Judging by how well the model fits the data, the model is successful in achieving this objective.

In the causal analyses, we shall focus on the ideational component of intellectual flexibility.[16] From the measurement model, we learn that the correlation between men's levels of ideational flexibility in 1964 and their levels of ideational flexibility in 1974, shorn of measurement error, is a very substantial 0.93. Clearly, there has been great consistency in men's levels of ideational flexibility over the ten-year period.

[15] We get slightly different estimates of the parameters of the measurement model, depending on whether we posit that the two underlying concepts are necessarily orthogonal to each other or that they are possibly correlated with one another. Because the non-orthogonal model is both conceptually more sensible and provides a significantly better fit to the data, we shall employ it in the causal analyses that follow.

[16] Why, if our analytic interest is solely in ideational flexibility, do we include perceptual flexibility in our measurement model? The answer is that, since the Embedded Figures test partakes of both dimensions, we believe we get a more precise measure of ideational flexibility by having both dimensions in the model. Certainly, nothing is lost thereby.

In analyzing the Polish data, we follow the same strategy for measuring intellectual flexibility – that is, we use the same variety of indicators of men's actual intellectual performance in the interview situation (see the lower half of figure 4.2). As with all the indices we employ, the question arises, do these procedures result in indices that are cross-nationally comparable, yet valid for Poland? Answering this question requires an item-by-item examination.

The first two measures are based on a semi-projective test, the Draw-a-Person test.[17] (As discussed in chapter 2, this test was administered only to a representative subsample of one-fourth of the men in the overall Polish sample.) There is no reason to think that such indicators are any less valid for Poland than for the United States; and in any case, neither indicator is of any import for the dimension of intellectual flexibility with which we are concerned in our causal analysis, ideational flexibility.

The third indicator, the Embedded Figures test (also administered only to the subsample), is relevant both to perceptual and to ideational flexibility. We have no data to demonstrate that such a measure is valid for Poland, nor anything to suggest that it is not; we rely here entirely on the empirical finding that it covaries with the other indicators of intellectual flexibility, much as it does for the United States.

The rationale for using the interviewer's appraisal of the respondent's intelligence is precisely the same for Poland as for the United States: although such measures are undoubtedly affected by the content of the interview, they do represent the appraisals of competent interviewers after long and demanding interviews in which the respondents were challenged to think about their jobs and their personal situations. Insofar as these judgments covary with other indicators of intellectual flexibility, there is every reason to employ them in both countries.

In using the frequency with which the respondent agreed with the many "agree–disagree" questions in our interview schedule as an indicator of intellectual flexibility, we reason – as we do for the United States – that, since some of the questions in our battery are stated positively and others are stated negatively, a consistently positive (or consistently negative) set of responses indicates that the respondent is not thinking carefully about the questions or his responses. This logic seems justifiable, for Poland as for the United States, even though there is reason to believe that Polish culture puts some pressure on polite Polish respondents to agree with their "guest," the interviewer. This, we believe, may make for cross-national differences in the absolute level of agreement but not in the correlations between agreeing with our set of questions and responses to other indicators of intellectual

[17] To assure cross-national comparability in our *coding* of the Draw-a-Person test, Carmi Schooler – who had supervised the coding of the US materials – recoded the Polish materials.

flexibility. As always, the logic of confirmatory factor analysis is that the ultimate test of an indicator is its covariation with other indicators.

In the Polish study, it proved necessary to modify the wording of the last two indicators of intellectual flexibility, the two cognitive problems. Since there are no hamburger stands in Poland, "kiosk" (news-stand) was substituted for "hamburger stand." Similarly, allowing the "advertisement of goods" on Polish TV was substituted as a debatable issue equivalent to banning "cigarette commercials" on US TV.[18] (Here again we were prescient; commercials are now allowed on Polish TV.) The pilot study, the field work, and confirmatory factor analyses all indicated that Polish men react to the modified questions much as do their US counterparts to the original questions.

These changes in question wording aside, the Polish model provides a cross-sectional analogue to the longitudinal US model, with only one real exception: the correlation between perceptual flexibility and ideational flexibility is much lower than in the US model. But, since our analytic interest is limited to the ideational component of intellectual flexibility, this difference in the measurement models should not impede our ability to make cross-national comparisons. These measurement models provide indices of ideational flexibility valid for cross-national analyses of the relationship between social structure and cognitive performance.

Since our analyses focus exclusively on the ideational component of intellectual flexibility, we shall throughout the remainder of this book use the terms intellectual flexibility and ideational flexibility as equivalents to the more precise but cumbersome term, the ideational component of intellectual flexibility.

Conceptualization and measurement of orientation to self and society

These measures, too, have a long history, only the essentials of which need be summarized here. Originally, they were an extension of Kohn and Schooler's interest in parental values: "[V]alues imply a great deal about conceptions of reality. Thus, if men value self-direction, they will tend to see the world and their own capacities in ways that make self-direction seem possible and efficacious. If they value conformity, they will tend to see the world and their own capacities in ways that make conformity seem necessary and appropriate" (Kohn, 1969, p. 73). In pursuit of this idea, Kohn and Schooler developed a large battery of questions, fifty-seven in all, designed to measure several dimensions of orientation to self and society

[18] The Polish-language version of these questions is given in Slomczynski and Kohn, 1988, pp. 70–2.

that they thought basic to valuation of self-direction or to valuation of conformity to external authority.[19]

These fifty-seven questions presented some of the greatest challenges for translation, for many were written in colloquial English. Again and again, Slomczynski found that some questions could be translated in two or more ways, with different connotations; which did we mean? All too often, a question had more than one connotation in English, too, and we were required to go back to pretest interviews and marginal notes on the actual interview schedules to be certain which connotation was understood by our US respondents. Slomczynski then translated the questions, not literally, but connotatively, to elicit the same meaning. When he returned to Poland, the survey research specialists of the Polish Academy of Sciences subjected the questions to further linguistic analysis, further modification, and intensive pretesting (see chapter 2). From this elaborate process, we have every confidence that the questions have similar meanings to US and Polish respondents.[20]

The issue for analysis, here as always, is how we can best utilize these questions to construct indices that are at once cross-nationally comparable and valid for each country.

In their original analyses of the 1964 US data, Kohn and Schooler used exploratory (orthogonal principal components) factor analysis to develop indices of nine dimensions of orientation (for the complete analysis, see Kohn, 1969, appendix D; or see the summary presentation in Kohn and Schooler, 1969). These dimensions are: authoritarian conservatism, standards of morality, trustfulness, receptivity to change, idea conformity, self-confidence, self-deprecation, anxiety, and fatalism.

In the present analysis, we again utilize exploratory factor analysis, this time for the limited purposes of verifying the existence of the same factors in both the US and Polish data, and of searching for the best indicators of each concept in each country. For comparability, we create cross-sectional models, using the entire sample of 3,101 men in the 1964 US survey, even though our causal analyses will be based on longitudinal models, using the subsample of 687 men in both the original and follow-up US surveys.

We therefore do exploratory factor analyses of the 1964 US data and the 1978 Polish data, extracting from each body of data as few as seven to as

[19] The actual wording of these questions is given in table 4.3. To see where they fit in the sequence of questions asked in the (1964) survey, see Kohn, 1969, appendix C, with appendix D providing a key to which questions are part of this battery. Appendix D also provides a history of the derivation of the items, many of which were taken from or adopted from previous batteries.

[20] For the actual question wording, in Polish, see Slomczynski and Kohn, 1988, appendix D, pp. 213–19.

many as fourteen factors. In such analyses, we find, for example, that authoritarian conservatism consistently emerges as a factor in both sets of data, with many of the same questions correlating substantially with this factor in both countries. Some questions, however, appear to be more strongly related to authoritarian conservatism in the US data and others appear to be more strongly related to authoritarian conservatism in the Polish data. Similarly for other dimensions: the core questions are much the same in both countries, but the strength of relationship of individual questions to any particular dimension differs in the two countries.

We thus face a dilemma: if we use *only* the indicators of a particular concept that prove to be consistently related to that concept for *both* countries, we guarantee cross-national comparability, but at the risk that we may lose important aspects of that concept for one or the other country. If we use *all* the indicators that are pertinent to the concept for *either* country, we guarantee that no nuance of meaning inherent in our data will be lost, but we may be imposing on one or both countries a set of indicators some of which are inappropriate to the particular country. If we use for each country those indicators that in the exploratory factor analyses prove most pertinent to that concept for that country, we achieve a compromise: because some indicators are shared, we do have a guarantee of very considerable, even if not perfect, cross-national comparability; and we also are able to make use of indicators that may have special meaning for a particular country. Since confirmatory factor analysis is based on shared variance, there is little danger that such a procedure will introduce any substantial cross-national dissimilarity, provided that the models of the concept for the two countries share important indicators. We therefore opt for the third approach; but, as will shortly be seen, we also build in some insurance to be certain of cross-national comparability.

Concretely, in constructing the "Polish model" of each concept, we use three criteria to determine whether a question is to be included in the measurement model for that concept. First, the question has to be *consistently* correlated with the factor, regardless of the number of factors extracted in the exploratory factor analyses. Second, the question has to be *substantially* correlated with that factor, no matter how many factors are extracted in the analysis. Third, the question cannot be substantially related to *more than one* factor in any of the solutions.

Employing these criteria, we have identified subsets of questions that measure five of the dimensions of orientation in the Polish data — authoritarian conservatism, anxiety, self-confidence, self-deprecation, and idea-conformity. Each subset of questions has then been used in a confirmatory factor analysis to produce a measurement model of the particular concept (see table 4.3). Since self-confidence and self-deprecation are closely related (being the two components of self-esteem), we produced a combined measurement model of these two concepts.

For two other concepts, standards of morality and trustfulness, there is no clear factor present in the exploratory factor analyses of the Polish data – probably because we started with too small a pool of likely indicators of each concept – but a priori selections of questions yield satisfactory measurement models of these concepts. We use indices based on these models tentatively and cautiously, recognizing that they do not meet our criteria as well as do the others. We shall judge them by the causal analyses to come.

Thus, we have indexed for Poland seven of the nine facets of orientation developed in the original US study (see table 4.3). These are:

1 Authoritarian conservatism: men's definitions of what is socially acceptable – at one extreme, rigid conformance to the dictates of authority and intolerance of nonconformity; at the other extreme, open-mindedness.
2 Standards of morality: a continuum of moral positions, from believing that morality consists of strict adherence to the letter of the law and keeping out of trouble, to defining and maintaining one's own moral standards.
3 Trustfulness: the degree to which men believe that their fellow man can be trusted.
4 Idea-conformity: the degree to which men believe that their ideas mirror those of the social entities to which they belong.
5 Self-confidence: the positive component of self-esteem; the degree to which men are confident of their own capacities.
6 Self-deprecation: the self-critical component of self-esteem; the degree to which men disparage themselves.
7 Anxiety: the intensity of consciously felt psychic discomfort.

All of the Polish measurement models fit the data well. We nevertheless have greater confidence in the indices based on the more rigorous selection procedure – those for authoritarian conservatism, anxiety, self-confidence, self-deprecation, and idea-conformity – and less confidence in the measurement models of standards of morality and trustfulness.

For the US data, not surprisingly, the exploratory factor analyses provide unequivocal subsets of questions for all seven of the concepts that we have been able to measure for Poland. Using these sets of questions, we have developed quite satisfactory measurement models – both cross-sectional models based on the data of the entire 1964 sample and longitudinal models based on the subsample of men included in the follow-up study of 1974 (again see table 4.3).

Table 4.3 *Measurement models of orientations to self and society for US and Polish men (standardized coefficients, all paths statistically significant, $p < 0.05$)*

	Standardized path: concept to indicator					
	Cross-sectional data				Longitudinal data (US men)	
	US men (1964) (N = 3,101)		Polish men (1978) (N = 1,557)		1964 (N=687)	1974 (N=687)
Concepts and indicators[a]	US model	Polish model	Polish model	US model		
Authoritarian conservatism						
The most important thing to teach children is absolute obedience to their parents.	0.65	0.71	0.73	0.66	0.61	0.68
In this complicated world, the only way to know what to do is to rely on leaders and experts. (M)	0.52	0.49	0.53	0.51	0.58	0.54
It's wrong to do things differently from the way our forefathers did. (M)	0.44	0.40	0.40	0.52	0.45	0.52
Any good leader should be strict with people under him in order to gain their respect.	0.46	0.52	0.53	0.54	0.41	0.54
No decent man can respect a woman who has had sex relations before marriage.	0.37	0.34	0.42	0.45	0.43	0.51
Prison is too good for sex criminals; they should be publicly whipped or worse. (M)	0.39	—	—	0.41	0.46	0.50
Young people should not be allowed to read books that are likely to confuse them.	0.44	—	—	0.33	0.50	0.46

There are two kinds of people in the world: the weak and the strong.	0.62	—	—	0.41	0.57	0.62
People who question the old and accepted ways of doing things usually just end up causing trouble. (M)	0.51	—	—	0.21	0.51	0.47
One should always show respect to those in authority.	—	0.31	0.62	—	—	—
You should obey your superiors whether or not you think they're right.	—	0.33	0.50	—	—	—
Do you believe that it's all right to do whatever the law allows, or are there some things that are wrong even if they are legal? (M)	—	0.17	0.42	—	—	—
Correlation: US model/Polish model	0.88		0.90			
χ^2 (d.f.)[b]	11.6 (17)	15.5 (15)	9.4 (13)	21.3 (18)		121.2 (111)
Ratio, χ^2/d.f.	0.68	1.03	0.72	1.18		1.09
Personally responsible standards of morality						
It's all right to do anything you want as long as you stay out of trouble.	−0.62	−0.60	−0.70	−0.61	−0.59	−0.64
If something works, it doesn't matter whether it's right or wrong.	−0.44	−0.44	−0.38	−0.44	−0.44	−0.30
It's all right to get around the law as long as you don't actually break it.	−0.60	−0.62	−0.30	−0.32	−0.58	−0.61
Do you believe that it's all right to do whatever the law allows, or are there some things that are wrong even if they are legal? (M)	−0.36	—	—	−0.31	−0.33	−0.26
Correlation: US model/Polish model	0.96		0.93			
χ^2 (d.f.)	0.0 (1)	d.f. = 0	d.f. = 0	4.4 (1)		12.9 (15)
Ratio, χ^2/d.f.	0.03	d.f. = 0	d.f. = 0	4.40		0.86

Table 4.3 cont.

Concepts and indicators[a]	Standardized path: concept to indicator					
	Cross-sectional data				Longitudinal data (US men)	
	US men (1964) (N = 3,101)		Polish men (1978) (N = 1,557)		1964 (N=687)	1974 (N=687)
	US model	Polish model	Polish model	US model		
Trustfulness						
Do you think that most people can be trusted?	0.75	0.49	0.31	—[c]	0.51	0.53
If you don't watch out, people will take advantage of you.	−0.31	−0.48	−0.33	—[c]	−0.52	−0.61
Human nature is really cooperative. (M)	0.15	0.15	0.31	—[c]	0.20	0.11
When you get right down to it, no one cares much what happens to you. (M)	—	−0.35	−0.35	—[c]	—	—
Correlation: US model/Polish model	0.84					
χ² (d.f.)	d.f. = 0	11.8 (2)	1.0 (1)	—[c]	5.3 (5)	
Ratio, χ²/d.f.	d.f. = 0	5.92	0.99	—[c]	1.06	
Idea conformity[d]						
According to your general impression, how often do your ideas and opinions about important matters differ from those of your relatives? (M)	−0.57		−0.41		−0.69	−0.64
How often do your ideas and opinions differ from those of your friends? (M)	−0.76		−0.55		−0.63	−0.51

Self-esteem, two-concept model and related measures

	C1	C2	C3	C4	C5	C6
How about from those of other people with your religious background?	−0.50	−0.58			−0.50	−0.44
Those of most people in the country? (M)	−0.40	−0.63			−0.68	−0.35
Correlation: US model/Polish model	—	—				
χ^2 (d.f.)	d.f. = 0	d.f. = 0				15.4(13)
Ratio, χ^2/d.f.	d.f. = 0	d.f. = 0				1.19
Self-confidence						
I take a positive attitude toward myself. (M)	0.55	0.41	0.39	0.38	0.60	0.71
I feel that I'm a person of worth, at least on an equal plane with others.	0.50	0.68	0.58	0.57	0.47	0.45
I am able to do most things as well as other people can.	0.36	0.50	0.53	0.55	0.43	0.34
I generally have confidence that when I make plans I will be able to carry them out.	0.58	—	—	0.33	0.54	0.45
Once I have made up my mind, I seldom change it.	—	0.14	0.41	—	—	—
Correlation: US model/Polish model		0.82	0.93			
Self-deprecation						
I feel useless at times.	0.46	0.52	0.53		0.43	0.40
At times I think I am no good at all.	0.57	0.80	0.71		0.49	0.51
There are very few things about which I'm absolutely certain.	0.39	0.26	0.29		0.29	0.43
I wish I could be as happy as others seem to be.	0.45	—	—		0.58	0.59
I wish I could have more respect for myself. (M)	0.60	—	—		0.76	0.71
Correlation: US model/Polish model	0.81	0.99				
χ^2 (d.f.)[c]	16.8(15)	4.8(4)	4.8(8)		6.1(11)	166.8(112)
Ratio, χ^2/d.f.	1.12	1.20	0.60		0.55	1.49
Correlation, self-confidence and self-deprecation	−0.38	−0.31	−0.27		−0.27	−0.28

Table 4.3 cont.

	Standardized path: concept to indicator					
	Cross-sectional data				Longitudinal data (US men)	
	US men (1964) (N = 3,101)		Polish men (1978) (N = 1,557)		1964 (N=687)	1974 (N=687)
Concepts and indicators[a]	US model	Polish model	Polish model	US model		
Anxiety						
How often do you feel that you are about to go to pieces? (M)	0.58	0.61	0.53	0.51	0.55	0.58
How often do you feel downcast and dejected? (M)	0.73	0.54	0.60	0.61	0.68	0.68
How frequently do you find yourself anxious and worrying about something? (M)	0.56	0.56	0.54	0.57	0.49	0.47
How often do you feel uneasy about something without knowing why?	0.55	0.54	0.58	0.57	0.45	0.50
How often do you feel so restless that you cannot sit still?	0.47	0.50	0.48	0.49	0.47	0.39
How often do you find that you can't get rid of some thought or idea that keeps running through your mind? (M)	0.40	0.52	0.47	0.48	0.41	0.44
How often do you feel bored with everything?	0.52	0.48	0.41	0.40	0.58	0.57

How often do you feel powerless to get what you want out of life? (M)	0.48	0.45	0.42	0.41	0.54	0.52
How often do you feel guilty for having done something wrong?	0.34	—	—	0.14	0.36	0.36
How often do you feel that the world just isn't very understandable?	0.46	—	—	0.46	0.48	0.44
How often do you feel there isn't much purpose to being alive?	0.50	—	—	0.37	0.45	0.37
Correlation: US model/Polish model	0.92		0.98			
χ^2 (d.f.)	14.5(19)	12.3(12)	15.8(13)	31.3(28)		213.9(159)
Ratio, χ^2/d.f.	0.76	1.03	1.22	1.12		1.35

[a] A high score on the indicator generally implies agreement or frequent occurrence; where alternatives are posed, the first alternative is scored high. "M" denotes a slight modification of US question wording in the Polish interview; for the Polish-language version of the questions, see Slomczynski and Kohn, 1988, appendix D, pp. 213–19.

[b] Correlations between residuals not shown.

[c] It was not possible to solve the "US model" with the Polish data.

[d] The US and Polish models of idea conformity have the same indicators.

[e] The chi-square of the two-concept model of self-esteem refers to the entire model.

To evaluate whether the Polish and US measurement models are indexing the same concepts, we have developed *two* sets of measurement models: the one described above, which measures each concept with the indicators suggested by the exploratory factor analyses of data for the country in question; and an alternative model, in which we measure each concept with the indicators suggested by the exploratory factor analyses of data for *the other* country. It was not possible to develop a "US model" of trustfulness that fits the Polish data. In every other instance, though, the alternative model fits the data well, albeit not quite as well as does the model derived from exploratory factor analyses of the country's own data. Moreover, the correlations between indices based on the two alternative operationalizations are uniformly high (table 4.3), especially for the indices based on larger numbers of overlapping indicators. The evidence is thus considerable that our measures of orientation to self and others are entirely consonant for the United States and Poland.[21]

Having used the full sample of US men to establish comparability between cross-sectional measurement models for US and Polish men, we shall in our causal analyses of the US data employ indices based on longitudinal measurement models of the subsample of men included in the follow-up study. As table 4.3 demonstrates in every detail, the relationships between concepts and indicators are very much the same for the cross-sectional and longitudinal US measurement models.

Second-order measurement models of orientation: self-directedness of orientation and distress

For detailed analysis, it will be useful to have at our disposal indices of all seven dimensions of orientation. It would give us a better overall grasp of the data, though, if we could deal also with a smaller number of fundamental dimensions that underlie these several facets of orientation.

---

[21] Further evidence of the reliability of the cross-sectional Polish measures of orientation is provided by the follow-up mail questionnaire, described in chapter 2. Four of the principal questions used to measure authoritarian conservatism – a key concept in our analyses – were repeated in the mail questionnaire, sent three months after the interviews. The correlation between measures of authoritarian conservatism based on these four questions as asked in the interview and in the mail questionnaire was 0.89, nearly as high as the correlation between this four-question measure of authoritarian conservatism and the full eight-question measure developed from all pertinent questions in the interview ($r = 0.94$). Moreover, the paths from concept to indicators are nearly identical for the interview and questionnaire responses to these four questions. (The four questions, all employing the agree–disagree format, are: "The most important thing to teach children is absolute obedience to their parents." "One should always show respect to those in authority." "You should obey your superiors whether or not you think they are right." and "Any good leader should be strict with people under him.")

We believe that there are two principal underlying dimensions: self-directedness of orientation versus conformity to external authority, and a sense of distress versus a sense of well-being.

Self-directedness of orientation implies the beliefs that one has the personal capacity to take responsibility for one's actions and that society is so constituted as to make self-direction possible. This, as we have noted, is precisely what Kohn and Schooler intended to measure in developing their set of questions. Admittedly, "self-directedness of orientation" is a cumbersome expression, but we have been unable to find a simpler term that does full justice to the range of phenomena encompassed. Antonovsky's (1979, 1984, 1987) term, "sense of coherence," is a possible alternative, but it does imply a somewhat different emphasis.[22] Another possible alternative is [perceived] "locus of control" (see Rotter, 1966), but we find the meaning of this concept rather elusive (see the discussion by Hoff, 1982). There are also characterizations of personality development that, although not entirely equivalent to our conceptualization, are in some respects analogous. The "stage" theories of moral development of Piaget (n. d.), Kohlberg (1976; Kohlberg and Gilligan, 1972), and Habermas (1979) certainly have much in common with what we mean by conformity to external authority versus self-directedness, even though ours is decidedly not a stage theory. Pertinent, too, is Bernstein's (1971, 1973) sociolinguistic distinction between the "restricted code" of the working class and the "elaborated code" of the middle class.

The hypothesis that distress versus a sense of well-being constitutes another underlying dimension of orientation to self and society also reflects Kohn and Schooler's original intent, in striving to measure not only people's sense of personal efficacy, but also their feelings of psychic comfort or pain. Self-directedness and conformity may each have distinct psychic costs and rewards.

Self-directedness of orientation and distress, then, are meant to be very general dimensions of orientation to self and society. Our measures of these concepts are based on "second-order" confirmatory factor analyses[23] testing our belief that these two dimensions underlie the several facets of

[22] Antonovsky (1979, p. 123) defines sense of coherence as "a global orientation that expresses the extent to which one has a pervasive, enduring though dynamic feeling of confidence that one's internal and external environments are predictable and that there is a high probability that things will work out as well as can reasonably be expected."

[23] We put quotation marks around "second-order" to indicate that this is not a true second-order measurement model, based on all fifty-seven indicators of self-conception and social orientation, but an approximation thereto, in which we use Bartlett-type factor scores of the first-order factors as the input to a confirmatory factor analysis. We use this procedure because it is much simpler to do where there is so large a number of indicators as we deal with here.

orientation to self and others that we have indexed in our research. The factor-analytic model for the United States (see the upper half of figure 4.3) certainly confirms these expectations.

Self-directedness is reflected in not having authoritarian conservative beliefs, in having personally responsible standards of morality, in being trustful of others, in not being self-deprecatory, in not being conformist in one's ideas, and in not being fatalistic – all of which is certainly in accord with our premises. It is hardly surprising that self-directedness of orientation is an underlying dimension of orientation; our analysis merely shows that Kohn and Schooler succeeded in measuring what they set out to measure. The importance of this result is not substantive but methodological: we have here the basis for a valid index of this theoretically important underlying dimension of orientation to self and others.

Distress is reflected in anxiety, self-deprecation, lack of self-confidence, nonconformity in one's ideas, and distrust – which certainly appears to be valid. Here, too, it is useful to have confirmation that the questions do measure what they were intended to measure, and to have an index that we can employ in our causal analyses.

The Polish model (see the lower half of figure 4.3) is entirely consonant with the US model in what it tells us about the relationships between the first-order factors and the underlying second-order factors.[24] The two models differ decidedly, though, in what they tell us about the relationship between self-directedness of orientation and distress. For US men, this relationship is negative; for Polish men, the relationship is positive. There appears, then, to be a fundamental difference: US men who are self-directed in their orientations tend also to have a sense of personal well-being; Polish men who are self-directed in their orientations tend also to have a sense of personal distress.[25] This difference will have important implications for our

[24] We could not develop an adequate measure of fatalism for Poland – probably because we have too few indicators. This means that the second-order models for the US and Poland differ in that fatalism is an indicator of self-directedness of orientation for the United States but is absent from the Polish model. We could of course re-estimate the US model leaving fatalism out of the model, but that would be carrying the quest for cross-national comparability to a mechanical extreme: fatalism enters the US model only insofar as it covaries with other indicators of self-directedness of orientation. Removing it from the model would have no substantive effect.

[25] This difference in the correlations of self-directedness of orientation and distress is not an artifact of how we constructed the second-order measurement models. Instead, it goes back to the zero-order correlations of the first-order factors and, beyond that, to the zero-order correlations of the indicators of the first-order factors. Thus, for example, the correlations between indicators of authoritarian conservatism and indicators of anxiety for US men are almost all positive and many of them are of at least moderate magnitude, while for Poland the corresponding correlations are almost all negative and many of them are of at least moderate magnitude; the exceptions in both countries are of trivial magnitude. We do find, though, that

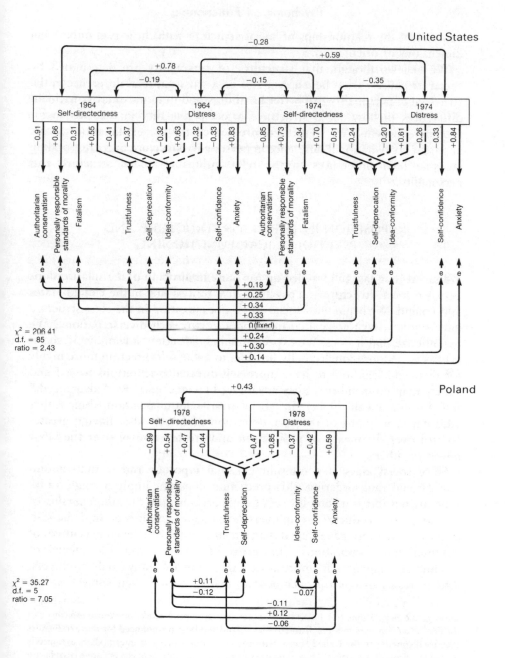

Figure 4.3 *"Second-order" measurement models of orientations to self and society. All non-zero parameters shown are statistically significant, $p \leq 0.05$.*

analyses of the relationships of social structure with these two underlying dimensions of orientation.

We believe, though, that structures of personality are determined by social structures; what here appears to be a cross-national difference in the structure of personality can better be understood in terms of cross-national differences in how social structures affect personality in the two socio-economic systems. We shall therefore search for the explanation of this apparent cross-national difference in personality structure in corresponding cross-national differences in the relationships of social structure and personality.

POSITION IN THE CLASS STRUCTURE AND PSYCHOLOGICAL FUNCTIONING

We are at long last fully tooled up for our examination of the relationships between social structure and psychological functioning in the United States and Poland. We begin with social class: does position in the class structure have similar psychological consequences in two such diverse nations? We hypothesize that it does. We expect members of more "advantaged" social classes to be more intellectually flexible, to value self-direction more highly for their children, and to have more self-directed orientations to self and society than do members of less advantaged social classes. By "advantaged," we do *not* mean higher in social-stratification position, but rather advantaged in terms of the very definition of social class: having greater control over the means of production and greater control over the labor power of others.

Since social class is a multidimensional typology rather than a uni-dimensional rank-ordering, this prediction does not imply a single rank-ordering but rather a complex set of comparisons. In terms of *ownership* of the means of production, employers (even small employers) and the self-employed are more advantaged than are any employees (even executives of multinational corporations). In terms of *control* over the means of production, managers are more advantaged than are many small employers. And in terms of *control over people*, managers and even some first-line

---

the negative correlations (for Poland) are somewhat more pronounced for those indicators of the first-order concepts that are distinctive to Poland and least pronounced for those indicators that are distinctive to the United States, with the correlations being of intermediate magnitude for the "common" indicators. Thus, it is possible that the magnitude of the negative correlation between self-directedness of orientation and distress would be somewhat lower if we were to base the second-order confirmatory factor analysis on the "US indicators" of the first-order concepts, but even then the correlation would be negative.

supervisors are clearly more advantaged than are small employers and the self-employed. We would expect employers and managers, who generally have greatest control over the means of production and the labor power of others, to value self-direction most highly and manual workers, who have least control over the means of production and the labor power of others, to value self-direction least highly. Similarly, we would expect employers and managers to have the most self-directed orientations and to be the most intellectually flexible of all the social classes; manual workers will be at the other extreme. But, since the other social classes are advantaged in some respects and disadvantaged in others, we have no a priori basis for predicting their relative ranking with respect to their values, orientations, or intellectual functioning. Moreover, we have no basis for expecting either cross-national similarity or dissimilarity in the relationships between social class and the sense of well-being or distress.

Our belief that position in the class structure has a generally similar psychological effect in the United States and Poland in no way denies that class structure differs in different economic and political systems. Nor do we dispute that the contemporary class structure of each country has been shaped by the history and culture of that country. Quite the contrary. None the less, we hypothesize that the psychological effects of social class, and the explanation of these effects, will be generally similar in all industrial societies, both capitalist and socialist.

We deal first with the relationships of social-class position with those facets of psychological functioning for which we have a priori expectations: parental valuation of self-direction, intellectual flexibility, and self-directedness of orientation. As hypothesized, in both countries these relationships are meaningful and the correlations (etas) are substantial (see table 4.4).

Consider first the US findings. The correlation (eta) between social-class position and parental valuation of self-direction was 0.38 in 1964, when the children were 3–15 years old, and increased to 0.47 ten years later, when the children were 13–25 years old. The pattern is the same at the two times, with managers and employers valuing self-direction most highly, followed by nonmanual workers, first-line supervisors and the self-employed, and finally – the most decidedly conformist in their values – manual workers. The correlation (eta) between social-class position and intellectual flexibility is even higher, at 0.53 in 1964 and 0.58 in 1974, with the rank-order of social classes quite similar to that for parental valuation of self-direction.

The correlation (eta) between social-class position and self-directedness of orientation is 0.44 in 1964 and 0.43 in 1974, with employers ranking highest, managers and nonmanual workers next, and manual workers lowest. The patterns are quite similar for those first-order dimensions of orientation that reflect self-directedness of orientation, particularly those

Table 4.4 Relationships of men's social-class positions with their values, intellectual flexibility, and orientations to self and society

	Parental valuation of self-direction			Intellectual flexibility		Second-order dimensions of orientation			
						Self-directedness of orientation		Distress	
	N (Fathers)	Mean[a]	N (All men)	Mean[a]		Mean[a]		Mean[a]	
A US men (1964)									
	(Children aged 3–15)								
Employers	(15)	0.57	(18)	0.37		0.62		−0.29	
Self-employed	(45)	−0.01	(73)	0.06		0.05		0.03	
Managers	(26)	0.60	(37)	0.69		0.60		0.03	
First-line supervisors	(77)	0.01	(120)	0.13		0.13		−0.15	
Nonmanual workers	(66)	0.26	(138)	0.53		0.43		−0.06	
Manual workers	(160)	−0.26	(301)	−0.42		−0.40		0.09	
Correlation (eta)[b] =		0.38*		0.53*		0.44*		0.13*	
Correlation, combining manual and nonmanual workers =		0.27*		0.26*		0.25*		0.11	

First-order dimensions of orientation to self and society

	Authoritarian conservatism	Standards of morality	Trustfulness	Idea-conformity	Self-confidence	Self-deprecation	Anxiety
				Means[a]			
Employers	-0.64	0.15	-0.03	-0.21	0.28	-0.51	-0.27
Self-employed	-0.02	0.08	0.05	-0.16	-0.01	0.04	-0.02
Managers	-0.68	0.20	0.27	-0.28	0.18	-0.08	-0.07
First-line supervisors	-0.13	0.08	0.06	0.00	0.15	-0.16	-0.12
Nonmanual workers	-0.43	0.23	0.33	-0.14	0.03	-0.14	-0.09
Manual workers	0.38	-0.20	-0.22	0.15	-0.11	0.16	0.12
Correlation (*eta*)[b] =	0.43*	0.23*	0.33*	0.18*	0.15*	0.20*	0.13*
Correlation, combining manual and nonmanual workers =	0.25*	0.11	0.12*	0.12*	0.14*	0.15*	0.09

Table 4.4 cont.

	Parental valuation of self-direction		N (All men)	Intellectual flexibility	Second-order dimensions of orientation	
					Self-directedness of orientation	Distress
	N (Fathers)	Mean[a]		Mean[a]	Mean[a]	Mean[a]
B US men (1974)						
	(Children aged 13–25)					
Employers	(20)	0.39	(32)	0.58	0.52	−0.20
Self-employed	(47)	0.06	(82)	0.01	−0.04	−0.08
Managers	(40)	0.42	(65)	0.59	0.41	−0.16
First-line supervisors	(72)	0.14	(122)	0.23	0.12	−0.16
Nonmanual workers	(60)	0.24	(106)	0.44	0.41	0.04
Manual workers	(128)	−0.41	(219)	−0.61	−0.45	0.18
Correlation (eta)[b] =	0.47*			0.58*	0.43*	0.18*
Correlation, combining manual and nonmanual workers =	0.34*			0.38*	0.26*	0.17*

First-order dimensions of orientation to self and society

	Authoritarian conservatism	Standards of morality	Trustfulness	Idea-conformity	Self-confidence	Self-deprecation	Anxiety
				Means[a]			
Employers	-0.44	0.09	0.26	-0.07	0.18	-0.54	-0.04
Self-employed	0.13	0.01	0.03	-0.10	-0.05	-0.11	-0.06
Managers	-0.39	0.25	0.34	-0.02	0.16	-0.27	-0.14
First-line supervisors	-0.19	0.01	0.07	0.03	0.01	-0.09	-0.21
Nonmanual workers	-0.35	0.39	0.27	-0.13	0.13	-0.10	-0.02
Manual workers	0.41	-0.28	-0.32	0.10	-0.13	0.30	0.20
Correlations (eta)[b] =	0.38*	0.32*	0.36*	0.12*	0.15*	0.29*	0.18*
Correlation, combining manual and nonmanual workers =	0.25*	0.12*	0.22*	0.06	0.09	0.24*	0.16*

Table 4.4 cont.

| | Parental valuation of self-direction | | N (All men) | Intellectual flexibility | Second-order dimensions of orientation | |
| | | | | | Self-directedness of orientation | Distress |
	N (Fathers)	Mean[a]		Mean[a]	Mean[a]	Mean[a]
C Polish men (1978)						
	(Children aged 3–15)					
Managers	(29)	0.45	(62)	0.92	0.77	0.10
First-line supervisors	(136)	0.26	(302)	0.41	0.30	0.05
Nonmanual workers	(108)	0.24	(266)	0.56	0.50	0.19
Production workers	(219)	−0.22	(526)	−0.36	−0.28	−0.09
Nonproduction workers	(138)	−0.19	(327)	−0.41	−0.35	−0.04
Self-employed	(30)	−0.01	(73)	−0.05	−0.14	−0.17
Correlation (eta)[b] =		0.36*		0.55*	0.42*	0.14*
Correlation, combining manual and nonmanual workers =		0.27*		0.36*	0.26*	0.06

First-order dimensions of orientation of self and society

	Authoritarian conservatism	Standards of morality	Trustfulness	Idea-conformity	Self-confidence	Self-deprecation	Anxiety
				Means[a]			
Managers	-0.73	0.66	0.61	-0.13	-0.21	-0.26	0.03
First-line supervisors	-0.27	0.25	0.16	-0.05	0.03	-0.09	0.07
Nonmanual workers	-0.48	0.39	0.19	-0.13	-0.18	-0.05	0.04
Production workers	0.27	-0.21	-0.12	0.09	0.08	0.06	-0.05
Nonproduction workers	0.32	-0.26	-0.21	0.04	-0.01	0.10	-0.02
Self-employed	0.13	-0.32	-0.05	-0.03	0.22	-0.10	0.03
Correlation (*eta*)[b] =	0.40*	0.39*	0.34*	0.11*	0.14*	0.12*	0.06
Correlation, combining manual and nonmanual workers =	0.24*	0.26*	0.26*	0.05	0.09*	0.10*	0.04

[a] Expressed as standardized differences from grand mean for the particular country at the particular time.
[b] Corrected for unreliability of measurement.
* Statistically significant, p<0.05.

that reflect self-directedness of orientation most closely – authoritarian conservatism, standards of morality, and trustfulness. All three are at least moderately correlated with class, with employers, managers, and nonmanual workers being less authoritarian, having more personally responsible standards of morality, and being more trustful; and manual workers evidencing a more conformist orientation.

Aside from there being no "employer" class in Poland at the time of the survey, the findings for Poland are very similar to those for the United States. Even the magnitudes of correlation are quite similar for socialist Poland and the capitalist United States. The relative positions of the several classes, too, are remarkably consistent with those for the United States, despite the very real differences in the circumstances of the classes in the two countries. Consider, for example, parental valuation of self-direction: managers value self-direction most highly, and by a wide margin; then follow first-line supervisors and nonmanual workers; the self-employed are in the middle; at the other extreme, valuing conformity to external authority most highly, are production workers and nonproduction workers, who are virtually identical in their values. This pattern is essentially repeated for intellectual flexibility, for self-directedness of orientation, and for those first-order dimensions of orientation that reflect self-directedness of orientation most closely – authoritarian conservatism, standards of morality, and trustfulness. The more advantaged social classes have more self-directed values and orientations, and are intellectually more flexible, than are disadvantaged social classes.

Since in both countries there are sizeable differences between nonmanual and manual workers, one must wonder whether our building this distinction into the index of social class has produced arguably exaggerated correlations between social class and these facets of psychological functioning. The question is readily answered: if we combine nonmanual and manual workers into a single category – the proletariat – the correlations between social class and these facets of psychological functioning are reduced in magnitude but remain substantial (again, see table 4.4). We have thus confirmed that in both countries members of more advantaged social classes are more intellectually flexible, value self-direction for their children more highly, and have more self-directed orientations to self and society, then do members of less advantaged social classes. Moreover, these findings are not simply an artifact of our building the distinction between manual and nonmanual work into the class schema.

Distress, though, is a striking exception to this otherwise cross-nationally consistent pattern. For the United States, the correlation (*eta*) between social class and distress, at 0.13 in 1964 and 0.18 in 1974, is much smaller than that between social class and other major dimensions of psychological functioning, but the pattern parallels that for the other dimensions: employers (followed by managers and first-line supervisors) are at one extreme – the least distressed; manual workers are at the other extreme – the most distressed. Much the same pattern is shown for the first-order dimensions of orientation that reflect distress – anxiety, self-deprecation, lack of self-confidence, nonconformity in one's ideas, and distrust.

The disadvantaged situation of manual workers in the United States is dramatically illustrated by the contrast between how they rank on the two underlying dimensions of orientation: they rank lowest of all social classes in self-directedness of orientation, highest of all social classes in distress.

The relationship of social class to distresss and to the first-order dimensions of orientation that reflect distress is decidedly different in Poland. The cross-national difference does not lie in the magnitudes of correlation: in both countries, the correlations (*etas*) of social class with distress and with the first-order dimensions of orientation that reflect distress are only small-to-moderate. The cross-national difference lies, instead, in the relative positions of the classes with respect to distress. In Poland, it is not the *manual* workers, but the *nonmanual* workers who are most distressed, with managers being next most distressed of all the social classes. Production workers and nonproduction workers are *less* distressed than are members of any other social class except the self-employed.

The relationships between social class and the first-order dimensions of orientation that reflect distress are weak and the patterns of relationship vary, but the relationships between social class and some of these dimensions – notably, (lack of) self-confidence – do seem to parallel that for distress. If our information were limited to these first-order dimensions, we would not be able to draw any firm conclusions as to whether the relationships of class to these facets of orientation are cross-nationally consistent or inconsistent, only that they are weak.

For the second-order dimension, though, the cross-national contrast is much sharper: there is a nearly complete reversal in the relationship of social class with distress for the two countries, with US managers being among the least distressed of all social classes, Polish managers being among the most distressed; and with US manual workers being the most distressed of all social classes, Polish manual workers being among the least distressed. We shall return repeatedly to these perplexing findings.

SOCIAL STRATIFICATION AND PSYCHOLOGICAL FUNCTIONING

The relationships of social-stratification position to parental values, to intellectual flexibility, and to self-directedness of orientation, like those for social class, are markedly similar in Poland and the United States (see table 4.5). For example, the correlation between social-stratification position and fathers' valuation of self-direction for their children is strongly positive in both countries: in both countries, higher stratification position is associated with valuing self-direction, lower stratification position with valuing conformity to external authority.

The correlations of social-stratification position with intellectual flexibility, with self-directedness of orientation, and with some of the component (first-order) facets of orientation that reflect self-directedness of orientation most closely – authoritarian conservatism, standards of morality, and trustfulness – are also very similar in the two countries. Holding a higher stratification position is consistently associated with valuing self-direction for one's children, being intellectually flexible, and being self-directed in one's orientations to self and society. The magnitudes of correlation would appear to be somewhat higher for the United States than for Poland, but this is almost entirely a consequence of the US measurement models being longitudinal; comparisons using cross-sectional measurement models for both countries yield nearly identical magnitudes of correlation (see Slomczynski et al., 1981).

Even analyses disaggregating the effects of social-stratification position into those for educational attainment, occupational status, and income, are quite consistent for the two countries. This is even more apparent when we disaggregate social-stratification position into only two components – educational attainment and occupational position (a composite of occupational status and job income) – thereby reducing collinearity. Either way, the analyses are consistent in showing that educational attainment is by far the strongest component of social stratification in terms of effect on these facets of psychological functioning. We hasten to add, though, that these findings do *not* mean that "education" is more important for psychological functioning than is "occupation." Occupational *status* is but one dimension of occupation; and, as our analyses will show, a large part of the reason why education affects psychological functioning is because education is determinative of job conditions, which in turn have a strong effect on psychological functioning.[26]

[26] Our analyses of the psychological effects of social stratification focus exclusively on what has been termed the "vertical" dimension of status, as indexed by the covariation of

Distress As we found for social class, the relationships between social-stratification position and distress are decidedly different in the two countries. In neither country is the correlation between social stratification and distress of any great magnitude, but the correlations are of opposite sign: for the United States, −0.09 in 1964, −0.18 in 1974; for Poland, +0.15. In the United States, men of higher position have a somewhat greater sense of well-being; in Poland, men of higher stratification position are more likely to be distressed. Similarly for some of the component (first-order) dimensions of orientation: in the United States, higher stratification position is associated with greater self-confidence (r's = +0.25 and +0.22), but in Poland the opposite is true (r = −0.12). Similarly, albeit less strikingly, for anxiety: in the United States, higher position is associated with somewhat less anxiety (r's = −0.12 and −0.21), but in Poland higher position is associated with slightly greater anxiety (r = +0.08). There is also a small difference between the two countries with respect to self-deprecation: although higher position is associated with less self-deprecation in both countries, the relationship is stronger in the United States (r = −0.24 in 1964 and −0.40 in 1974) than in Poland (r = −0.12).

The cross-national differences in the relationships of class and stratification with distress, it will be seen, are the crucial cross-national differences that our investigations have discovered.

THE INDEPENDENT EFFECTS OF SOCIAL CLASS AND SOCIAL STRATIFICATION

Might the relationships between social class and psychological functioning result from the close relationship between social class and social stratification? Conversely, might the relationships between social stratification and psychological functioning result from that same close relationship? To test

---

educational attainment, occupation status, and job income. Utilizing Hope's (1975) interpretation of Lenski's (1954) original conceptualization, Slomczynski (1989) has also assessed the psychological effects of status inconsistency. He defines status inconsistency as a "non-vertical" dimension of social stratification, orthogonal to the vertical dimension. For both the United States and Poland, this non-vertical dimension of social stratification contrasts people whose incomes are lower than is typical for those of their educational attainment and occupational status (the "under-rewarded") with those whose incomes are higher than is typical for those of their educational attainment and occupational status (the "over-rewarded"). Slomczynski finds that status inconsistency has only modest psychological effects, above and beyond those of the "vertical" dimension of social stratification, but that these effects are statistically significant and they add meaningfully to our understanding of the psychological effects of social stratification: in both the United States and Poland, the under-rewarded are more intellectually flexible and less authoritarian conservative than are the over-rewarded.

Table 4.5 Relationships of men's social-stratification positions with their values, intellectual flexibility, and orientations to self and society

	Zero-order correlation, social stratification	Regression coefficients			Regression coefficients	
		Education	Occupational status	Income	Education	Occupational position
A US men (1964)						
Values						
Parental valuation of self-direction	0.56*	0.41*	0.14*	0.06	0.37*	0.21*
Intellectual flexibility	0.87*	0.61*	0.22*	0.07*	0.54*	0.35*
Orientations to self and society						
Second-order dimensions						
Self-directedness	0.68*	0.53*	0.09*	0.12*	0.48*	0.21*
Distress	-0.09*	0.08	-0.14*	-0.06	0.10	-0.19*
First-order dimensions						
Authoritarian conservatism	-0.65*	-0.51*	-0.09*	-0.09*	-0.46*	-0.20*
Standards of morality	0.41*	0.24*	0.10	0.16*	0.19*	0.24*
Trustfulness	0.49*	0.41*	0.03	0.13*	0.37*	0.14*
Idea-conformity	-0.30*	-0.32*	0.02	-0.01	-0.31*	0.00
Self-confidence	0.25*	0.19*	-0.03	0.14*	0.16*	0.08
Self-deprecation	-0.24*	-0.18*	-0.02	-0.08	-0.16*	-0.08
Anxiety	-0.12*	0.09	-0.20*	-0.03	0.12*	-0.24*
B US men (1974)						
Values						
Parental valuation of self-direction	0.66*	0.55*	0.09*	0.07	0.52*	0.17*
Intellectual flexibility	0.85*	0.55*	0.25*	0.11*	0.48*	0.40*

Nov. 1996 - Cont. Soc.

Strozier 305 C761

Orientations to self and society						
Second-order dimensions						
Self-directedness	0.70*	0.52*	0.13*	0.11*	0.47*	0.25*
Distress	−0.18*	0.00	−0.17*	−0.03	0.03	−0.22*
First-order dimensions						
Authoritarian conservatism	−0.64*	−0.54*	−0.08	−0.07*	−0.49*	−0.17*
Standards of morality	0.47*	0.23*	0.19*	0.08*	0.19*	0.28*
Trustfulness	0.56*	0.40*	0.10*	0.10*	0.35*	0.22*
Idea-conformity	−0.18*	−0.17*	0.02	−0.03	−0.17*	0.00
Self-confidence	0.22*	0.17*	−0.01	0.10*	0.16*	0.06
Self-deprecation	−0.40*	−0.20*	−0.17*	−0.08	−0.16*	−0.26*
Anxiety	−0.21*	−0.03	−0.18*	0.00	−0.01	−0.20*
C Polish men (1978)						
Values						
Parental valuation of self-direction	0.44*	0.45*	0.02	0.06	0.44*	0.06
Intellectual flexibility	0.69*	0.62*	0.14*	0.06*	0.60*	0.19*
Orientations to self and society						
Second-order dimensions						
Self-directedness	0.50*	0.52*	0.04	0.04	0.51*	0.06
Distress	0.15*	0.28*	−0.08*	−0.02	0.29*	−0.10*
First-order dimensions						
Authoritarian conservatism	−0.48*	−0.52*	−0.02	−0.04	−0.51*	−0.05
Standards of morality	0.43*	0.28*	0.19*	−0.01	0.25*	0.21*
Trustfulness	0.42*	0.18*	0.23*	0.07*	0.15*	0.30*
Idea-conformity	−0.12*	−0.18*	0.06	−0.08*	−0.19*	0.03
Self-confidence	−0.12*	−0.08*	−0.05	0.01	−0.07	−0.05
Self-deprecation	−0.12*	0.01	−0.10*	−0.06*	0.02	−0.14*
Anxiety	0.08*	0.17*	−0.07	0.01	0.18*	−0.08*

Note: The N for US men is 687, except for parental values, where it is 339. The N for Polish men is 1,557, except for parental values, where it is 660.
* Statistically significant, $p<0.05$.

these possibilities, we re-examine the correlations of social class with psychological functioning, statistically controlling social stratification, and the correlations of social stratification with psychological functioning, statistically controlling social class.

Our concern here is not with testing the theoretical claims of either the proponents of class or the proponents of stratification, but only with ensuring that what we conclude about the psychological effects of social class is not merely a reflection of the psychological effects of social stratification, and that what we conclude about the psychological effects of social stratification is not merely a reflection of the psychological effects of social class. This heuristic exercise in no way tests the validity of either concept. Nor does it tell us which is the more important concept. Not only do we not deal with that facet of psychological functioning of greatest concern to class theorists – class consciousness (see Vallas, 1987) – but we in no way evaluate the long-term historical consequences of either class structure or the stratification order.

What this analysis does tell us – and this is precisely why we engage in such an exercise – is whether social class has an *independent* effect on psychological functioning, even if we arbitrarily assign all joint variance to social stratification, and whether social stratification has an *independent* effect on psychological functioning, even if we arbitrarily assign all joint variance to social class.

We find (see table 4.6) that the correlations of social stratification with parental valuation of self-direction, intellectual flexibility, self-directedness of orientation, and the first-order components of self-directedness of orientation are somewhat reduced when social class is statistically controlled, but that these correlations remain statistically significant, cross-nationally consistent, and substantial in magnitude.[27] The correlations of social stratification with distress and with the first-order dimensions that reflect distress, of course, were neither substantial nor cross-nationally consistent even before social class was statistically controlled; controlling social class

[27] Social stratification being treated as an interval scale, we express its correlations with psychological phenomena as Pearsonian correlations and employ partial-correlational analysis to statistically control social class, using dummy variables for all but one of the class categories. Social class being a nominal variable, we use multiple regression analysis (again using dummy variables for all but one of the class categories) to compute the correlations (*etas*) of social class with psychological phenomena and to compute the (multiple-) partial correlations of social class with psychological phenomena, statistically controlling social stratification. Since the *signs* of the correlations for social stratification are meaningful, we show negative correlations (and partial correlations) by a bracketed minus sign [−], the bracket used as a cautionary, lest an unwary reader not realize that the corresponding correlations (*etas*) for social class can be neither positive nor negative.

does not change that situation. Thus, the effects of social stratification on psychological functioning cannot by any stretch of imagination be attributed to social class.

The correlations of social class with parental valuation of self-direction, intellectual flexibility, self-directedness of orientation, and the first-order dimensions of self-directedness of orientation – which were smaller than those for social stratification to begin with – are markedly reduced when social stratification is statistically controlled. Consonant with the correlation between social class and social stratification being higher for Poland than for the United States, the effect of controlling social stratification may be somewhat greater for Poland than for the United States. In any case, there is no gainsaying that, for both countries, the correlations between social class and these facets of psychological functioning are decidedly reduced when social stratification is statistically controlled. Nevertheless, most of these (multiple–partial) correlations remain statistically significant and non-trivial in magnitude. (For distress and its first-order components, of course, the relationships with social class were small to begin with.) At minimum, social class has some, in a few instances substantial, psychological effect, entirely above and beyond that of social stratification.

We thought that the reason why controlling social stratification has so much more dramatic an effect on the magnitudes of the correlations between social class and psychological functioning than controlling social class has on the magnitudes of the correlations between social stratification and psychological functioning might be because education is one of the components of social stratification, but not of social class. We know from table 4.5 that education accounts for a good share of the effects of social stratification; more important still, as we shall see in later chapters, education is a major determinant of job conditions, which in turn greatly affect psychological functioning. Might it be, then, that a principal reason why controlling social stratification greatly reduces the correlations of social class with psychological functioning is because social stratification includes education as one of its components?

To test this hypothesis, we re-did the analyses, substituting occupational position (a composite of occupational status and job income) for social stratification. The hypothesis was not supported (table not shown). The general conclusions are not much changed when we substitute occupational position for social stratification. It is not that education, *per se*, is so potent, but that the organization of occupations into the social stratification hierarchy is more closely related to psychological functioning than is the organization of occupations into social-class groupings. Perhaps, when we consider the heterogeneity of some of the social classes – nonmanual

Table 4.6 (Multiple-) partial correlations of social stratification and of social class with psychological functioning

	Zero-order correlation with social stratification	Partial correlation, controlling social class[a]	Multiple-correlation with social class[a]	Multiple-partial correlation, controlling social stratification
A US men (1964)				
Values				
Parental valuation of self-direction	0.56*	0.50*	0.38*	0.22*
Intellectual Flexibility	0.87*	0.84*	0.53*	0.35*
Orientations to self and society				
Second-order dimensions				
Self-directedness of orientation	0.68*	0.59*	0.44*	0.13*
Distress	[−]0.09*	[−]0.04	0.13*	0.10*
First-order dimensions				
Authoritarian conservatism	[−]0.65*	[−]0.55*	0.43*	0.12*
Standards of morality	0.41*	0.36*	0.23*	0.12*
Trustfulness	0.49*	0.41*	0.33*	0.14*
Idea-conformity	[−]0.30*	[−]0.26*	0.18*	0.09*
Self-confidence	0.25*	0.24*	0.15*	0.13*
Self-deprecation	[−]0.24*	[−]0.18*	0.20*	0.11*
Anxiety	[−]0.11*	[−]0.05	0.13*	0.07
B US men (1974)				
Values				
Parental valuation of self-direction	0.66*	0.54*	0.47*	0.14*
Intellectual flexibility	0.85*	0.77*	0.58*	0.23*
Orientations to self and society				
Second-order dimensions				
Self-directedness of orientation	0.70*	0.63*	0.43*	0.19*
Distress	[−]0.18*	[−]0.13*	0.18*	0.12*

First-order dimensions

Authoritarian conservatism	[−]0.64*	[−]0.59*	0.38*	0.24*
Standards of morality	0.47*	0.38*	0.32*	0.11*
Trustfulness	0.56*	0.46*	0.36*	0.08*
Idea-conformity	[−]0.18*	[−]0.15*	0.12	0.07
Self-confidence	0.22*	0.17*	0.15*	0.05
Self-deprecation	[−]0.40*	[−]0.32*	0.29*	0.14*
Anxiety	[−]0.21*	[−]0.16*	0.18*	0.12*

C Polish men (1978)

Values

Parental valuation of self-direction	0.44*	0.28*	0.36*	0.09*
Intellectual flexibility	0.69*	0.50*	0.55*	0.10*

Orientations to self and society

Second-order dimensions

Self-directedness of orientation	0.50*	0.31*	0.42*	0.08*
Distress	0.15*	0.10*	0.14*	0.09*

First-order dimensions

Authoritarian conservatism	[−]0.48*	[−]0.30*	0.40*	0.08*
Standards of morality	0.43*	0.23*	0.39*	0.14*
Trustfulness	0.42*	0.28*	0.34*	0.08*
Idea-conformity	[−]0.12*	[−]0.08*	0.11*	0.04
Self-confidence	[−]0.12*	[−]0.07*	0.14*	0.11*
Self-deprecation	[−]0.12*	[−]0.05*	0.12*	0.05*
Anxiety	0.08*	0.06*	0.06	0.04

Note: Correlations of social stratification with psychological functioning are positive or negative, but *multiple* correlations of class dummies with psychological functioning cannot have a sign.

a Using dummy variables for all but one class category.

* Statistically significant, p<0.05.

workers, first-line supervisors, and the self-employed, to take some prime examples – this should not be surprising.

Still, despite social stratification having a decidedly greater independent effect on psychological functioning than does social class, there is not only theoretical, but also empirical, utility in employing both concepts in our continuing analyses. As we shall see, having both concepts at our disposal will be particularly useful in trying to interpret the cross-nationally inconsistent relationships of social structure with distress.

CONCLUSION

Much of this chapter has been devoted to developing indices of psychological functioning suitable for cross-national comparison. We developed such indices for parental valuation of self-direction, intellectual flexibility, several first-order dimensions of orientation to self and society, and two fundamental underlying dimensions of orientation: self-directedness of orientation and distress.

Using those indices, we have established that both social class and social stratification have cross-nationally consistent effects on most dimensions of psychological functioning that we have examined. In both the capitalist United States and socialist Poland, a more advantaged position in the class structure, and a higher position in the social-stratification order, result in valuing self-direction more highly, in greater intellectual flexibility, and in a more self-directed orientation. Moreover, even though class and stratification are substantially correlated with each other, each has a significant effect on these dimensions of psychological functioning, independent of the other. We have not yet empirically addressed the question, why class and stratification have such effects. That is the subject of the next chapter.

We have also found one major cross-national difference: in the effects of class and stratification on another major dimension of orientation, distress. In the United States, a more advantaged class position and a higher position in the stratification order result in a greater sense of well-being; in Poland, quite the reverse. Explicating and explaining this difference will be a major concern, not only of the next chapter, but of the entire book.

5

Occupational Self-direction as a Crucial Explanatory Link between Social Structure and Personality

In this chapter, we attempt to answer the question, *why* do men's positions in the class structure and in the hierarchical organization of the society affect their values, their intellectual functioning, and their orientation to self and others? We advance the same hypothesis for both class and stratification: that position in the social structure – whether the class structure or the stratification order – affects psychological functioning primarily because such position greatly affects one's opportunities to be self-directed in one's work.

This interpretation of the relationships of social class and social stratification with men's values, intellectual flexibility, and self-directedness of orientation has its origins in Kohn's speculations of a quarter-century ago, when he proposed that, among the "different conditions of life" that affect people's aspirations, hopes, fears, and conceptions of reality, differences in occupational conditions may be of particular importance. At that time, he was trying to explain why middle-class parents are more likely to value self-direction for their children; working-class parents, conformity to external authority:

That middle-class parents are more likely to espouse some values, and working-class parents other values, must be a function of differences in their conditions of life. . . . The logical place to begin is with occupational differences, for these are certainly pre-eminently important, not only in defining social classes in urban, industrialized society, but also in determining much else about people's life conditions. There are at least three respects in which middle-class occupations typically differ from working-class occupations, above and beyond their obvious status-linked differences in security, stability of income, and general social prestige. One is that middle-class occupations deal more with the manipulation of interpersonal relations, ideas, and symbols, while working-class occupations deal more with the manipulation of things. The second is that middle-class occupations are more subject to self-direction, while working-class occupations are more subject to standardization and direct supervision. The third is that getting ahead in middle-class occupations is more dependent upon one's own actions, while in working-class occupations it is more dependent on collective action, particularly in unionized industries. . . . Middle-class occupations require a greater degree of self-direction; working-class occupations, in larger measure, require that one follow explicit rules set down by someone in authority.

Obviously, these differences parallel the differences we have found between the two social classes in the characteristics valued by parents for children. At minimum, one can conclude that there is a congruence between occupational requirements and parental values. It is, moreover, a reasonable supposition, although not a necessary conclusion, that middle- and working-class parents value different characteristics in children *because* of these differences in their occupational circumstances. This supposition does not necessarily assume that parents consciously train their children to meet future occupational requirements; it may simply be that their own occupational requirements have significantly affected parents' conceptions of what is desirable behavior, on or off the job, for adults or for children. (Kohn, 1963, pp. 475-6)

In subsequent work, Kohn (1969) and Kohn and Schooler (1983) refined and expanded this formulation in several ways. The three job conditions were redefined: the distinction between the "manipulation of interpersonal relations, ideas, and symbols," in contrast to "the manipulation of things," was redefined as "the substantive complexity of the work," because empirical analyses (Kohn, 1969) demonstrated that the essential difference in the substance of the work lies not in the realm in which the work is performed, but in the complexity of that work, in whatever realm it is performed. The distinction between "self-direction," in contrast to "standardization and direct supervision," was redefined as two distinguishable differences in job conditions: "closeness of supervision" and "routinization." And "getting ahead" on the basis of one's own actions or on the basis of collective action was dropped from the formulation, mainly because "getting ahead" is not really a condition of work. The term, "self-direction" was broadened to *occupational* self-direction, meaning not only freedom from close supervision and non-routinized conditions of work, but also, and of central importance, doing substantively complex work.

Of equal importance, the formulation was greatly expanded, from occupational self-direction providing the crucial link to explain the effects of social stratification on parental values, to occupational self-direction explaining the effects of social structure (both class and stratification), not only on values, but also on intellectual flexibility and orientations to self and society.

Kohn and Schoenbach (1983) have tested this expanded formulation for the United States. In this book, we refine their formulation, extend their empirical analyses, and incorporate those analyses into a cross-national comparison, asking whether occupational self-direction is equally pertinent for explaining the psychological impact of social structure in capitalist and socialist society.

Ideally, one should address this question by assessing not only whether the job conditions facilitative or restrictive of occupational self-direction provide an empirically convincing explanation of the effects of class and stratification on psychological functioning, but also whether other job conditions (and other conditions of life) provide an equally convincing explanation. Kohn and Schooler (1969; Kohn, 1969) have provided substantial evidence for the United States that a considerable range of job conditions *other* than those directly related to occupational self-direction are not nearly as important for explaining the relationships of social stratification with psychological functioning as are those directly related to occupational self-direction. Similar (unpublished) analyses show the same to be true for social class.

Unfortunately, we do not have data for Poland about job conditions other than the substantive complexity of work, closeness of supervision, and routinization.[1] And, although we do have information about the social characteristics of both our US and Polish respondents, we do not have the systematic information about other conditions of life that would permit us to assess their utility for explaining the psychological effects of social structure. Thus, our analyses will enable us to assess how effective an explanation of the psychological effects of class and stratification is provided by occupational self-direction, but not whether other conditions of life might provide an alternative explanation.

---

[1] Our intent in the Polish survey, as in the US survey, was to ask about a broad range of job conditions, thus to be able to compare the explanatory power of occupational self-direction to that of other job conditions. But the survey research specialists of the Polish Academy of Sciences objected to including questions about job conditions that did not meet their criteria of objectivity. The criticism of the subjectivity of some of our questions about job conditions is apt, but the loss is none the less great. Even subjective questions about job conditions provide some basis for assessing whether occupational self-direction is singularly important for explaining the psychological effects of class and stratification, or whether other job conditions might be equally important. The US analyses clearly show occupational self-direction to be much more important for values, cognitive functioning, and self-directedness of orientation than are such other job conditions as position in the organizational structure, job pressures, and extrinsic risks and rewards (Kohn and Schooler, 1983, particularly chapters 1, 3, and 6). But we have no evidence from the Polish study as to the cross-national validity of this conclusion.

CONCEPTUALIZATION AND MEASUREMENT OF
OCCUPATIONAL SELF-DIRECTION

By "occupational self-direction," we mean the use of initiative, thought, and independent judgment in work. We see three job conditions as crucial in facilitating or restricting the exercise of occupational self-direction: the substantive complexity of the work, closeness of supervision, and routinization. Being closely supervised and doing routinized work limit opportunities for occupational self-direction; doing substantively complex work facilitates, even requires, the exercise of occupational self-direction.

By "the substantive complexity of work," we mean the degree to which performance of the work requires thought and independent judgment. Substantively complex work by its very nature requires making many decisions that must take into account ill-defined or apparently conflicting contingencies. For both the United States and Poland, our information about the substantive complexity of work is based on detailed questioning of each respondent about his work with things, with data or ideas, and with people. These questions provide the basis for seven ratings of each man's job: our appraisals of the complexity of his work with things, with data, and with people; our appraisal of the overall complexity of his work, regardless of whether he works primarily with data, with people, or with things; and his estimates of the number of hours he spends each week working at each of the three types of activity.[2] In both the US and Polish models (see figure 5.1 for the United States and figure 5.2 for Poland), we treat these seven ratings as indicators of the underlying but not directly measured construct, the substantive complexity of that job.[3]

"Close supervision" limits one's opportunities for occupational self-direction: workers cannot exercise occupational self-direction if they are closely supervised, although not being closely supervised does not necessarily mean that they are required or even free to use initiative, thought, and independent judgment. In both studies, closeness of supervision is measured by a worker's subjective appraisals of his freedom to disagree with his supervisor, how closely he is supervised, the extent to which his supervisor

---

[2] For the exact wording of the questions in English, see Kohn, 1969, pp. 153–5, 271–6; or Kohn and Schooler, 1983, pp. 24–5; for the exact wording of the questions in Polish, see Slomczynski and Kohn, 1988, appendix C. The classifications of complexity of work with data, with people, and with things, and of the overall complexity of the work, are given in Kohn, 1969, appendix E and in Kohn and Schooler, 1983, appendix B.

[3] For a more detailed discussion of the US measurement model of the substantive complexity of work, see Kohn and Schooler 1983, pp. 106–10; for a more detailed discussion of the Polish measurement model of work complexity see Janicka et al., 1983.

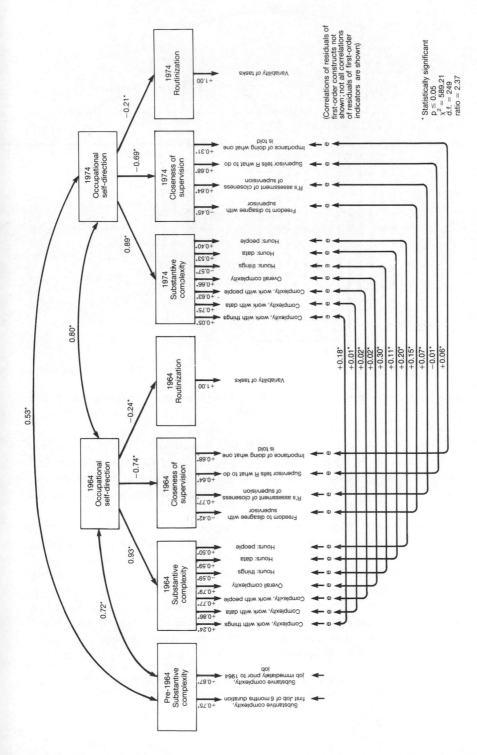

Figure 5.1 *Second-order measurement model of occupational self-direction: US men.*

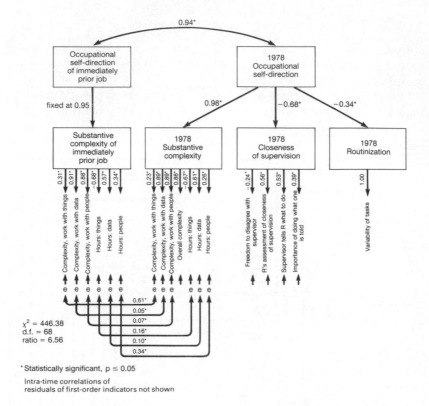

Figure 5.2 *Second-order measurement model of occupational self-direction: Polish men.*

tells him what to do rather than discussing it with him, and the importance in his job of doing what one is told to do.[4] In our measurement models of occupational self-direction (again, see figures 5.1 and 5.2) these questions are treated as "indicators" of an underlying concept, the closeness of supervision of work.

"Routinization" is the final facet of occupational self-direction; highly routinized (repetitive and predictable) jobs restrict possibilities for exercising initiative, thought, and judgment, while jobs with a variety of unpredictable tasks may facilitate or even require the use of self-direction. We use slightly different measures of routinization for the United States and Poland. For the United States, respondents' work was coded from most variable (the work involves doing different things in different ways and one cannot predict what may come up) to least variable (the work is unvaryingly repetitive). For Poland, we do not include predictability in the index, since it adds

[4] For the exact wording of the questions in English, see Kohn and Schooler, 1983, p. 23; for the wording in Polish, see Slomczynski and Kohn, 1988, appendix C.

nothing to the explanatory power of variability. Having only one indicator of routinization for each country, we treat this concept as if it were perfectly measured.

In the second-order portion of the measurement model, we treat the three first-order concepts – the substantive complexity of the work, closeness of supervision, and routinization – as "indicators" of an underlying but not directly measured concept, occupational self-direction (again, see figures 5.1 and 5.2). Aside from our using retrospective information to index the substantive complexity of pre-1964 jobs (see the rationale in Kohn and Schooler, 1973), the US model is longitudinal: information about the 1964 job was secured during the baseline interview that year, information about the 1974 job was secured during the follow-up interview ten years later. The Polish model is quasi-longitudinal, in that information about the 1978 job was secured at the time of the interview that year, but information about the immediately prior job was necessarily retrospective. That the information is retrospective, and that we asked about the job the man held immediately before his present job (rather than about the job he held ten years before, which may be harder to remember), probably explains the higher over-time correlation for Poland than for the United States.

Both the US and Polish measurement models for occupational self-direction fit their respective variance–covariance matrices well. The parameters of the models are quite similar in the two countries, with the substantive complexity of work by far the most powerful component of occupational self-direction. Even the relationships between the first-order concepts and their indicators are remarkably similar for the United States and Poland. There is, then, a decided similarity in the structuring of work in the two countries, despite the obvious and important contrast in ownership of economic enterprise. We can have considerable confidence that the concept, occupational self- direction, is equally valid for the two countries and that our indices of this concept are altogether comparable.

THE RELATIONSHIP BETWEEN SOCIAL CLASS AND OCCUPATIONAL SELF-DIRECTION

We hypothesize that the explanation for the effects of social class on values, intellectual flexibility, and self-directedness of orientation will lie – in substantial degree – in particular job conditions associated with social-class position. We expect to find that men who are more advantageously located in the class structure have greater opportunity to be self-directed in their work and, in turn, that the experience of occupational self-direction has profound effects on their values, orientations, and cognitive functioning.

This is a very strong hypothesis. We define social class in terms of ownership and control over the means of production and control over the labor power of others; but we hypothesize that the reason why social class affects personality is that class position is determinative of how much control one has over the conditions of one's *own* work. There is nothing in the classic definition of social class, nor in the criteria we employ to index social class, that speaks directly to the issue of control over the conditions of one's own occupational life. Yet, on the basis of extensive previous analyses of job conditions and psychological functioning (Kohn and Schooler, 1983), we believe that what is psychologically crucial about control in the work place is not control over others, but control over the conditions of one's own life – occupational self-direction. We therefore hypothesize that what is psychologically important about having an advantaged class position is not the power over others that it affords, nor even the socioeconomic rewards that it confers, but the opportunity it provides to be self-directed in one's own occupational life. Conversely, the psychological importance of a disadvantaged class position lies primarily in the limits it imposes on the opportunity to be self-directed in one's occupational life.

The hypothesis that occupational self-direction will provide the key to explaining the relationships between social class and psychological functioning will prove to be valid if, and only if, there are differential opportunities for occupational self-direction available to members of the several social classes. We find, in fact, that the relationship between social class and occupational self-direction is very strong in both countries (table 5.1). The correlation (*eta*) between social class and occupational self-direction is, for the United States, 0.78 as measured at the time of the baseline interviews in 1964 and 0.74 as measured at the time of the follow-up interviews in 1974; for Poland, it is 0.83 as measured at the time of the interviews in 1978. Even the correlations of social class with two of the three component job conditions are strong: correlations (*etas*) in the 0.70s for the substantive complexity of work and in the 0.40s and 0.50s for closeness of supervision.[5]

[5] We faced a dilemma in deciding how to evaluate closeness of supervision for employers and the self-employed. We could not ask them our standard interview questions about how closely they are supervised, since they have no formal supervisor. We might, none the less, have placed them in the least closely supervised category, on the rationale that, having no supervisor, they could not be closely supervised. To do so, however, would have confounded social class and occupational self-direction, since the classification of these men with respect to occupational self-direction would be made, in part, on the basis of their class position. This would favor our principal hypothesis, that the psychological effects of social class will be greatly reduced when occupational self-direction is statistically controlled. The alternative procedure, which we followed, is to risk understating the relationship between social class and occupational self-direction by treating closeness of supervision as "missing data" for employers

In both countries, managers are the class whose members are most self-directed in their work. Nonmanual workers (a class that includes non-supervisory professionals), rank substantially above the mean for their country in occupational self-direction, as do first-line supervisors. In the United States, employers also rank fairly high. The self-employed rank relatively low, and manual workers lowest of all. (In Poland, the difference between production workers and nonproduction workers is minimal.) These patterns hold not only for occupational self-direction *in toto*, but also, with only minor variations, for its three components – the substantive complexity of the work, closeness of supervision, and routinization. Clearly, class is strongly and meaningfully related to occupational self-direction.[6]

Clearly, too, the strong relationship between class and occupational self-direction results in part, but only in part, from manual workers' being, on the average, less occupationally self-directed than are nonmanual workers. If we combine manual and nonmanual workers into a single social class, the proletariat, the correlations (*etas*) between class and occupational self-direction remain strong, even if not as strong as when we differentiate between manual and nonmanual workers: 0.47 for the United States in 1964, 0.50 for the United States in 1974, and 0.53 for Poland in 1978.[7] (For Poland, it should be noted, combining manual and nonmanual workers necessarily means that we are also combining production and nonproduction workers.)

---

and the self-employed. Re-analyses of our data, treating employers and the self-employed as being in the least closely supervised category, yield the same substantive conclusions as do those presented in this book, except that (1) they show employers to be somewhat more self-directed than nonmanual workers and (2) they imply that occupational self-direction plays an even larger part in explaining the psychological effects of social class than is demonstrated by our more conservative procedures.

[6] This conclusion begs the question of whether class is related to occupational self-direction because class position affects opportunities to be self-directed in one's work, because the exercise of occupational self-direction affects one's class placement, or some combination of the two. We shall address this issue in chapter 6.

[7] Might the correlations of social class with occupational self-direction reflect the strong correlations of social class with social stratification? The answer is a decided "no": if we statistically control, and thereby attribute all shared variance to, social stratification, the correlations between social class and occupational self-direction remain substantial in both countries. (The correlations between social stratification and occupational self-direction also remain substantial when social class is statistically controlled.)

Table 5.1 Relationship of social class to occupational self-direction

	N	Occupational self-direction	Substantive complexity	Closeness of supervision	Routinization
		Means[a]			
A US men (1964)					
Employers	(18)	0.42	0.61	xx[b]	−0.06
Self-employed	(73)	0.20	0.21	xx	−0.14
Managers	(37)	1.17	1.21	−0.80	−0.45
First-line supervisors	(120)	0.51	0.46	−0.43	−0.12
Nonmanual workers	(138)	0.75	0.77	−0.50	−0.03
Manual workers	(301)	−0.76	−0.77	0.49	0.15
Correlation (eta)[c]		0.78*	0.76*	0.51*	0.16*
Correlation, combining manual and nonmanual workers		0.47*	0.46*	0.33*	0.15*
B US men (1974)					
Employers	(32)	0.41	0.67	xx[b]	−0.25
Self-employed	(82)	−0.01	−0.02	xx	−0.13
Managers	(65)	0.91	0.88	−0.54	−0.34
First-line supervisors	(122)	0.34	0.29	−0.21	−0.07
Nonmanual workers	(106)	0.56	0.65	−0.23	0.01
Manual workers	(219)	−0.79	−0.83	0.39	0.22
Correlation (eta)[c]		0.74*	0.74*	0.41*	0.19*
Correlation, combining manual and nonmanual workers		0.50*	0.48*	0.34*	0.17*

C Polish men (1978)

Managers	(62)	1.70	1.64	−0.63	−0.51
First-line supervisors	(302)	0.74	0.71	−0.49	−0.28
Nonmanual workers	(266)	0.98	0.94	−0.50	−0.28
Production workers	(526)	−0.65	−0.62	0.41	0.19
Nonproduction workers	(327)	−0.71	−0.71	0.32	0.34
Self-employed	(73)	−0.16	−0.05	xx[b]	−0.25
Correlation (eta)[c]		0.83*	0.78*	0.57*	0.28*
Correlation, combining manual and nonmanual workers		0.53*	0.52*	0.40*	0.20*

[a] Expressed as standardized differences from grand mean for the particular country at the particular time.

[b] Self-employed are treated as "missing data."

[c] Corrected for unreliability of measurement.

* Statistically significant, $p < 0.05$.

OCCUPATIONAL SELF-DIRECTION AS AN EXPLANATION OF THE RELATIONSHIPS OF SOCIAL CLASS AND PSYCHOLOGICAL FUNCTIONING

It is, then, an entirely plausible hypothesis that position in the class structure affects psychological functioning in substantial degree because of the differential opportunities for occupational self-direction afforded to men variously located in the class structure. To test this hypothesis, we statistically control the substantive complexity of work, closeness of supervision, and routinization. Insofar as the correlations between social class and psychological functioning are thereby reduced, we can tentatively infer that social class affects psychological functioning because of the differential opportunities for occupational self-direction available to members of the several social classes.[8] (We shall examine the issue of directionality of effects in chapter 6.)

Values, intellectual flexibility, and self-directedness of orientation

Consider, first, the cross-nationally consistent relationships of social class with parental valuation of self-direction, intellectual flexibility, self-directedness of orientation, and the principal first-order component dimensions of self-directedness of orientation – authoritarian conservatism, standards of morality, and trustfulness. We find, for both countries, that the magnitudes of the correlations of social class with all these facets of psychological functioning are substantially reduced when the substantive complexity of the work, closeness of supervision, and routinization are statistically controlled (see table 5.2). For example, the correlation between social class and parental valuation of self-direction is reduced by 39 percent for the United States at the time of the baseline interviews, when the respondents' offspring were 3–15 years old, by 78 percent ten years later, when the offspring were 13–25 years old, and by 79 percent for Poland, the offspring being 3–15 years old at the time of the interviews. Similarly for intellectual flexibility, self-directedness of orientation, and the first-order components of self-directedness of orientation: in both countries, all the

---

[8] In these analyses, we compute the multiple correlation between some facet of psychological functioning and dummy variables for all but one of the class categories, then compute the multiple–partial correlation, statistically controlling the substantive complexity of work, closeness of supervision, and routinization. Assessing reductions in correlations is distinctly less precise than assessing reductions in total effects (as we shall do in our analyses of social stratification), but since class is a nominal variable, we can do no better.

Table 5.2 *Effects on class-correlations of statistically controlling occupational self-direction and social characteristics*

	US men (1964)	US men (1974)	Polish men (1978)
Values			
Parental valuation of self-direction			
(a) Correlation (*eta*) with social class	0.38	0.47	0.36
(b) Proportional reduction, controlling:			
— occupational self-direction	39%	78%	79%
— social characteristics[a]	21%	10%	0%
— both occupational self-direction and social characteristics	38%	65%	68%
Intellectual flexibility			
(a) Correlation (*eta*) with social class	0.53	0.57	0.55
(b) Proportional reduction, controlling:			
— occupational self-direction	62%	87%	83%
— social characteristics[a]	17%	3%	0%
— both occupational self-direction and social characteristics	63%	75%	78%
Orientations to self and society			
Second-order dimensions			
Self-directedness of orientation			
(a) Correlation (*eta*) with social class	0.44	0.43	0.42
(b) Proportional reduction, controlling:			
— occupational self-direction	73%	70%	77%
— social characteristics[a]	23%	13%	4%
— both occupational self-direction and social characteristics	72%	67%	74%
Distress			
(a) Correlation (*eta*) with social class	0.13	0.18	0.14
(b) Proportional reduction, controlling:			
— occupational self-direction	27%	35%	38%
— social characteristics[a]	3%	7%	10%
— both occupational self-direction and social characteristics	28%	31%	44%
First-order dimensions			
Authoritarian conservatism			
(a) Correlation (*eta*) with social class	0.43	0.38	0.40
(b) Proportional reduction, controlling:			
— occupational self-direction	73%	70%	72%
— social characteristics[a]	22%	21%	4%
— both occupational self-direction and social characteristics	74%	80%	70%

Table 5.2 Cont.

	US men (1964)	US men (1974)	Polish men (1978)
Standards of morality			
(a) Correlation (*eta*) with social class	0.23	0.32	0.39
(b) Proportional reduction, controlling:			
— occupational self-direction	55%	53%	57%
— social characteristics[a]	27%	17%	11%
— both occupational self-direction and social characteristics	51%	54%	64%
Trustfulness			
(a) Correlation (*eta*) with social class	0.33	0.36	0.34
(b) Proportional reduction, controlling:			
— occupational self-direction	64%	77%	62%
— social characteristics[a]	35%	19%	5%
— both occupational self-direction and social characteristics	61%	59%	59%
Idea-conformity			
(a) Correlation (*eta*) with social class	0.18	0.12	0.11
(b) Proportional reduction, controlling:			
— occupational self-direction	26%	10%	60%
— social characteristics[a]	20%	8%	7%
— both occupational self-direction and social characteristics	16%	0%	65%
Self-confidence			
(a) Correlation (*eta*) with social class	0.15	0.15	0.14
(b) Proportional reduction, controlling:			
— occupational self-direction	19%	67%	26%
— social characteristics[a]	18%	19%	9%
— both occupational self-direction and social characteristics	15%	72%	28%
Self-deprecation			
(a) Correlation (*eta*) with social class	0.20	0.29	0.12
(b) Proportional reduction, controlling:			
— occupational self-direction	43%	47%	37%
— social characteristics[a]	23%	17%	17%
— both occupational self-direction and social characteristics	46%	47%	38%

Anxiety

(a) Correlation (*eta*) with social class	0.13	0.18	0.06
(b) Proportional reduction, controlling:			
— occupational self-direction	56%	46%	49%
— social characteristics[a]	0%	5%	11%
— both occupational self-direction and social characteristics	58%	36%	50%

[a] For the United States, the pertinent social characteristics are age, race, national background, religious background, mother's and father's education, father's occupational status, maternal and paternal grandfathers' occupational statuses, urbanness and region of the country of the principal place where respondent was raised, and the number of brothers and sisters he had; for parental values, also child's age and sex. For Poland, the pertinent social characteristics are year of birth, urbanness of principal place raised, father's education and occupational status; for parental values, also child's age and sex.

class-correlations are substantially reduced – in many instances, by two-thirds or more – when occupational self-direction is statistically controlled.

Occupational self-direction does not completely explain the effect of class on psychological functioning; even with occupational self-direction statistically controlled, most of the partial correlations remain statistically significant, albeit much diminished in magnitude. Occupational self-direction does, however, provide a cross-nationally consistent explanation of the lion's share of the psychological effects of social class.

Since we have seen (in table 5.1) that manual workers are distinctly less self-directed in their work than are nonmanual workers, we must ask whether these findings are an artifact of our using the distinction between manual and nonmanual work as a desideratum of class. The answer is a decided "no": if we combine manual and nonmanual workers into a single social class, the proletariat, then occupational self-direction continues to explain nearly as large a proportion of the correlations between social class and psychological functioning as it does when manual and nonmanual workers are treated as separate classes.

An obvious alternative hypothesis is that social class is related to these facets of psychological functioning, not because of differential opportunities for occupational self-direction, but because of the social compositions of the several social classes – the varying proportions of men from higher and lower socioeconomic backgrounds, rural or urban origins, and the like. To test this possibility, we statistically control all pertinent social characteristics about which we have information. For the United States, these social characteristics are age, race, national background, religious background, mother's and father's education, maternal and paternal grandfathers' occupational statuses, urbanness and region of the country of the principal place where the respondent was raised, and the number of brothers and sisters he had; for parental values, also child's age and sex. For Poland, the pertinent social characteristics are age, the urbanness of the principal place raised, and father's education and occupational status; for parental values, also child's age and sex.

For both countries, statistically controlling the pertinent social characteristics results in decidedly smaller reductions in the correlations between social class and these facets of psychological functioning than does statistically controlling the job conditions facilitative or restrictive of occupational self-direction. For example, the correlations between social class and parental valuation of self-direction are reduced by 21 percent for US fathers of younger children, by 10 percent for US fathers of older children, and not at all for Polish fathers, when the pertinent social characteristics are statistically controlled. Similarly for intellectual flexibility, for self-directedness of orientation, and for the first-order components of self-directedness of orientation: the reductions in the class-correlations are decidedly smaller when social characteristics are statistically controlled than when the substantive complexity of work, closeness of supervision, and routinization of work are controlled. Moreover, controlling *both* social characteristics *and* occupational self-direction generally does not reduce the class correlations any more than does controlling occupational self-direction alone.

Clearly, the explanation of the relationship between social class and these facets of psychological functioning does not rest in the social compositions of the classes. Instead, the explanation would seem to be that social-class position markedly affects men's opportunities to exercise occupational self-direction; and that the exercise of occupational self-direction in turn markedly affects these pivotal facets of psychological functioning.

Does occupational self-direction explain (even if incompletely) *all* of the class differences in these facets of psychological functioning, or does it explain only *some* of the class differences? Might it be, for example, that occupational self-direction accounts for psychological differences between manual and nonmanual workers, but that psychological differences, say, between managers and non-managerial employees are to be explained in some other way?

To answer this question, we use analysis of covariance to adjust the means of each facet of psychological functioning for each class category, statistically controlling occupational self-direction (see table 5.3, which provides information about the principal facets of psychological functioning). The results are entirely consistent for both countries: the rank-orders of social classes with respect to parental valuation of self-direction, intellectual flexibility, and self-directedness of orientation remain almost exactly as they

Table 5.3 Relationships of men's social-class positions with their values, intellectual flexibility, self-directedness of orientation, and distress – adjusted for occupational self-direction

| | Parental valuation of self-direction | | Intellectual flexibility | | Second-order dimensions of orientation | | | |
| | | | | | Self-directedness of orientation | | Distress | |
	Unadjusted Mean[a]	Adjusted Mean[b]	Unadjusted Mean[a]	Adjusted Mean[b]	Unadjusted Mean[a]	Adjusted Mean[b]	Unadjusted Mean[a]	Adjusted Mean[b]
A US men (1974)								
Employers	+0.39	+0.33	+0.58	+0.41	+0.52	+0.36	−0.20	−0.13
Self-employed	+0.06	+0.08	+0.01	0.00	−0.04	−0.03	−0.08	−0.06
Managers	+0.42	+0.19	+0.59	+0.20	+0.41	+0.07	−0.16	−0.01
First-line supervisors	+0.14	+0.03	+0.23	+0.08	+0.12	−0.01	−0.16	−0.10
Nonmanual workers	+0.24	+0.16	+0.44	+0.20	+0.41	+0.19	+0.04	+0.13
Manual workers	−0.41	−0.23	−0.61	−0.26	−0.45	−0.15	+0.18	+0.04
B Polish men (1978)								
Managers	+0.45	+0.15	+0.92	+0.25	+0.77	+0.26	+0.10	−0.10
First-line supervisors	+0.26	+0.12	+0.41	+0.10	+0.30	+0.05	+0.05	−0.05
Nonmanual workers	+0.24	+0.04	+0.56	+0.16	+0.50	+0.18	+0.19	+0.06
Production workers	−0.22	−0.09	−0.36	−0.10	−0.28	−0.07	−0.09	−0.01
Nonproduction workers	−0.19	−0.05	−0.41	−0.10	−0.35	−0.10	−0.04	+0.06
Self-employed	−0.01	+0.01	−0.05	−0.04	−0.14	−0.13	−0.17	−0.17

[a] Expressed as standardized difference from grand mean for the particular country at the particular time.
[b] Expressed as standardized difference from grand mean, adjusted for occupational self-direction.

had been; but the magnitudes of the differences among the means for the several classes diminish sharply. Occupational self-direction provides a quite general, even if incomplete, explanation of class differences in these facets of psychological functioning.

The one partial exception to this generalization is that, for the United States, the differences between employers and members of other social classes are not much diminished. Something more than occupational self-direction is involved in explaining why employers are as intellectually flexible and as self-directed in their values and orientations as they are. The larger lesson of this analysis, none the less, is that occupational self-direction provides a quite general explanation of class differences in these facets of psychological functioning.

Distress

Once again, distress is the exception to an otherwise consistent pattern. We have seen that the correlations (*etas*) of social class with distress and with its principal components are not very large in either country; nor is the nature of the relationship consistent from country to country. This means that we have to explain not only what accounts for the cross-national differences in the relationships between social class and distress but also – and perhaps more important – why the magnitudes of these relationships are so much smaller than those between social class and other facets of psychological functioning.

Part of the explanation for the relationships' being weak and cross-nationally inconsistent – and also part of the interpretive problem – is that occupational self-direction does not provide a cross-nationally consistent explanation of the relationship between social class and distress.

Even for the United States – where the relationship between class and distress is in accord with our expectations – statistically controlling the job conditions facilitative or restrictive of occupational self-direction reduces the correlation of social class with distress by only 27 percent in 1964 and 35 percent in 1974 – far less than the reductions in the correlations of social class with intellectual flexibility and with self-directedness of orientation (again, see table 5.2). Similarly for the first-order components of distress. Moreover, even for the United States the adjusted means (table 5.3) suggest that occupational self-direction does not provide the general explanation of class differences in distress that it provides for other dimensions of psychological functioning. These adjusted means do suggest that manual workers are distressed primarily because they lack occupational self-direction, and that managers have a strong sense of well-being primarily because they do enjoy occupational self-direction. But the adjusted means also imply that nonmanual workers, who are only a little more distressed than the average for the population as a whole, would be distinctly more distressed were it not for their rather substantial level of occupational self-direction. And occupational self-direction provides only a modest part of the explanation of employers' being the least distressed social class. More than occupational self-direction is involved in explaining the class–distress relationship, even for the United States.

For Poland, where the social classes whose members enjoy the greatest opportunities for occupational self-direction are among those whose members evidence the greatest degree of distress, the only way that occupational self-direction could explain the relationship of social class to distress would be if the exercise of occupational self-direction were conducive to, rather than ameliorative of, distress. Although such a possibility is contrary both to our general interpretation and to all other known effects of occupational self-direction both in Poland and in the United States, we must consider it seriously.

Table 5.2 does suggest that occupational self-direction may account for at least a moderate proportion (38 percent) of the relationship between social class and distress, and for similar proportions of the (very small) relationships of class with anxiety and with self-confidence. An examination of the adjusted class means for distress in table 5.3, though, suggests contradictory processes at work. Occupational self-direction contributes nothing to our understanding of why the self-employed are the least distressed social class. It contributes a great deal to explaining (in the statistical sense) why it is that nonmanual workers are the most distressed social class. But why should it be that occupational self-direction *exacerbates* Polish nonmanual workers' distress but *ameliorates* US nonmanual workers' distress? And, as for the Polish managers, the adjusted means suggest that they too suffer distress *because of* occupational self-direction. Can this really be? We are left in a quandary, not to be resolved until chapter 8, when we shall bring more extensive analyses of job conditions and distress to bear on these issues.

If occupational self-direction does not provide a cross-nationally consistent explanation of the relationships between social class and distress, might such an explanation lie in the social composition of the classes? Table 5.2 clearly shows, for both the United States and Poland, that statistically controlling the pertinent social characteristics has only a small effect on the magnitudes of the class–distress relationships. The explanation of the class–distress relationships lies elsewhere.

For now we simply conclude that neither occupational self-direction nor the social composition of the classes provides a cross-nationally consistent explanation of the relationships between social class and distress.

CONCEPTUALIZING THE RELATIONSHIP BETWEEN SOCIAL STRATIFICATION AND OCCUPATIONAL SELF-DIRECTION

Our hypothesis for explaining the relationship between social stratification and psychological functioning is exactly parallel to our hypothesis for explaining the relationship between social class and psychological functioning: that occupational self-direction explains – at least in substantial part – the relationships of social-stratification position with values, intellectual flexibility, and self-directedness of orientation. Since social stratification is an interval scale, though, we no longer need assume that position in the social structure has unidirectional effects on occupational self-direction. Instead, we can develop and test models that allow for the possibility that social-stratification position not only affects, but also is affected by, occupational self-direction.

The assumption of unidirectionality of effects may be appropriate for one dimension of stratification – educational attainment – at least in the United States, because formal education ends for most men in the United States before their occupational careers get under way.[9] In Poland, where many men continue their formal educations well into their occupational careers, an assumption of unidirectionality may be unwarranted. In both countries, the appropriate assumption for occupational status and job income is that they may both affect and be affected by occupational self-direction.

We therefore disaggregate social stratification into two components – education and occupational position. Occupational position is depicted as a second-order concept, with job income and occupational status as its first-order component concepts.[10]

Since occupational position signifies a job's placement in the system of social stratification, it can affect the actual conditions of work experienced in that job. But, since occupational position – and, in particular, the indicators we use to measure occupational position, i.e., status and income – is a reward, distributed in accordance with critical aspects of the work

[9] There is a correlation of 0.97 between men's educational levels at the time of the first interview, in 1964, and at the time of the follow-up interview, ten years later. The correlation is of essentially the same magnitude for the oldest, intermediate, and youngest segments of the work force.

[10] This can readily be done by modifying the measurement models of social-stratification position depicted in figure 3.3 (see p. 46). Instead of education, job income, and occupational status being treated as three "indicators" of social-stratification position, education is treated as a separate concept and job income and occupational status are treated as "indicators" of occupational position. Even though a two-indicator measurement model is ordinarily under-identified, the presence of education in this measurement model provides the necessary identification for solving the model.

performed, it can be affected by job conditions.[11] We therefore consider the relationship between occupational position and occupational self-direction to be reciprocal.

This being our first presentation in this book of a model of reciprocal effects, we shall digress somewhat to address in general terms the issues in estimating such a model. Our intention here is to discuss in entirely nonmathematical terms the issues that one encounters when one abandons the assumption of unidirectionality of effects. For those readers who would like an intuitive understanding of a method on which we shall repeatedly rely, and which we regard as the method of choice for cross-national analysis, the following may help.[12]

The problem of identification in reciprocal-effects causal modelling

Even with longitudinal data, modelling reciprocal effects is difficult, the source of the problem being insufficient information to estimate all the parameters that should be estimated in a well-specified model. The nature of the problem is illustrated in a heuristic model (figure 5.3) depicting the heart of our intended analysis of the reciprocal effects of occupational position and occupational self-direction. In principle, we should like to estimate eight parameters, but we have sufficient information to estimate only six.

The eight parameters are numbered in the heuristic figure. The first parameter to be estimated is the correlation between occupational position and occupational self-direction at the time of the baseline interviews. In this model, we treat these concepts as "exogenous," that is, as givens. We make no attempt to explain them in the model. By contrast, we treat occupational position and occupational self-direction at the time of the follow-up interview as "endogenous," that is, to be explained in the model. We use the terms "exogenous" and "endogenous," rather than the more familiar terms, "independent" and "dependent," because an endogenous variable may be an independent variable in some equations and a dependent variable in another equation.

The second and third parameters to be estimated are the "stabilities" of occupational position and occupational self-direction, that is, the path

---

[11] Even though our measures of occupational status refer to the status of an entire occupation rather than to the status of a particular job, we are treating our index of occupational status as if it measured the status of an individual's own job. Job income is of course specific to the particular job.

[12] Ours is a heuristic treatment. For rigorous discussions of this complex topic, see Duncan, 1967 and 1975, pp. 81–90; and Heise 1975, pp. 160–81. Still pertinent is Simon's (1957) classic essay on the subject.

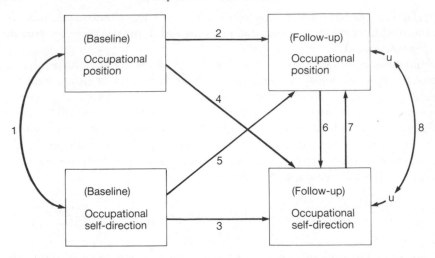

Figure 5.3   *Heuristic model of the reciprocal relationship between occupational
position and occupational self-direction.*

from occupational position measured at the time of the baseline interview to occupational position measured at the time of the follow-up interview, and the path from occupational self-direction measured at the time of the baseline interview to occupational self-direction measured at the time of the follow-up interview. These paths are essential to longitudinal analysis – perhaps the main reason for doing longitudinal analysis – for they serve as essential statistical controls. The path from earlier to later occupational self-direction enables us to statistically control earlier occupational self-direction when assessing the effect of occupational position on occupational self-direction. Similarly, the path from earlier to later occupational position serves as a statistical control for assessing the effect of occupational self-direction on occupational position.

The fourth and fifth parameters, which are called "cross-lagged" effects, are the effect of occupational position as measured in the baseline interview on occupational self-direction as measured in the follow-up interview, and the effect of occupational self-direction as measured in the baseline interview on occupational position as measured in the follow-up interview. Wherever an effect is a priori possible, it should in principle be estimated in the model. Both of these effects are a priori possible: the position held at the time of the baseline interview might affect the opportunities afforded for occupational self-direction in the same or another job at the time of the follow-up interview. And the exercise of self-direction in an earlier job might well affect subsequent career mobility.

The sixth and seventh parameters are the "contemporaneous" effects of occupational position on occupational self-direction and of occupational self-direction on occupational position. These paths represent ongoing and continuous effects, as distinct from the longer-term effects of past jobs on present jobs depicted in the cross-lagged paths. The a priori rationale for these paths is that current occupational position might affect the degree of occupational self-direction afforded by a job; and the exercise of occupational self-direction might affect the income and status of a job.[13] Here, again, the critical issue is not whether there *are* such effects but whether it is reasonable to assume that there *might be* such effects. If there might be such effects, then they should be estimated in the model.

The eighth and final parameter is the correlation of the residuals of the two endogenous variables, occupational position and occupational self-direction, both variables as measured at the time of the follow-up study. No causal model is ever complete; one can never explicitly include in the model all variables that might affect the endogenous variables. Thus, there are always residuals, and since some left-out variable might affect both variables in a reciprocally related pair, their residuals might be correlated. To allow for this possibility, we should estimate the correlation of their residuals.

Eight parameters to be estimated; and the information we have consists of the set of intercorrelations among four variables, six correlations in all – too little information to solve the set of simultaneous equations required to estimate the eight parameters we want to estimate. When there is too little information to estimate a model, that model is termed "under-identified." If there is just enough information to provide a unique solution (the model then being called, appropriately enough, "just-identified"), the model can usually be solved. When there is more information than needed (so that the model is "over-identified"), so much the better: extra information adds to the robustness of the model.

How then does one transform an under-identified model, such as our heuristic model, to a just-identified or, better yet, an over-identified model? Some simplifying assumptions must be made, usually in conjunction with adding further information.

Where possible, the best simplifying assumptions involve the use of "instruments." An instrument is a variable that identifies an equation by *not*

---

[13] One might argue that occupational self-direction cannot have a contemporaneous effect on occupational position, for that would signify a change in job. We think it more conservative to allow the possibility that small changes in occupational status and in income do not necessarily signify a change in job. In any case, as will shortly be seen, in our actual model we are unable to differentiate lagged from contemporaneous effects, but are only able to assess total effects.

being allowed to have a *direct* effect on the dependent variable of that equation. (In practice, this means that the path from the instrument to that endogenous variable is fixed at zero.) For an instrument to identify an equation meaningfully, there must be good a priori justification that its effect on that endogenous variable should only be indirect. The critical issue in causal modelling is always whether or not there is a priori reason to think that some direct effect *could* occur. If an effect is logically possible, then that path should be estimated in the model. Only when one has good a priori reason *not* to allow a path is it legitimate to fix that path at zero.

In addition, if the instrument is to be efficacious, it must be correlated at least moderately with the endogenous variable that it is not allowed to affect directly. The stronger the correlation between the instrument and that endogenous variable, the more efficacious the instrument. The *degree* of identification depends on how strong are the correlations between the instruments and the endogenous variables that they are not allowed to affect directly. Lacking an instrument that is strongly correlated with the endogenous variable that it is not allowed to affect directly, it may strengthen identification to employ several less-strongly correlated instruments. This is a principal reason why over-identification is desirable.

In this model (and in many other models that we shall employ in this book), we use as an instrument a measure of the substantive complexity of pre-1964 jobs (derived from retrospective interviewing). The substantive complexity of pre-1964 jobs is allowed to directly affect occupational self-direction at both the time of the baseline interview in 1964 and the time of the follow-up interview, but is allowed to directly affect occupational position only at the time of the baseline interview. The rationale for not allowing a direct effect of the substantive complexity of pre-1964 jobs on occupational position at the time of the follow-up interview is that we believe that any effect of the substantive complexity of these earlier jobs on the occupational position of jobs held much later in men's occupational careers could only be indirect, either through its effect on occupational self-direction at the time of the baseline interview, or through its effect on occupational self-direction at the time of the follow-up interview, or through its effect on occupational position at the time of the baseline interview, or through some combination of these processes. Using the substantive complexity of pre-1964 jobs as an instrument identifies the equation for occupational position and also means that our deficit of information is down from two to one: we have added four more correlations to the information we have, but we are estimating only three more paths.

In later models, we shall introduce other instruments; but since these are not applicable to this model, we defer their consideration. For this model, we are still under-identified. How else, then, can one gain identification? The two principal methods that are used for achieving identification in this type of model are either to fix the contemporaneous reciprocal paths at zero, thus identifying the cross-lagged paths, or to fix the cross-lagged paths at zero, thus identifying the contemporaneous reciprocal paths.

Many analysts do the former, which is simpler to do: the model can be estimated as a set of ordinary least squares equations and does not require solving simultaneous equations. If the time-interval between our baseline and follow-up interviews were short, a matter of weeks or even months rather than a decade, we might do the same. But, since the time-interval is long, and magnitudes of cross-lagged paths are a function not only of the effects one wishes to measure but also of the reliability of whichever is the independent variable in the equation, this method does not tell us what we want to learn.

The alternative, of fixing the cross-lagged paths at zero and estimating the contemporaneous reciprocal effects, does provide most of the information we want: it tells us the relative magnitudes of the reciprocal effects of occupational position and occupational self-direction.[14] However, in models that do not estimate both cross-lagged and contemporaneous reciprocal effects, what appear to be *contemporaneous* reciprocal effects are actually *total* effects, representing both lagged and contemporaneous effects. When we use this method for identifying a model, then, we cannot say anything about the timing of effects, whether lagged or contemporaneous, but can only assess the total effects of the variables on each other. This is unfortunate, but it is a small price to pay to achieve well-identified, robust models. We shall pay this price in most of our models.

And then, finally, one can achieve identification in a way that we would prefer not to have to use but which often must be employed, fixing the correlation of the residuals of the endogenous variables at zero. This violates our a priori belief that these residuals may actually be correlated, but often one has no choice: lacking adequate instruments, one may have to use this method to achieve identifications. And even if one has sufficient instruments for the model to be just-identified (or even over-identified), many models cannot be solved without making the assumption of uncorrelated residuals.[15]

[14] For a discussion of the rationale and also the dangers of using the cross-lagged paths to identify the reciprocal effects of the endogenous variables, see Heise, 1975, pp. 184–5.

[15] Throughout this book, we test the correlations of the residuals of reciprocally related variables whenever it is possible to do so, generally fixing them at zero only when the correlations are statistically nonsignificant. But, for some models, we get statistically equivocal results unless we fix one or another correlation of residuals at zero.

A model of the reciprocal effects of occupational position and occupational self-direction

In the actual models for both the United States and Poland (figure 5.4), occupational position is a second-order concept, the first-order concepts that serve as its indicators being occupational status and job income. Occupational self-direction, too, is a second-order concept, the first-order concepts that serve as its indicators being the substantive complexity of the work, routinization, and closeness of supervision.

In the model for the United States (the upper half of figure 5.4), education is depicted as exogenous to both occupational position and occupational self-direction and is permitted to affect both directly, in 1964 and also in 1974. To provide identification for assessing the reciprocal effects of occupational position and occupational self-direction, we permit the occupational position of the job held in 1964 to directly affect the present job's occupational position but not its occupational self-direction; correspondingly, the occupational self-direction of the 1964 job is allowed to directly affect the present job's degree of occupational self-direction but not its occupational position. The relationship between occupational position and occupational self-direction is undoubtedly the outgrowth of longer-term processes of selective recruitment into and retention in particular jobs, individual career mobility, and changes in how work is organized. Our model depicts the outcomes of these ongoing processes.[16]

Those social characteristics that might be pertinent to the job placement of men who are well into their careers are permitted to affect both occupational position and occupational self-direction. For the United States, the relevant characteristics are age, race, national background, and religious background. We include these social characteristics primarily as statistical controls.

The model for Poland (the lower half of figure 5.4) is similar in most respects, the differences being mainly in our treatment of education, in the social characteristics that are statistically controlled, and in our data for the earlier job being retrospective information about the job immediately

[16] In this model, the correlation of the residuals of 1974 occupational position and occupational self-direction is fixed at zero. When we estimate this correlation, it is statistically nonsignificant. Even though statistically nonsignificant, we might nevertheless prefer to allow such a correlation – since the model is better specified when the correlation is allowed than when it is fixed at zero – except that doing so results in the standardized path from 1974 occupational self-direction to 1974 substantive complexity being slightly greater than 1.0 (a statistical anomaly known as a Heywood problem). Since such a model produces *stronger* paths from occupational position to occupational self-direction, and the reverse, than does the model that fixes the correlation of residuals at zero, it seems more conservative to fix the statistically nonsignificant correlation of residuals at zero.

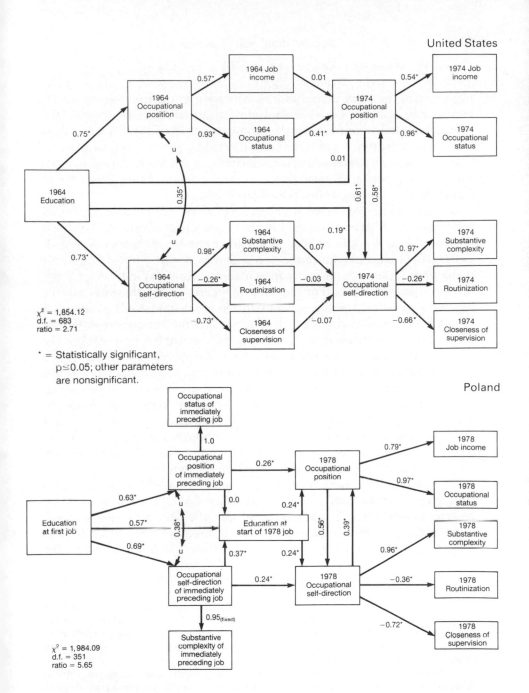

Figure 5.4 *Actual models of the relationship between social-stratification position and occupational self-direction. (First-order measurement parameters, paths from social characteristics to endogenous variables, and some correlations among residuals not shown.)*

preceding the job that the respondent held at the time of the interview in 1978. For Poland, we include both the respondent's education at the beginning of his work career and his education at the time he started his current job. The initial level of education is treated as exogenous, but the educational level at the time the respondent began his current job is endogenous, because it can have been affected by previous job experience. The only social characteristic that is controlled in this model is respondent's age, the other social characteristics in the US model being irrelevant in culturally more homogeneous post-war Poland.

We find that, for both countries, much of education's effect on occupational self-direction occurs during earlier stages of career. The effects of prior education on the level of occupational self-direction of early or mid-career jobs is quite similar in the two countries: for the United States, the path from education to the occupational self-direction of the 1964 job[17] is a very pronounced 0.73. For Poland, the path from education at the beginning of the occupational career to the occupational self-direction of the job held immediately prior to the one at which the respondent worked at the time of the interview in 1978 is nearly the same, at 0.69. Thereafter, the processes diverge, but the end results are much the same: for the United States, even though most men do not go on in their formal educations once they have embarked on their occupational careers, education continues to have a fairly substantial direct effect on their continuing levels of occupational self-direction – a statistically significant, non-trivial path (of 0.19) on occupational self-direction in the 1974 job. The cumulative effect of education on current occupational self-direction is 0.72, most of this effect indirect, through education's effect on earlier jobs.[18]

For Poland, where many men continue their formal educations well into their occupational careers, educational attainment is part of an ongoing process, in which the educational level attained before the work career begins affects the degree of occupational self-direction experienced early in the career, which in turn affects further education, which in turn affects the

[17] Since the 1964 job is the earliest job depicted in this model, the model makes it appear that education has strong effects on the occupational self-direction and occupational position of the job held in that particular year. But, if we were to treat the job conditions of pre-1964 jobs as endogenous, the effects of education would be shown to occur even earlier. For present purposes, the important point is that education's greatest effects on occupational self-direction occur earlier in men's careers than the mid- or later-career job held when men have been employed for at least ten years.

[18] Calculating direct, indirect, and total effects in reciprocal-effects models is more difficult than in recursive models because of feedback effects. The MILS computer program calculates total and indirect effects, following Fox (1980). This information makes possible the computation of particular indirect effects, e.g., the indirect effect of education on the occupational self-direction of the 1974 job via the occupational self-direction of the 1964 job.

occupational self-direction of the current job. Nevertheless, the long-term effect of education on occupational self-direction is substantially the same in both countries: the cumulative effect of initial level of education on current occupational self-direction is 0.73 for Poland and 0.72 for the United States.

Despite our statistically controlling education, prior occupational self-direction, and relevant social characteristics, the effect of occupational position on occupational self-direction is substantial in both countries, the direct effect being 0.61 in the United States and 0.56 in Poland. Moreover, the reciprocal effect of occupational self-direction on occupational position is also substantial, a direct effect of 0.58 for the United States and 0.39 for Poland. These mutually reinforcing processes result in extraordinarily high correlations between occupational position and occupational self-direction: 0.96 for the United States and 0.94 for Poland.

The high correlation between occupational position and occupational self-direction is no mere artifact of the level of aggregation in our analysis. Occupational status and the substantive complexity of work are themselves highly correlated, at 0.85 in the United States and 0.88 in Poland; adding job income, closeness of supervision, and routinization to the equations simply increases already high correlations to near-identities. Nor does the particular causal model we have employed exaggerate the degree of relationship. Simply computing zero-order correlations, adjusted for un-reliability of measurement, of factor scores based on the measurement models of occupational position and occupational self-direction yields the same conclusion. No matter what method we employ for assessing the magnitude of correlation, the result is very much the same – a near-unity correlation.

These findings confirm a central tenet of our interpretation: for both the United States and Poland, not only is social stratification highly correlated with occupational self-direction, but men's social-stratification positions have a decisive causal effect on their levels of occupational self-direction. (We again emphasize, though, that having a decisive causal effect does not mean having a unidirectional effect. Unidirectionality of effect is not essential to our interpretation.) It is therefore plausible to think that the psychological effects of social-stratification position might result in good part from the close relationship between social stratification and occupational self-direction.

OCCUPATIONAL SELF-DIRECTION AS AN EXPLANATORY LINK IN THE RELATIONSHIPS OF SOCIAL STRATIFICATION AND PSYCHOLOGICAL FUNCTIONING

Values, intellectual flexibility, and self-directedness of orientation

Distinguishing the direct effects of social-stratification position on values, orientations, and intellectual flexibility from its indirect effects through occupational self-direction is a matter of considerable importance to our interpretation. Do education and occupational position *directly* affect men's psychological functioning? Or is it, rather, that education and occupational position matter not for their own sakes but because they markedly influence a worker's opportunities to be self-directed in his work? Not even a near-unity correlation between occupational position and occupational self-direction necessarily means that social-stratification position and occupational self-direction have the same causal dynamics *vis-à-vis* other variables.

Because of the extremely high correlation between occupational position and occupational self-direction, a causal model that permitted both of them to directly affect some facet of psychological functioning would be afflicted with overwhelming problems of multicollinearity. To sidestep such problems, we disaggregate occupational position and occupational self-direction into their components and allow these components to affect one or another facet of psychological functioning. This is accomplished by extending the models depicted in figure 5.4 to allow occupational status, income, the substantive complexity of the work, routinization, and closeness of supervision, as well as education and pertinent social characteristics, to directly affect some specified facet of psychological functioning. It must be emphasized that this analysis does not yet take into account the stability of psychological functioning. Nor does it yet take into account that both occupational position and occupational self-direction may not only affect, but may also be affected by, psychological functioning.

Figure 5.5 provides an example that shows the effects of education, occupational position, and occupational self-direction on fathers' valuation of self-direction for children.[19] We also allow social characteristics that

---

[19] Since it would be exceedingly expensive and would serve no useful purpose to estimate anew a combined measurement and causal model for each facet of psychological functioning, we now impose the (unstandardized) parameters of the model depicted in figure 5.4 on causal models that use factor scores to index first-order concepts. Because factor scores are not entirely reliable, we correct the correlations of factor scores with each other and with other

might be pertinent to current job placement to affect both occupational position and occupational self-direction. These social characteristics, as well as others that might affect psychological functioning, are also allowed to affect whichever facet of psychological functioning is being assessed in the particular model[20] – in this case, parental valuation of self-direction. In the model for Poland, only educational level at the time of beginning the *current* job – not educational level as of the time of beginning the first job – is modelled as directly affecting parental valuation of self-direction. Thus, the modelling of direct effects on parental values is exactly comparable to that for the United States, even though the earlier part of the model is different.

In the model for the United States, education has a sizeable and statistically significant direct effect (0.47) on parental valuation of self-direction, but neither occupational status nor job income significantly affects parental valuation of self-direction. By contrast, two components of occupational self-direction – the substantive complexity of the work and closeness of supervision – have modest but none the less statistically significant effects (+0.19 and −0.11, respectively). Thus, education affects parental valuation of self-direction both directly and indirectly through occupational self-direction, but occupational position affects parental valuation of self-direction only indirectly.

In the model for Poland, *none* of the components of social stratification has a statistically significant direct effect on parental valuation of self-direction, but all three components of occupational self-direction significantly affect parental valuation of self-direction. Hence, the effects of social stratification on parental valuation of self-direction are preponderantly indirect through occupational self-direction.

Similar models for intellectual flexibility and for self-directedness of orientation and its principal first-order component dimensions (see table

---

variables, using information provided by MILS about the correlations of the factor scores with the "true" scores for the constructs. We fix the paths from concepts to indicators and the principal causal paths at the (unstandardized) values found in the more detailed model but (to put no undue constraints on the model) re-estimate the residuals and the correlations among residuals.

[20] For the United States, the pertinent social characteristics are age, race, national background, religious background, parental family socioeconomic status (a construct based on mother's and father's education, father's occupational status, and maternal and paternal grandfathers' occupational statuses), the urbanness and region of the country of the principal place where the respondent was raised, and the number of brothers and sisters he had. Some of the social characteristics in the US model are omitted from the Polish model because they are irrelevant in the culturally more homogeneous Polish society (namely, race, religious background, and national background) and others are omitted because we do not have the pertinent information (namely, mother's education, grandfathers' occupational statuses, region of origin, and number of children in the family of orientation).

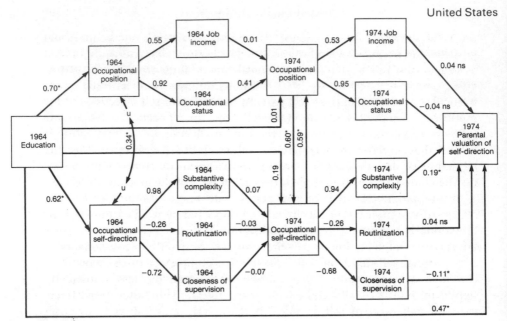

χ^2 (for causal model) = 424.17
d.f. = 213
ratio = 1.99

* Statistically significant,
  $p \le 0.05$ ns,
  nonsignificant; other
  parameters are fixed

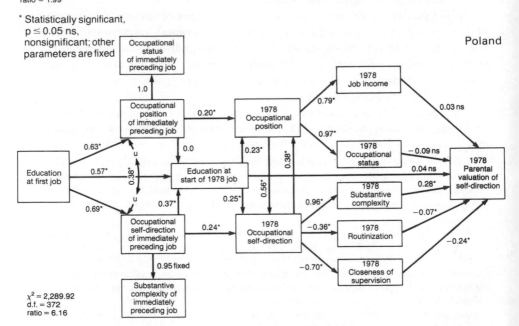

Poland

χ^2 = 2,289.92
d.f. = 372
ratio = 6.16

Figure 5.5 *The effects of education, occupational position, and occupational self-direction on parental valuation of self-direction. (Paths from social characteristics to endogenous variables and correlations among residuals not shown.)*

5.4) yield the general conclusion that, in both countries, one or another component of occupational self-direction significantly affects all these facets of psychological functioning, despite education and occupational position being statistically controlled. In particular, for the United States, the substantive complexity of work has a statistically significant effect, not only on parental valuation of self-direction, but also on intellectual flexibility and on self-directedness of orientation and three of its first-order components – authoritarian conservatism, standards of morality, and self-deprecation. Where substantive complexity does not have a significant effect, closeness of supervision fills the breach. In short, occupational self-direction, particularly the substantive complexity of work, is of considerable importance for all these facets of psychological functioning, independent of its close association with education and with occupational position.

It is equally clear, though, that occupational self-direction does not completely explain the effects of social-stratification position, particularly of education, on these facets of psychological functioning. Education has a statistically significant direct effect, not only on parental valuation of self-direction, but also on intellectual flexibility and on self-directedness of orientation and many of its components, above and beyond its indirect effects through occupational self-direction. Income, too, significantly affects some aspects of orientation, namely self-directedness of orientation and one of its components, trustfulness. Occupational status, however, is overwhelmed by the other independent variables in the equations, its regression coefficients being either statistically nonsignificant or reversed in sign from the zero-order correlations.

The models for Poland (see the second half of table 5.4) yield very similar conclusions. For Poland, we find that the substantive complexity of work has a statistically significant direct effect, not only on parental valuation of self-direction, but also on intellectual flexibility and on self-directedness of orientation and its three principal components – authoritarian conservatism, standards of morality, and trustfulness. Moreover, closeness of supervision, routinization, or both have statistically significant effects on parental valuation of self-direction, intellectual flexibility, and self-directedness of orientation and its three principal components. Still, for Poland as for the United States, occupational self-direction does not completely explain the effects of the educational component of social stratification on these facets of psychological functioning. Education has a statistically significant direct effect on intellectual flexibility and on self-directedness of orientation and its three principal components.

Where Poland may well differ from the United States is in the relative importance of the substantive complexity of work and closeness of supervision. Closeness of supervision is of *relatively* greater importance for

Table 5.4 The effects of social-stratification position and occupational self-direction on values, intellectual flexibility, and orientations to self and society

| | Standardized regression coefficients | | | | | |
| | Social-stratification position | | | Occupational self-direction | | |
	Education	Job income	Occupational status	Substantive complexity	Closeness of supervision	Routinization
A United States						
Values						
Parental valuation of self-direction	0.47*	0.04	−0.04	0.19*	−0.11*	0.04
Intellectual flexibility	0.29*	0.03	−0.08*	0.53*	−0.02	0.06*
Orientations to self and society						
Second-order dimensions						
Self-directedness	0.36*	0.06*	−0.13*	0.37*	−0.03	0.03
Distress	0.05	−0.01	0.06	−0.30*	0.05	0.02
First-order dimensions						
Authoritarian conservatism	−0.37*	−0.01	0.06	−0.23*	0.04	−0.02
Standards of moraltiy	0.18*	0.04	−0.19*	0.50*	−0.01	0.09*
Trustfulness	0.33*	0.07*	0.05	−0.09	−0.13*	−0.06
Idea-conformity	−0.09	−0.02	0.09	−0.05	0.25*	0.10*
Self-confidence	0.09	0.09*	−0.13	0.25*	0.04	0.02
Self-deprecation	−0.07	−0.03	0.12	−0.49*	−0.05	0.00
Anxiety	−0.01	0.00	−0.01	−0.15	0.15*	0.02

B *Poland*
Values

Parental valuation of self-direction	0.04	0.03	−0.09	0.28*	−0.24*	−0.07*
Intellectual flexibility	0.23*	−0.04	0.02	0.49*	−0.09*	−0.02
Orientations to self and society						
Second-order dimensions						
Self-directedness	0.15*	−0.03	−0.08	0.24*	−0.32*	−0.05*
Distress	0.00	0.02	0.17	0.07	0.02	−0.01
First-order dimensions						
Authoritarian conservatism	−0.14*	0.02	0.10	−0.24*	0.32*	0.04
Standards of moraltiy	0.18*	−0.09*	0.10	0.15*	−0.09	−0.06*
Trustfulness	−0.08*	−0.04	0.11	0.34*	−0.07	−0.12*
Idea-conformity	0.12*	−0.06	−0.19	−0.09	0.06	−0.02
Self-confidence	−0.08	−0.11*	0.02	−0.04	−0.09	0.02
Self-deprecation	−0.16*	−0.00	0.11	0.08	0.12	0.03
Anxiety	0.13*	0.00	−0.10	0.05	0.00	−0.06

* Statistically significant, 0.05 level or better.

Poland than for the United States in explaining the relationships of social stratification with parental valuation of self-direction, intellectual flexibility, self-directedness of orientation, and one pivotal component dimension of self-directedness of orientation – authoritarian conservatism. The overall conclusion for both countries is nevertheless the same: either the substantive complexity of work or closeness of supervision (or both) has a statistically significant direct effect on all these facets of psychological functioning.

Distress

The two countries differ dramatically, though, precisely where our analyses of chapter 4 would lead us to expect them to differ: in the relationships of social stratification and of occupational self-direction to distress.

For the United States, the picture is not much different for distress from what we found it to be for values, intellectual flexibility, and self-directedness of orientation: the substantive complexity of work has a statistically significant and rather substantial negative effect (of -0.30); no other component of occupational self-direction or of social stratification has a statistically significant effect. The picture is consistent for the first-order components of distress: the substantive complexity of the work, or closeness of supervision, or both, have statistically significant direct effects on all five component dimensions: trustfulness, idea-conformity, self-confidence, self-deprecation, and anxiety. In some instances, so too does education or income. From the US data alone, we would come to the same conclusion for distress and its component dimensions as for values, intellectual flexibility, and self-directedness of orientation: the effects of social stratification on distress are substantially attributable to occupational self-direction, with the lack of opportunity for occupational self-direction of those lower in the stratification hierarchy contributing to their greater degree of distress.

Not so for Poland. We found, as we reported in chapter 4, a major cross-national inconsistency in the relationship between social stratification and distress: a negative relationship for the United States, a positive relationship for Poland. Now we see part of the explanation. For the United States, as we have just learned, greater opportunity for occupational self-direction is associated with lower levels of distress; in particular, the more substantively complex the work, the less distressed the worker; *hence* the negative relationship between social stratification and distress. For Poland, we now learn, the substantive complexity of work does *not* bear such a negative relationship to distress; instead, the substantive complexity of work bears only a small, statistically nonsignificant, positive relationship to distress. Nor does either closeness of supervision or routinization significantly affect distress. Part of the explanation for social stratification not having a negative effect on distress for Poland, as it does for the United States, is that in Poland occupational self-direction somehow fails to ameliorate distress, as it does in the United States.

The same is true for the principal first-order components of distress – self-deprecation, anxiety, self-confidence, and idea-conformity: neither the substantive complexity of work, nor either of the other job conditions conducive to occupational self-direction, has a statistically significant direct effect on any of these dimensions of orientation. The relationships between social stratification and these dimensions of orientation, such as they are, do *not* result from opportunities, or lack of opportunities, to exercise occupational self-direction. We shall have to search elsewhere for the explanation of the cross-nationally inconsistent relationships between social stratification and distress.

It may be pertinent to note that closeness of supervision – which we have seen to be more important for explaining the effects of social stratification on some other facets of psychological functioning for Poland than for the United States – fails to have any significant effect on distress or its component dimensions for Poland. Why does close supervision have such decided effects on parental values and on authoritarian beliefs but fail to cause distress?

Assessing the role of occupational self-direction in explaining the psychological effects of social stratification

Whatever the explanation of the cross-nationally inconsistent relationships between social stratification and distress, we do have strong evidence in support of a crucial role for occupational self-direction in explaining the cross-nationally consistent effects of social stratification on values, intellectual flexibility, and self-directedness of orientation. Clearly, for both countries, much but not all of the psychological effect of social stratification is indirect, through social stratification's effect on occupational self-direction. It would appear, then, that the answer to our question, does social-stratification position affect values, intellectual flexibility, and self-directedness of orientation because of, or independent of, its close association with occupational self-direction is – both.

How much of the effect of social stratification on psychological functioning can be attributed to occupational self-direction? By re-aggregating the processes depicted in table 5.4, it is possible to assess the degree to which the effects of education, of occupational position, and of social-stratification position occur indirectly via occupational self-direction (see table 5.5). To make this assessment, we note the total effect of education, occupational position, or of social-stratification position on each

Table 5.5 *Effects of social-stratification position attributable to occupational self-direction*

	Social-stratification position			Education			Occupational position		
	Total effect	Indirect effect[a]	Indirect as %	Total effect	Indirect effect[a]	Indirect as %	Total effect	Indirect effect[a]	Indirect as %
A United States									
Values									
Parental valuation of self-direction	0.67	0.34	50%	0.63	0.16	26%	0.20	0.21	100%
Intellectual flexibility	0.82	0.67	81%	0.59	0.32	54%	0.37	0.43	100%
Orientations to self and society									
Second-order dimensions									
Self-directedness	0.63	0.46	73%	0.54	0.22	40%	0.19	0.29	100%
Distress	-0.34	-0.43	100%	-0.14	-0.20	100%	-0.23	-0.27	100%
First-order dimensions									
Authoritarian conservatism	-0.52	-0.30	57%	-0.50	-0.14	28%	-0.14	-0.19	100%
Standards of morality	0.49	0.52	100%	0.38	0.24	64%	0.16	0.33	100%
Trustfulness	0.45	0.11	25%	0.41	0.06	15%	0.16	0.07	43%
Idea-conformity	-0.27	-0.28	100%	-0.20	-0.13	65%	-0.10	-0.18	100%
Self-confidence	0.22	0.24	100%	0.17	0.12	68%	0.06	0.14	100%
Self-deprecation	-0.49	-0.54	100%	-0.30	-0.25	85%	-0.24	-0.34	100%
Anxiety	-0.38	-0.36	96%	-0.18	-0.17	94%	-0.25	-0.24	96%

B *Poland*

Values

Parental valuation of self-direction	0.44	0.47	100%	0.24	0.22	88%	0.25	0.32	100%
Intellectual flexibility	0.71	0.56	79%	0.48	0.26	53%	0.36	0.38	100%
Orientations to self and society									
Second-order dimensions									
Self-directedness	0.48	0.48	99%	0.34	0.21	62%	0.21	0.32	100%
Distress	0.31	0.12	40%	0.07	0.02	30%	0.30	0.12	40%
First-order dimensions									
Authoritarian conservatism	−0.46	−0.48	100%	−0.32	−0.21	65%	−0.20	−0.32	100%
Standards of morality	0.41	0.26	62%	0.31	0.12	38%	0.20	0.23	100%
Trustfulness	0.47	0.34	73%	0.15	0.21	100%	0.39	0.32	82%
Idea-conformity	−0.42	−0.18	44%	0.00	0.00	—	−0.42	−0.18	44%
Self-confidence	−0.15	−0.02	13%	−0.10	0.00	0%	−0.08	0.01	0%
Self-deprecation	0.02	—	—	−0.14	0.00	0%	0.14	0.04	28%
Anxiety	0.03	—	—	0.12	0.02	13%	−0.08	0.02	0%

[a] "Indirect effect" refers to only those effects that are indirect *through* occupational self-direction.

facet of psychological functioning; we calculate the indirect effects of each via occupational self-direction; and finally, we calculate the proportion of the total effect that is attributable to occupational self-direction.[21]

As shown in table 5.5, for both the United States and Poland, the effects of social-stratification position on parental valuation of self-direction, intellectual flexibility, and self- directedness of orientation and its component dimensions are very substantially attributable to occupational self-direction, the proportions generally ranging from one-half to two-thirds or more. Moreover, for almost all these facets of psychological functioning, the effects of occupational position are entirely attributable to occupational self-direction. The effects of education are in varying degree attributable to occupational self-direction, albeit generally not to the same extent as for occupational position, the discrepancy being larger for the United States than for Poland. Thus, we have firm evidence that the effects of social-stratification position – and of one of its two principal components, occupational position – on values, intellectual flexibility, and self-directedness of orientation are very substantially attributable to occupational self-direction. Even the effects of education on these facets of psychological functioning are in some substantial measure attributable to occupational self-direction.

For the United States, the same is true of the effects of social-stratification position on distress and its component dimensions: occupational self-direction explains the entire effect of social stratification, of occupational position, and of education on distress. In fact, the indirect effects of occupational self-direction are larger than the total effects of social-stratification position; the relatively modest negative effects of social-stratification position on distress would be greater if something else were not constraining the ameliorative effects of occupational self-direction.

For Poland, we have equivocal results. Forty percent of the (positive) effect of social stratification on distress is attributable to occupational self-direction, but this is based on what we have seen to be statistically nonsignificant effects of the substantive complexity of work, closeness of supervision, and routinization on distress. As for the component dimensions of distress, the total effects of social stratification on the two most important

---

[21] The total, direct, and indirect effects of education and of occupational position are provided by the MILS program, and from this information we calculate those indirect effects that are attributable specifically to occupational self-direction. Social-stratification position is not explicitly included in the model, but the MILS program does provide the intercorrelations of education, occupational status, and job income implied by the model. Using this information, we calculate the paths from an implicit second-order social-stratification construct to these three first-order constructs and, alternatively, to education and occupational position. This provides the data for computing the total and the indirect effects of social-stratification position on any particular facet of psychological functioning.

components – anxiety and self-deprecation – are trivial, too small for it to make any sense to ask what proportion of these effects may be attributed to occupational self-direction; and only 13 percent of the effect of social stratification on self-confidence is attributable to occupational self-direction. One could hardly conclude that this constitutes strong evidence for occupational self-direction providing much of the explanation of the positive effect of social stratification on distress in Poland; but neither does it provide unequivocal evidence against such an interpretation. We shall deal with the issue more frontally in chapter 8, when we examine the reciprocal effects of occupational self-direction and distress.

SOCIAL CLASS, SOCIAL STRATIFICATION, OCCUPATIONAL SELF-DIRECTION, AND PSYCHOLOGICAL FUNCTIONING

Whatever the explanation of the cross-nationally inconsistent effects of position in the social structure on distress, we have found that occupational self-direction substantially explains the effects of both class position and stratification position on values, intellectual flexibility, and self-directedness of orientation. But, since social class, social stratification, and occupational self-direction are so highly interrelated, we should take pains to be certain that occupational self-direction affects these facets of psychological functioning independently of *both* class and stratification. Otherwise, there would be the possibility of an alternative interpretation: that in examining the interrelationship of class, occupational self-direction, and psychological functioning, we have mistakenly attributed to occupational self-direction psychological effects that are really a consequence of social stratification; and that in examining the interrelationship of stratification, occupational self-direction, and psychological functioning, we have mistakenly attributed to occupational self-direction psychological effects that are really a consequence of social class. The best way to be certain that we have not done so is to include class, stratification, and occupational self-direction in the same regression equations.[22]

When we do, we find (table 5.6) that for both countries the standardized regression coefficients for the substantive complexity of work, closeness of

[22] In these multiple-regression equations, we include as independent variables (*vis-à-vis* one or another facet of psychological functioning) occupational status, educational attainment, income, dummy variables for all but one of the class categories, the substantive complexity of work, closeness of supervision, and routinization. In table 5.6 we present the standardized regression coefficients for only the substantive complexity of work, closeness of supervision, and routinization. (Since the regression coefficients for the class dummies have no meaning except by reference to the left-out class category, a full presentation of the regression coefficients would be both unwieldy and confusing.)

Table 5.6 *Standardized regression coefficients for the substantive complexity of work, closeness of supervision, and routinization in regression equations that include social stratification and social class*[a]

	United States Standardized regression coefficient for:			Poland Standardized regression coefficient for:		
	Substantive complexity	Closeness of supervision	Routinization	Substantive complexity	Closeness of supervision	Routinization
Vis-à-vis						
1 Parental valuation of self-direction	0.10	−0.11*	0.04	−0.03	−0.21*	−0.09*
2 Intellectual flexibility	0.50*	−0.06*	0.04	0.10*	−0.12*	−0.05*
3 Self-directedness of orientation	0.37*	−0.07*	0.00	0.02	−0.24*	−0.07*
4 Distress	−0.35*	0.04	−0.01	0.09	−0.04	−0.03

[a] In these equations, the dimension of psychological functioning in the left-hand column is the dependent variable; the independent variables are the substantive complexity of work, closeness of supervision, routinization of work, occupational status, job income, educational attainment, and dummy variables for all but one of the class categories.

* Statistically significant, $p < 0.05$.

supervision, or both remain statistically significant and non-trivial in magnitude in the regression equations for parental valuation of self-direction, intellectual flexibility, and self-directedness of orientation.

There is, as always, a cross-national difference with respect to distress: for the United States, the standardized beta coefficient for the substantive complexity of work is a substantial and statistically significant -0.35. This we see as compelling evidence that doing substantively complex work ameliorates distress. For Poland, the standardized beta coefficients for all three components of occupational self-direction are small and statistically nonsignificant — the most compelling evidence yet that the explanation of the effects of class and stratification on distress in Poland is not to be found in occupational self-direction.

There is another notable difference between the United States and Poland, this one not so much a sharp contrast as a variation on theme. The cross-nationally consistent theme is the importance of occupational self-direction for explaining the effects of social-structural position on parental valuation of self-direction, intellectual flexibility, and self-directedness of orientation. The variation on theme, once again, is the differential importance for the United States and Poland of the substantive complexity of work and of closeness of supervision. For the United States, the substantive complexity of work is decidedly more important for intellectual flexibility and for self-directedness of orientation, albeit not for parental valuation of self-direction. For Poland, closeness of supervision is more important for all three of these facets of psychological functioning.

In any case, whether the substantive complexity of work or closeness of supervision is the more important component of occupational self-direction, we have here impressive evidence that the psychological effects of occupational self-direction are no mere reflection of the close relationships of occupational self-direction with both class and stratification.

CONCLUSION

This chapter partially tests the fundamental hypothesis of our inquiry: that the cross-nationally consistent relationships of class and stratification with parental valuation of self-direction, intellectual flexibility, and self-directedness of orientation can be largely explained in terms of the greater opportunities for occupational self-direction afforded men who are more advantageously located in the class structure or more highly placed in the stratification order. The hypothesis is strikingly confirmed. Occupational self-direction clearly plays a major part in explaining the effects of class and stratification on these facets of psychological functioning. Admittedly, this might not be the case for facets of psychological functioning that we have not examined in our analyses, such as class consciousness. But, for the broad spectrum encompassed in our indices of values, self-directedness of orientation, and cognitive functioning, class and stratification affect psychological functioning in large part because of their close relationship to occupational self-direction.

There is one apparent anomaly in our findings: occupational self-direction provides little or no help in understanding the cross-nationally inconsistent relationships of both social class and social stratification with distress. Even here, though, we have further evidence of the great importance of occupational self-direction as a principal vehicle by which social structure affects psychological functioning. Our analyses clearly demonstrate that wherever occupational self-direction has cross-nationally consistent effects on psychological functioning, so too do social class and social stratification. The converse is also true: wherever occupational self-direction fails to have cross-nationally consistent psychological effects, class and stratification, too, fail to have cross-nationally consistent effects.

The implications of these findings are considerable. Social class is defined and indexed primarily in terms of ownership and control over the means of production and control over the labor powers of others, and secondarily in terms of the employment situation. Social stratification is defined in terms of a hierarchy of power, privilege, and prestige; it is indexed in terms of occupational status, education, and income. Neither class nor stratification is defined or indexed in terms of control over the conditions of one's own work. Nevertheless, position in the class structure affects psychological functioning, not primarily because of ownership or control over resources, nor because of control over other people, nor because of the employment situation, but primarily because class position affects opportunities for occupational self-direction. Stratification position affects psychological functioning not because of the status the job confers, nor because of the income that it affords, but because higher stratification position affords greater opportunities for occupational self-direction.

Occupational self-direction thus provides an incomplete, but powerful, explanation of the psychological effects of both major facets of social structure. We have thus strengthened the basic premise on which all our analyses of social structure and personality are premised: that social structure affects individual psychological functioning mainly by affecting the conditions of people's own lives.

We stated at the beginning of this book that we see class and stratification as alternative conceptualizations of social structure, both conceptualizations theoretically useful, albeit not necessarily for answering the same questions. We have seen (in chapter 4) that class and stratification have independent, albeit overlapping, and altogether parallel psychological effects: more advantaged position in the class structure and higher position in the stratification order lead to higher valuation of self-direction, greater intellectual flexibility, and a more self-directed orientation to self and society. We now see that this "parallelism" is more than coincidental. It happens for essentially the same reason – because both higher stratification position and more advantaged class position afford greater opportunity for occupational self-direction.

6

Issues of Causal Directionality in the Relationships of Class and Stratification with Occupational Self-direction and Psychological Functioning

We have to this point established a prima facie case that both social class and social stratification have decided effects on men's valuation of self-direction for their children, their intellectual functioning, and the self-directedness of their orientations. We have, moreover, established a similarly prima facie case that a principal reason why class and stratification have these psychological effects is because they are very important in determining how much opportunity men have to be self-directed in their work.

The argument, however, has thus far rested on untested assumptions about the directions of effects in the relationships between social structure and occupational self-direction, and between occupational self-direction and psychological functioning. Although we have shown that social stratification does indeed have a substantial effect on occupational self-direction, we have to this point only assumed that social class similarly affects occupational self-direction. Moreover, and more crucial, we have only assumed that occupational self-direction does affect parental values, intellectual flexibility, and self-directedness of orientation.

It could be argued, though, that the process is not one of class and stratification affecting psychological functioning, but of psychological functioning affecting attained position in the class structure and in the stratification order. It is essential that we reassess our assumptions about causal directionality.

It is *not* essential to our interpretation that the effects be unidirectional, from social structure to occupational self-direction, and from occupational self-direction to psychological functioning. It is, however, essential that the effects not be unidirectional in the opposite direction, or else what we have been interpreting as the psychological effects of social structure would in reality be nothing more than a reflection of processes of occupational mobility and of job molding. Our intent, then, is to ascertain whether position in the social structure actually affects or merely reflects psychological functioning.

We see three interrelated issues: the relationship between position in the social structure and occupational self-direction; the relationship between occupational self-direction and psychological functioning; and the possibility that psychological functioning could affect position in the social structure quite aside from whatever effects it might have on occupational self-direction. This chapter is addressed to an empirical assessment of these three issues.

THE RELATIONSHIP BETWEEN POSITION IN THE SOCIAL STRUCTURE AND OCCUPATIONAL SELF-DIRECTION

In our analysis of the relationship between social stratification and occupational self-direction, we found it useful to disaggregate social stratification into two principal components, occupational position and educational attainment. We found strong effects of occupational position on occupational self-direction and, reciprocally, of occupational self-direction on occupational position. We also found strong effects of educational attainment on occupational self-direction in both countries – the only cross-national difference being in whether the educational process continues into the occupational career. It therefore seems entirely justified to conclude that social stratification does have a strong effect on occupational self-direction, quite apart from occupational self-direction also affecting one's placement in the stratification order.

We cannot do this type of statistical analysis for social class, because social class is not an interval variable; there is no sensible way to model the reciprocal effects of six class categories with occupational self-direction. It is possible, however, to treat two of the principal occupational dimensions linked to social class, ownership and hierarchical position, as interval variables and to assess their reciprocal relationships with occupational self-direction.

In doing such an analysis, we must keep in mind that any change from being an owner to not being an owner, or the reverse, and any substantial change in hierarchical position (for example, from not being a supervisor to becoming a first-line supervisor, or from being a manager to becoming a first-line supervisor) constitutes a change in class position. Therefore, it is not possible for occupational self-direction (or anything else) to have a *contemporaneous* effect on ownership or on hierarchical position. There is no reason, however, why occupational self-direction could not have lagged effects on both ownership and hierarchical position. Thus, in modelling the reciprocal effects of ownership, hierarchical position, and occupational self-direction, it is a priori sensible to depict all effects on ownership and hierarchical position as lagged; effects on occupational self-direction can in principle be either contemporaneous or lagged.

Kohn and Schooler (1983, pp. 134–5)[1] did such an analysis for the United States in a longitudinal analysis of job structure; the pertinent parts of their analysis are reproduced in table 6.1. This analysis shows modest effects, both of ownership on the substantive complexity of work and of the substantive complexity of work on ownership. The analysis also shows more substantial effects of hierarchical position on the substantive complexity of work and, reciprocally, of the substantive complexity of work on hierarchical position, as well as unidirectional effects of hierarchical position on closeness of supervision and on routinization. All this suggests that class position decidedly affects opportunities for occupational self-direction, albeit not unidirectionally: over time, the exercise (or the failure to exercise) occupational self-direction also affects class placement.

This type of analysis requires longitudinal data about job conditions. Unfortunately, for Poland we do not have information about ownership and hierarchical position in earlier jobs and thus cannot carry out a comparable analysis. On the issue of whether class position actually affects, or only reflects, occupational self-direction, we must therefore rely on US data.

[1] Their causal model depicts the reciprocal relationships among some fourteen job conditions, the pertinent ones for our purposes being ownership, hierarchical position, and the conditions determinative of occupational self-direction – the substantive complexity of the work, closeness of supervision, and routinization. The other job conditions included in the overall model (namely, bureaucratization, time-pressure, heaviness, dirtiness, hours of work, the probability of being held responsible for things outside of one's control, the risk of loss of job or business, job protections, and job income) can for present purposes be regarded as statistical controls, along with the standard set of social characteristics. In this model, contemporaneous effects (i.e., of job conditions as measured at the time of the follow-up interviews in 1974 on other job conditions as measured at that same time) were tested, using cross-lagged effects as instruments. Any contemporaneous effect that proved to be statistically nonsignificant was then set to zero and the corresponding cross-lagged effect tested. If that effect proved to be nonsignificant, it too was set to zero. The one major exception to these procedures is that nothing was allowed to have a contemporaneous effect on ownership, hierarchical position, or bureaucratization, for such an effect, by definition, would mean a job change; as noted in the text, it might also be a change in class position. Instead, all effects on ownership, hierarchical position, and bureaucratization were depicted as lagged.

Table 6.1 *The reciprocal effects of ownership, hierarchical position, and occupational self-direction: US men*[a]

	Statistically significant effects of:				
On:	Ownership	Hierarchical position	Substantive complexity of work	Closeness of supervision	Routinization
Ownership	0.55(L)[b]	0.0[d]	0.08(L)	0.0	0.0
Hierarchical position	0.0	0.30(L)	0.20(L)	0.0	0.0
Substantive complexity of work	0.09(C)[c]	0.18(C)	0.36(L)	−0.24(C)	−0.11(C)
Closeness of supervision	0.0	−0.15(C)	−0.31(L)	0.08(L)	0.0
Routinization	0.0	−0.09(C)	0.0	0.0	0.27(L)

[a] Taken from a larger model of job structure in Kohn and Schooler, 1983 (table 6.1, pp. 134–5).
[b] "L" means a "lagged" effect, i.e. an effect of some variable as measured at the time of the baseline interview in 1964 on itself or on some other variable as measured at the time of the follow-up interview in 1974. The lagged effect of some variable on itself is the "stability" of that variable.
[c] "C" means a "contemporaneous" effect, i.e. an effect of some variable as measured at the time of the follow-up interview in 1974 on some other variable as measured at that same time.
[d] "0,0" means a statistically nonsignificant effect that has subsequently been fixed at zero.

Given the similarity of the US and Polish findings about the reciprocal relationships between social stratification and occupational self-direction, though, it seems improbable that the association between social class and occupational self-direction could result in large degree from class position affecting opportunities for occupational self-direction in the United States but solely from the exercise of occupational self-direction affecting class placement in Poland.

THE RECIPROCAL EFFECTS OF OCCUPATIONAL SELF-DIRECTION AND PSYCHOLOGICAL FUNCTIONING

The second issue – the crucial issue – is the relationship of occupational self-direction with values, intellectual flexibility, and self-directedness of orientation. We have thus far assumed that occupational self-direction actually affects these facets of psychological functioning. But what if the relationships between occupational self-direction and psychological functioning result predominantly from self-directed, intellectually flexible men seeking out, or being selected for, or molding their jobs to achieve maximum opportunities to be self-directed in their work?

We employ linear structural-effects causal modelling to assess the reciprocal effects of occupational self-direction and each facet of psychological functioning. Since a thorough appraisal of reciprocal effects requires longitudinal data, our ability to assess the reciprocal effects of occupational self-direction and psychological functioning for Poland is somewhat constrained. We can, however, make longitudinal assessments for the United States and we can develop simulated longitudinal models that provide tolerably good approximations for Poland.

Consider first the fully longitudinal models for the United States – illustrated for parental valuation of self-direction in the upper half of figure 6.1. In these models, occupational self-direction in the job held at the time of the baseline interview in 1964 is permitted to affect occupational self-direction in the job held at the time of the follow-up interview in 1974, and the particular facet of psychological functioning measured at the time of the baseline interview is permitted to affect that same facet of psychological functioning measured ten years later. Cross-lagged effects, however, are fixed at zero – they are used as instruments. This means that what appear in the models to be contemporaneous effects of occupational self-direction on psychological functioning and of psychological functioning on occupational self-direction are actually total effects, both lagged and contemporaneous.

Because nearly all of the men had completed their formal educations

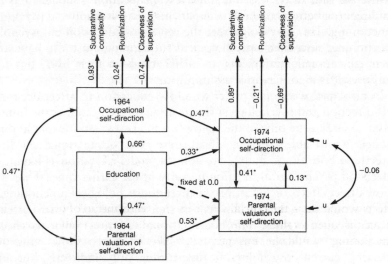

χ^2 (for the causal model) = 311.14
d.f. = 167
ratio = 1.86

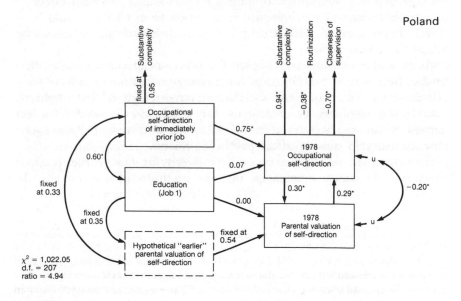

Poland

χ^2 = 1,022.05
d.f. = 207
ratio = 4.94

Figure 6.1 *The reciprocal effects of occupational self-direction and parental valuation of self-direction. (Paths from social characteristics to endogenous variables not shown.)* *Statistically significant, $p \leq 0.05$.

before the time of the baseline interviews, education is modelled as having unidirectional effects on both occupational self-direction and psychological functioning. This may exaggerate the effects of education on psychological functioning, since men's psychological functioning must also have affected their educational attainments at earlier times in their lives, but for our purposes it is a conservative assumption.

In principle, we would prefer to allow education to affect occupational self-direction and psychological functioning directly, both at the time of the baseline and at the time of the follow-up interviews. In the longitudinal US models, we are able to permit education to affect occupational self-direction directly at both times. But we are able to model education as having direct effects on psychological functioning only at the earlier time. If we were to allow direct effects of education on current psychological functioning, these effects would be mainly inconsistent in sign with the zero-order correlations. As a consequence, the effects of occupational self-direction on psychological functioning would be exaggerated.[2] We therefore show education as affecting current psychological functioning only indirectly, through its effects on earlier psychological functioning and on (earlier and current) occupational self-direction. Allowing education to have only indirect effects on current psychological functioning does not reduce the total effect of education on current psychological functioning from what it would be if direct effects were allowed; it simply depicts differently the processes by which this comes about.

As in earlier models (see chapter 5), other social characteristics that might affect current psychological functioning are permitted to have such effects and a subset of those social characteristics, those that might be seen by an employer as credentials for a job, are allowed to affect current occupational self-direction. Allowing non-credentialling social characteristics to directly affect psychological functioning, but to affect current occupational self-direction only indirectly (through earlier occupational self-direction) strengthens the identification of the models. In

---

[2] The one exception is the model for parental valuation of self-direction, where a direct path from education to parental valuation of self-direction as of the time of the follow-up survey would be significantly positive, and the path from occupational self-direction to parental valuation of self-direction would be reduced in magnitude (from 0.41 as shown in figure 6.1 to 0.14). For this general assessment of the relationship between men's occupational self-direction and psychological functioning, it seems preferable to treat parental values in the same way that we treat all other facets of psychological functioning. When we develop a model of the transmission of values in the family, in chapter 7, it will be more important to make the model as consonant as possible for fathers and for mothers; then we shall allow each parent's educational level to directly affect that parent's current values.

particular, it strengthens the identification for assessing the effects of psychological functioning on occupational self-direction.[3]

As shown for the United States in the upper half of figure 6.1, occupational self-direction both affects and is affected by men's valuation of self-direction for their children, with the predominant direction of effect from occupational self-direction to parental values. We find, too, that education has substantial, even if indirect, effects on parental values through its effects on earlier values and on occupational self-direction.

The causal models for Poland (illustrated for parental values in the lower half of figure 6.1) are similar to those for the United States, with two exceptions.

First, the Polish data about the occupational self-direction of the earlier job refer to the immediately prior job, not to the job held ten years earlier. Moreover, these data are limited and retrospective; we use retrospective accounts of the substantive complexity of work in the prior job as a proxy for the occupational self-direction of that job, fixing the path from occupational self-direction to the substantive complexity of work at the same (unstandardized) value as we find it to be for the 1978 job.

Second, and much more important, we have no data about earlier psychological functioning. We attempt to deal with this deficiency by simulating such a measure. To do so requires that we estimate the covariances of this hypothetical construct with other exogenous variables, i.e. social characteristics and earlier occupational self-direction. This we do by extrapolating from the covariances of these same variables with current psychological functioning, adjusting these covariances to take account of over-time changes as inferred from our longitudinal data for US men. We also fix the "stability" (that is, the path from earlier to later psychological functioning), initially, to be the same as we find it to be for US men. In further analyses, we shall subject these estimates to sensitivity analyses.

As figure 6.1 shows, for Poland as for the United States, occupational self-direction both affects and is affected by parental valuation of self-direction. For Poland, though, education – which in the Polish models is permitted to directly affect current psychological functioning – does not significantly affect fathers' values.

Similar models (summarized in table 6.2) show occupational self-direction to have statistically significant, generally substantial, effects on intellectual flexibility and on self-directedness of orientation and its first-

---

[3] These models impose the parameters from the measurement model of occupational self-direction on causal models that use factor scores as their indices of first-order concepts. The residual of occupational self-direction is allowed to correlate with the residual of the facet of psychological functioning being examined in the particular model. This correlation is retained if statistically significant; otherwise, it is fixed at zero.

Table 6.2 The reciprocal effects of occupational self-direction and psychological functioning

	Standardized path coefficients		
	Occupation self-direction to psychological functioning	Psychological functioning to occupational self-direction	Education to psychological functioning[a]
Values			
Parental valuation of self-direction			
(a) US men	0.41*	0.13*	0.47*
(b) Polish men	0.30*	0.29*	0.00
Intellectual flexibility			
(a) US men	0.27*	0.63*	0.64*
(b) Polish men	0.26*	0.11*	−0.01
Orientations to self and society			
A Second-order dimensions			
Self-directedness of orientation			
(a) US men	0.43*	0.28*	0.53*
(b) Polish men	0.31*	0.07*	0.00
Distress			
(a) US men	−0.21*	−0.04	−0.06
(b) Polish men	0.00	0.00	0.19*

B First-order dimensions

Authoritarian conservatism			
(a) US men	−0.29*	−0.21*	−0.50*
(b) Polish men	−0.23*	−0.08*	−0.01
Standards of morality			
(a) US men	0.32*	0.17*	0.40*
(b) Polish men	0.23*	0.06*	−0.01
Trustfulness			
(a) US men	0.22*	0.01	0.40*
(b) Polish men	0.21*	0.03	−0.05
Idea-conformity			
(a) US men	−0.12*	−0.18*	−0.28*
(b) Polish men	−0.14*	0.03	0.04
Self-confidence			
(a) US men	0.12*	0.15*	0.23*
(b) Polish men	−0.05	0.00	−0.02
Self-deprecation			
(a) US men	−0.27*	−0.15*	−0.23*
(b) Polish men	0.06	−0.04*	−0.09*
Anxiety			
(a) US men	−0.23*	−0.02	−0.09*
(b) Polish men	0.03	−0.01	0.06

[a] For the United States, where data are longitudinal, path is from education to baseline psychological functioning; for Poland, where data are cross-sectional, path is from education to current psychological functioning.

* Statistically significant, $p < 0.05$.

order components in both countries. Several facets of psychological functioning, in turn, affect occupational self-direction; the relationships are mainly reciprocal. Thus, our expectation that occupational self-direction does affect these facets of psychological functioning, albeit not necessarily unidirectionally, is impressively borne out by these analyses.

Before fully accepting this conclusion, though, we must consider whether the assumptions made in estimating the quasi-longitudinal Polish models are fully tenable. What if the "stabilities" (the paths from hypothetical earlier to later actual psychological functioning) should be higher – or lower – for Poland than for the United States? If so, does our importing these values from the US model distort the Polish reality? Similarly for the assumptions made about the covariances of the hypothetical earlier measures of psychological functioning with other exogenous variables: these are based on the actual Polish covariances of psychological functioning with these same variables, adjusted to take account of over-time change in these relationships as extrapolated from what we know from the US longitudinal data. But what if these adjustments are too large – or too small? Does our making such adjustments on the basis of US information distort the Polish reality?

To test both possibilities, we do "sensitivity" analyses, in which we systematically raise and lower the estimates, thus testing the robustness of the models. We have done this for parental valuation of self-direction, for intellectual flexibility, and for the two second-order dimensions of orientation to self and society – self-directedness of orientation and distress. The results are so consistent that it hardly seems necessary to go through these tedious procedures to test the robustness of the models for the first-order dimensions of orientation. All the models that we did test proved to be highly robust (see table 6.3), the conclusions we draw being changed to only a minor degree when the estimated stabilities and the estimated covariances are increased or decreased by even as much as 25 percent.

Thus, our expectation that occupational self-direction really does affect parental valuation of self-direction, intellectual flexibility, and self-directedness of orientation is fully borne out by these analyses, both for the United States and for Poland. The analyses also demonstrate that the effects are mainly reciprocal.

Distress

The one real difference between the two countries is precisely where we should by now expect to find it: in the reciprocal relationship between occupational self-direction and distress (as well as in the relationships of occupational self-direction and the component dimensions of distress). In the model for the United States (again, see table 6.2), occupational self-direction has a modest but statistically significant, negative effect on distress, while education has only a small, statistically nonsignificant negative effect on (1964) distress. In the model for Poland, occupational self-direction has no effect at all on distress, while education has a modest but statistically significant *positive* effect on distress. We do not interpret education's positive effect on distress as necessarily meaning that educational attainment *per se* increases distress; since education is the only component of social stratification included in this model, and since no job conditions other than those directly involved in occupational self-direction are included in the model, education may be playing the role of proxy for social stratification or for job conditions (or other conditions of life) not explicitly included in the model. The model therefore is inconclusive in telling us what actually does cause distress; but it is conclusive – as no unidirectional analysis could be – in telling us that occupational self-direction is not the culprit.

Similar models for the first-order components of distress yield similar conclusions: for the United States, occupational self-direction decreases self-deprecation, anxiety, and idea-conformity, and increases self-confidence and trustfulness. With the singular exception of idea-conformity, these are all consistent with the conclusion that occupational self-direction decreases distress. Even the apparent exception is no real exception. Since idea-conformity is negatively related to both self-directedness of orientation and distress, the hypothesis that occupational self-direction increases self-directedness of orientation leads us to expect a *negative* effect of occupational self-direction on idea-conformity, but the hypothesis that occupational self-direction decreases distress leads us to expect a *positive* effect of occupational self-direction on idea-conformity. Both cannot happen; the self-directedness component of idea-conformity prevails.

For Poland, occupational self-direction *decreases* idea-conformity, *increases* trustfulness, and fails to have a statistically significant effect on self-confidence, self-deprecation, or anxiety. The effect of occupational self-direction on trustfulness is opposite in sign to the hypothesis of occupational self-direction increasing distress, but consistent with trustfulness' reflecting not only distress but also self-directedness of orientation.

Thus, the only possible evidence for occupational self-direction increasing distress in Poland is that occupational self-direction decreases idea-conformity, and idea-conformity is negatively related to distress. With this single exception, there is no evidence at all of occupational self-direction actually increasing distress – not for Poland, and certainly not for the United States. And even the exception does not constitute a cross-national inconsistency; as we have seen, occupational self-direction has a negative

Table 6.3 Sensitivity analyses for quasi-longitudinal Polish models

	Standardized path coefficients		
	Occupational self-direction to psychological functioning	Psychological functioning to occupational self-direction	Education to psychological functioning
A *Stability of psychological functioning*			
Parental valuation of self-direction			
(a) Decrease stability by 25%	0.33*	0.29*	0.03
(b) Decrease stability by 10%	0.31*	0.29*	0.01
(c) Stability as in US model	0.30*	0.29*	0.00
(d) Increase stability by 10%	0.29*	0.29*	−0.01
(e) Increase stability by 25%	0.27*	0.29*	−0.02
Intellectual flexibility			
(a) Decrease stability by 25%	0.36*	0.08*	0.02
(b) Decrease stability by 10%	0.30*	0.10*	0.00
(c) Stability as in US model	0.26*	0.11*	−0.01
(d) Increase stability by 10%	0.22*	0.13*	−0.02
(e) Increase stability by 25%	0.16*	0.15*	−0.04
Self-directedness of orientation			
(a) Decrease stability by 25%	0.35*	0.06*	0.02
(b) Decrease stability by 10%	0.33*	0.07*	0.01
(c) Stability as in US model	0.31*	0.07*	0.00
(d) Increase stability by 10%	0.30*	0.07*	−0.01
(e) Increase stability by 25%	0.28*	0.08*	−0.02

Distress			
(a) Decrease stability by 25%	0.06	−0.01	0.14*
(b) Decrease stability by 10%	0.02	0.00	0.17*
(c) Stability as in US model	0.00	0.00	0.19*
(d) Increase stability by 10%	−0.03	0.01	0.21*
(e) Increase stability by 25%	−0.06	0.01	0.24*
B *Covariations of hypothetical measure of "early" psychological functioning with other exogenous variables*			
Parental valuation of self-direction			
(a) Covariations increased by 25%	0.27*	0.29*	−0.02
(b) Covariations as calculated by a priori procedures	0.30*	0.29*	0.00
(c) Covariations decreased by 25%	0.33*	0.29*	0.03
Intellectual flexibility			
(a) Covariations increased by 25%	0.16*	0.15*	−0.04
(b) Covariations as calculated by a priori procedures	0.26*	0.11*	−0.01
(c) Covariations decreased by 25%	0.36*	0.08*	0.02
Self-directedness of orientation			
(a) Covariations increased by 25%	0.28*	0.08*	−0.02
(b) Covariations as calculated by a priori procedures	0.31*	0.07*	0.00
(c) Covariations decreased by 25%	0.35*	0.06*	0.02
Distress			
(a) Covariations increased by 25%	−0.06	0.01	0.24*
(b) Covariations as calculated by a priori procedures	0.00	0.00	0.19*
(c) Covariations decreased by 25%	0.06	−0.01	0.14*

* Statistically significant, $p < 0.05$.

effect on idea-conformity for the United States, too. The reciprocal-effects models thus make it reasonably certain that occupational self-direction does not actually increase distress in Poland. The story, instead, is that occupational self-direction ameliorates distress in the United States but somehow fails to do so in Poland. We shall pursue this issue further in chapter 8.

Distress aside, though, it would appear that occupational self-direction truly does provide a cross-nationally consistent explanation of the psychological effects of both social stratification and social class: occupational self-direction is not merely correlated with, but has an actual causal effect on men's values, intellectual flexibility, and self-directedness of orientation.[4]

In finding that, for both the United States and Poland, occupational self-direction has an actual causal effect on men's values, intellectual flexibility, and self-directedness of orientation, we provide solid evidence for the interpretation that self-direction in one's work leads to valuing self-direction more generally — as measured here, it leads to valuing self-direction for one's children — to greater intellectual flexibility, and to having a more open, flexible orientation to society. Lack of opportunity for self-direction in one's work leads to valuing conformity to external authority, to diminished intellectual flexibility, and to having a generally conformist orientation to self and society. In short, the lessons of the job are generalized to one's stance toward the larger society, in socialist as well as in capitalist society.

Herein lies the core explanation of the cross-nationally consistent relationships of both social stratification and social class with values, intellectual flexibility, and self-directedness of orientation. We have here as

---

[4] Since these models test only contemporaneous, but not cross-lagged, effects, they do not tell us whether the effects of occupational self-direction on values, orientations, and intellectual flexibility are ongoing and continuous or occur only over some longer interval of time. Nor do they tell us whether the effects of values, orientations, and intellectual flexibility on occupational self-direction result primarily from men molding their jobs to fit their values (primarily a contemporaneous process) or from the selection of men into jobs for which they are suited and out of jobs for which they are not suited (a lagged process). Using the longitudinal US data, Kohn and Schoenbach (1983, pp. 173–4) attempted to estimate models that simultaneously assess the contemporaneous and lagged reciprocal effects of occupational self-direction and psychological functioning. They were only partially successful. A model of the reciprocal effects of occupational self-direction and ideational flexibility clearly and unambiguously shows that the effect of occupational self-direction on ideational flexibility is contemporaneous, while that of ideational flexibility on occupational self-direction is lagged. A similar model for self-directedness of orientation is somewhat equivocal, but the results are consonant: occupational self-direction has a significant contemporaneous effect on self-directedness of orientation, while a self-directed orientation has a significant lagged effect on occupational self-direction. Unfortunately, the identification of this type of model is not strong enough to reach statistically sensible solutions for other facets of psychological functioning.

well part (but only part) of the explanation of why class and stratification do not have cross-nationally consistent effects on distress: it is because occupational self-direction fails to have cross-nationally consistent effects on that important facet of psychological functioning.

THE DIRECT EFFECTS OF PSYCHOLOGICAL FUNCTIONING ON CLASS PLACEMENT AND STATUS ATTAINMENT

The final issue of causal directionality is the possibility that psychological functioning might affect class placement and status attainment by selection processes *other than* by affecting occupational self-direction. More intellectually flexible men, or men who value self-direction more highly, for example, might be promoted into jobs with more supervisory or administrative responsibility, or might open their own businesses. Thus, values, intellectual flexibility, self-directedness of orientation, and even distress might over time have possibly substantial *direct* effects on position in the class structure and in the stratification order – above and beyond their indirect effects through occupational self-direction.

To test this possibility we rely on longitudinal analysis of the reciprocal effects of ownership, hierarchical position, and the principal facets of psychological functioning. An analysis focused on ownership and hierarchical position is of course directly pertinent to issues of class placement, only inferentially pertinent to issues of status attainment. But since, as we have seen, the correlation between occupational self-direction and occupational position is nearly unity, it would be impossible to control occupational self-direction in a reciprocal-effects assessment of the relationship between occupational position and psychological functioning. The substantive implication of this methodological fact is that it would be nearly impossible for psychological functioning to affect status attainment other than by affecting occupational self-direction. The question to be answered, then, is how psychological functioning might affect class placement.

Kohn and Schooler (1983, table 6.4, p. 149) have, for the United States, included the analysis that concerns us in their assessment of the reciprocal relationships among major dimensions of job structure, intellectual flexibility, self-directedness of orientation, and distress.[5] The pertinent parts of

---

[5] This model is an extension of the model of job structure (from which table 6.1 is excerpted), containing all the job conditions and social characteristics included in that model, plus the three dimensions of psychological functioning and additional pertinent social characteristics. In testing the reciprocal effects of job conditions and psychological functioning, and of the three dimensions of psychological functioning on one another, they used essentially the same methods of identification, first testing contemporaneous effects, using the cross-lagged

Table 6.4   *The effects of psychological functioning on ownership, hierarchical position, and occupational self-direction: US men[a]*

	Statistically significant direct effects of:		
	Intellectual flexibility	Self-directedness of orientation	Distress
On:			
Ownership	0.06(L)[b]	0.0	0.0
Hierarchical position	0.0[d]	0.0	0.0
Substantive complexity of work	0.26(L)	0.0	0.0
Closeness of supervision	0.0	−0.13(L)	0.0
Routinization	0.0	0.0	0.0
Intellectual flexibility	0.57(L)	0.24(C)[c]	0.0
Self-directedness of orientation	0.13(C)	0.43(L)	−0.08(C)
Distress	0.0	−0.25(C)	0.54(L)

[a] Taken from a larger model of the reciprocal effects of job conditions and psychological functioning in Kohn and Schooler, 1983 (table 6.4, p. 149).

[b] "L" means a "lagged" effect, i.e. an effect of some variable as measured at the time of the baseline interview in 1964 on itself or on some other variable as measured at the time of the follow-up interview in 1974. The lagged effect of some variable on itself is the "stability" of that variable.

[c] "C" means a "contemporaneous" effect, i.e. an effect of some variable as measured at the time of the follow-up interview in 1974 on some other variable as measured at that same time.

[d] "0.0" means a statistically nonsignificant effect that has subsequently been fixed at zero.

their analysis are reproduced in table 6.4. Here again (as in table 6.1), nothing is allowed to have a contemporaneous effect on either ownership or hierarchical position, for a change in ownership or a substantial change in hierarchical position would constitute a change in class position. But psychological functioning may have lagged effects on both ownership and hierarchial position. These turn out to be insubstantial. Although there is a statistically significant direct effect of intellectual flexibility (at the time of the baseline interview) on ownership (at the time of the follow-up interview), this effect is quite small (0.06) and there is no significant effect of intellectual flexibility on hierarchical position, nor of either self-directedness of orientation or distress on either ownership or hierarchical position.

effects as instruments; then, for any contemporaneous effect found to be statistically nonsignificant, setting that effect to zero and testing the corresponding cross-lagged effect. As before, they allowed nothing to have a contemporaneous effect on ownership or on hierarchical position – for that would constitute a new job – but instead depicted all effects on those variables as lagged.

This does not mean that psychological functioning does not affect class placement. Instead, it suggests that the principal mechanism by which psychological functioning affects class position is by affecting occupational self-direction.

Taking into account both personality's direct effects on ownership and hierarchical position and its indirect effects through occupational self-direction, we conclude that these effects are not so large as to dwarf those of class position or of stratification position on personality. Quite the contrary: position in the class structure and in the stratification order decidedly affect psychological functioning.

For Poland, we lack the longitudinal data to do a comparable analysis. Since, at the time of our interviews, ownership was of only minor importance as a determinant of class position in Poland (and that only with respect to becoming a petty bourgeois), we need not be concerned about the possible effects of personality on ownership. The issue, then, is whether personality might have dramatically greater importance for attaining a supervisory or management position in the centralized economy of Poland than in the less centralized economy of the United States.

Some might argue that this was indeed possible, that political loyalty (as distinct from political, educational, and other credentials) played an important part in class placement in Poland at that time. If so, was political loyalty so dominant a criterion for class placement as to dwarf the effects of class position on personality? And was political loyalty so closely tied to personality, even to the dimension of personality we have termed self-direction versus conformity to external authority, as to amount to personality having an essentially unidirectional effect on class placement? We greatly doubt it.

CONCLUSION

The central issue for this chapter is whether position in the social structure actually affects, or merely reflects, personality. Our interpretation requires the former. It does *not* require that the effects be unidirectional, only that position in the social structure have appreciable effects on occupational self-direction and that occupational self-direction, in turn, have appreciable effects on personality. It is entirely consonant with our interpretation that personality should also have appreciable effects on position in the class structure and in the stratification order, either directly or indirectly through occupational self-direction – provided that these effects are not so large as to dwarf those of class and stratification on personality.

Our analyses demonstrate that there are important effects both of position in the social structure on psychological functioning and of psychological functioning on position in the social structure. These analyses do not tell us, with any degree of precision, to what degree the relationships of class and stratification with parental valuation of self-direction, intellectual flexibility, and self-directedness of orientation result from the effects of men's class and stratification positions on their psychological functioning, and to what degree the relationships result from the effects of men's psychological functioning on their class positions and status attainments. Not only do we lack the longitudinal data to make a complete assessment of the issues for Poland, but there is no way, even for the United States, for us to take account of selection procedures that occurred before the time of the baseline interviews. The analyses do demonstrate, however, that there are decided effects of class and stratification on personality. The relationships between social structure and personality most certainly do not result solely or even predominantly from personality determining class placement and status attainment.

These analyses also demonstrate that occupational self-direction plays the pivotal role in explaining both the effects of social structure on personality and the effects of personality on achieved position in the social structure. Position in the class structure and in the stratification order affect men's values, intellectual flexibility, and self-directedness of orientation primarily *because* they affect occupational self-direction; occupational self-direction, in turn, affects these facets of psychological functioning. These facets of psychological functioning affect men's positions in the social structure mainly *because* they affect occupational self-direction, which then affects class placement and status achievement.

7

Social Structure and the Transmission of Values in the Family

In this chapter, we extend our analysis intergenerationally. Having learned how fathers' positions in the class structure and the stratification order affect their values for their children, we are impelled to ask, what effect, if any, do fathers' values have on their children's values?

In considering the effects of parental values on children's values, it is imperative that we bring mothers' values into play. Moreover, since mothers' values presumably are affected by their social-structural positions and their job conditions, just as are fathers' values, we must greatly enlarge our interpretation. Our analyses must now encompass the effects of the family's social-structural position and of both parents' job conditions on parental values, as well as the effects of parental values upon offspring's values.

Fortunately, we have the requisite data to conduct such analyses. For the United States, we have interviews with the wives of those men who were married at the time of the follow-up interview and with the very child about whom the parental values questions had been asked in the baseline interview and were asked again in the follow-up interview. For Poland, we have interviews with the wives and children of a subsample of the fathers interviewed in the original survey, these interviews conducted one-and-a-half to two years after the interviews with the fathers.

These data permit us to address two major issues: *to what extent* do the social-class and social-stratification positions of the parental family affect the values of its adolescent and young-adult offspring; and *what are the processes* by which these social-structural positions affect offspring's values? Both questions, of course, are classic issues for the sociology and social psychology of socialization.

The evidence of our own research, presented in earlier chapters, clearly demonstrates that class and stratification have substantial effects on fathers' values. There is little evidence, though, that the family's class and stratification positions have appreciable effects on the values of its adolescent and young-adult *offspring* (Bengtson and Lovejoy, 1973). Nor, for that matter, is there much evidence that parents' values have an appreciable effect on their children's values. Quite the contrary: past research has indicated surprisingly weak relationships between parents' and children's values (Jennings and Niemi, 1968; Furstenberg, 1971; Clausen, 1974; Bengtson, 1975; Niemi et al., 1978; Skvoretz and Kheoruenromne, 1979; Gecas, 1980; Nowak, 1981; Hoge et al., 1982; Looker and Pineo, 1983; Sulek, 1985; see also Jalowiecki, 1978; Troll and Bengtson, 1979; Adamski, 1981; Kohn, 1983; Smith 1983). And yet, as Clausen (1974) put it, "[a] basic tenet of socialization theory – almost all socialization theory – is that the child's core value orientations are learned in the family . . ."

We believe that it is not socialization theory but the empirical evidence that is deficient. We therefore hypothesize that the class and stratification positions of the parental family appreciably affect the values of adolescent and young-adult offspring and, furthermore, that this occurs mainly because the family's social-structural position affects the parents' own values and parents' values, in turn, affect their children's values.

We further hypothesize that the effect of social class and social stratification on children's values, as mediated through parents' values, is not peculiar to any particular economic or political system, but is built into the structure of industrial society. Comparative analyses of the United States and Poland will not test this hypothesis definitively, but will certainly add greatly to its plausibility or challenge it frontally.

Our further intent is to explicate the mechanisms by which the family's class and stratification positions affect children's values. Here we build on the analyses of chapters 5 and 6, which point to the pivotal role of occupational experience, specifically the opportunity to exercise self-direction in one's work. We extend those analyses in several ways: by simultaneously examining the relationship between the exercise of self-direction in one's work and the values of husband, wife, and child; by assessing the influence of each family member's values on the values of the others; and, basic to all the rest, by treating the family as a subsystem of the larger social system.

THE DATA ON WHICH THE TRANSMISSION-OF-VALUES ANALYSES ARE BASED

Both the US and Polish samples consist of triads: father, mother, and one randomly selected child.

At the time of the US baseline interview in 1964, every man who was the father of at least one child living at home and aged 3–15 years was asked about his values *vis-à-vis* a child of the age and sex of a randomly selected child of his own. Ten years later, in 1974, when NORC re-interviewed a representative subsample of 25 percent of the men in the baseline survey, the interviewers again asked the fathers about their values *vis-à-vis* someone of the age and sex of the same child (now ten years older) on whom the 1964 inquiry had been focused. At that time, NORC also interviewed the wives of those men who were then married and the child who was the referent of the values questions – these "children" now 13–25 years old. These interviews were conducted separately, with no respondent present during any other respondent's interview. There are 352 families in the US sample of families.

In 1978, using the same procedures as those used in the US baseline survey, the interviewers of the Polish Academy of Sciences asked each Polish father who had at least one child aged 3–15 living at home about his values *vis-à-vis* a child of the age and sex of a randomly selected child of his own. In 1979–80, one-and-a-half to two years after these fathers were inter- viewed, the Polish Academy of Sciences interviewed those children who were then 13–17 years old (N = 177) and, separately, their mothers. This age-range was intended to maximize the overlap with the age-range of the US offspring. Although the data from mothers and children were secured one-and-a-half to two years after those from fathers, we are treating the Polish data as if the interviews with father, mother, and child were contemporaneous.

Because the US and Polish surveys are methodologically different – one partially longitudinal, the other entirely cross-sectional – we are limited in our ability to make direct US–Polish comparisons. But that is not our purpose. In studying the effects of social structure on the values of adolescent and young-adult offspring in a capitalist and a socialist society, our intent is to see whether these effects – and the processes that produce them – are similar in the two types of societies. For this purpose, the surveys need not be exactly comparable, so long as both are appropriate to the task.

Since both the US and Polish samples are based on intact families, we cannot generalize our findings to families from which either parent is absent. Nor can we safely generalize to children outside the age-range of those in the families studied. It is quite possible that parents' values have a greater effect on the values of younger children, before they are subject to the possibly conflicting values of school and peers or, conversely, that the effects of parents' values on children's values come to full fruition only as the children mature. And, since the size of our samples is limited, we are not able to explore the theoretically important issue of whether the correlations of parents' and children's values may be higher for same-sex or opposite-sex pairs.

A MEASUREMENT MODEL OF PARENTS' AND CHILDREN'S VALUES

There is no change in our conceptualization of parental values: by parental values we mean the values that parents would most like to see embodied in their children's behavior. Parent-to-child value-transmission implies that children come to hold the same values for themselves that their parents think desirable for them. We therefore asked parents about their values for children; we asked children about their values for themselves.

Our analyses continue to focus on one primary dimension of values, namely valuation of self-direction versus conformity to external authority – self-direction emphasizing internal standards for behavior; conformity, externally imposed rules. We select this dimension for three reasons. The analyses of previous chapters demonstrate that valuation of self-direction is closely related to both social class and social stratification. Furthermore, valuation of self-direction is of considerable theoretical importance in its own right, underlying many facets of self-conception and social orientation. Finally, extensive cross-national analyses have found self-direction versus conformity to be a "universal" dimension of parental values (Kohn and Schoenbach, 1980).

Our method for asking mothers about their values for their children is identical to that for asking fathers about their values: we asked both parents to partially rank a standard set of thirteen characteristics in terms of how desirable they consider these characteristics to be for a child of the age and sex of a randomly selected child of their own. Since some of the characteristics about which we inquired were intended to apply to younger children, we modified the question wording slightly when asking about older offspring.[1]

We then asked that very child – the subject of the present inquiry – to partially rank that same set of characteristics in terms of how desirable he or she considered each of them to be.

As we have seen, this mode of inquiry results in a linear dependency of each of the value-choices on the set of all the others. We again sidestep this problem, by omitting some of the characteristics from the variance–

---

[1] In particular, "that he acts like a boy should" (or "that she acts like a girl should") was changed to "that he acts like a man should" (or "that she acts like a woman should") and "that he (she) gets along well with other children" was changed to "that he (she) gets along well with others."

covariance matrices on which the confirmatory factor analyses are based. We deliberately do not follow our earlier procedure of covarying child's age out of these matrices, because it is more appropriate to the causal analyses that follow to include child's age as an independent variable.

The characteristics included in the US measurement model are the items that, in exploratory factor analyses of fathers', mothers', and children's values, related most consistently to the first factor, which reflects valuation of self-direction versus conformity to external authority; similarly for the Polish measurement model. Since an extensive multinational comparison of factor analyses of mothers' and fathers' values (Kohn and Schoenbach, 1980) shows that linguistic and cultural differences may make particular characteristics more indicative of self-direction versus conformity in some studies than in others, it is not surprising that the resulting sets of characteristics are not identical for the United States and Poland. In fact, though, six of the eight characteristics thus selected are the same for both countries. These are "good manners," "neatness and cleanliness," "good sense and sound judgment," "obedience to parents," "responsibility," and "being interested in how and why things happen" (curiosity). The US measurement model includes, also, "consideration" and "acts as a boy or girl (man or woman) should;" the Polish model includes "self-control" and "being a good student," the latter of course being more appropriate to the younger age-range of the Polish children.

Since our unit of analysis is the family, we develop for each country a three-person model that measures fathers', mothers', and children's valuations of self-direction (see table 7.1). A perplexing issue in constructing these models is how to take into account that members of a family may not only share the same underlying values, but may also impute idiosyncratic connotations to one or another component characteristic. What is the most appropriate way to differentiate shared valuation of self-direction from shared, family-specific, interpretations of the meaning of particular characteristics?

In practice, this comes down to a decision about how to treat inter-person correlations of the residuals of the same characteristic. (Remember that in confirmatory factor analysis, the residual of an indicator represents that portion of the variance of the indicator that is not "explained" by the underlying concept. In this case, the residual of a characteristic is that portion of its variance that does not reflect valuation of self-direction versus conformity to external authority.) If we constrain to zero a correlation of the residuals of, for example, father's and child's valuations of "responsibility," this is tantamount to saying that, if both father and child value "responsibility", it is because they both value self-direction; their both valuing "responsibility" should therefore contribute to the correlation between fathers' and children's valuations of self-direction. If, however, we allow a correlation of the residuals of father's and child's valuations of "responsibility" – which can decrease the correlation of fathers' and children's valuations of self-direction – we ensure that we do not infer a higher father–child correlation than may actually be the case.

Since it is always preferable to load the methodological dice *against* our hypotheses, we want to be certain that we do not overestimate the correlations between parents' and children's (or between mothers' and fathers') valuation of self-direction, even at the risk of underestimating

Table 7.1　*Measurement models of fathers', mothers', and offspring's valuation of self-direction*

A　US families (children aged 13–25 years when interviewed)

	Fathers 1964	Fathers 1974	Mothers 1974	Children 1974
	Paths from concept, valuation of self-direction, to "indicators" of that concept			
Indicators:				
1　Good manners	−0.34*	−0.31*	−0.35*	−0.21*
2　Neat and clean	−0.32*	−0.38*	−0.25*	−0.31*
3　Good sense and sound judgment	0.24*	0.23*	0.31*	0.29*
4　Acts as a boy/girl (man/woman) should	−0.21*	−0.25*	−0.24*	−0.49*
5　Obedient to parents	−0.37*	−0.32*	−0.39*	−0.18*
6　Responsible	0.40*	0.49*	0.38*	0.16*
7　Considerate	0.34*	0.35*	0.22*	0.19*
8　Interested in how and why things happen	0.37*	0.25*	0.31*	0.23*
(Correlations of residuals not shown)				
	Intercorrelations of fathers', mothers', and children's valuation of self-direction vs conformity to external authority			
Valuation of self-direction by:				
1　Fathers, 1964	1.00			
2　Fathers, 1974	0.79*	1.00		
3　Mothers, 1974	0.34*	0.48*	1.00	
4　Children, 1974	0.59*	0.58*	0.52*	1.00

* Statistically significant, $p \leq 0.05$.
$\chi^2/\text{d.f.} = 1.96$.
N = 352.

B   Polish families (children aged 13–17 years when interviewed)

	Fathers 1978	Mothers 1979–80	Children 1979–80
	Paths from concept, valuation of self-direction, to "indicators" of that concept		

Indicators:

		Fathers 1978	Mothers 1979–80	Children 1979–80
1	Good manners	−0.36*	−0.34*	−0.54*
2	Neat and clean	−0.24*	−0.26*	−0.39*
3	Good sense and sound judgment	0.49*	0.42*	0.49*
4	Self-control	0.22*	0.42*	0.56*
5	Obedient to parents	−0.38*	−0.43*	−0.26*
6	Responsible	0.25*	0.29*	0.09
7	Interested in how and why things happen	0.26*	0.42*	0.47*
8	Good student	0.38*	−0.44*	−0.49*

(Correlations of residuals not shown)

Intercorrelations of fathers', mothers', and children's valuation of self-direction vs conformity to external authority

Valuation of self-direction by:

1	Fathers, 1978	1.00		
2	Mothers, 1979–80	0.49*	1.00	
3	Children, 1979–80	0.37*	0.55*	1.00

* Statistically significant, p ≤ 0.05.
χ^2/d.f. = 1.74.
N = 177.

those correlations. We therefore allow all inter-person correlations of residuals of the same characteristics that prove to be statistically significant. We also allow all intra-person correlations of residuals that are statistically significant, not because doing so greatly affects the parent–child value-correlations, but because it improves the fit of models to data. In the US model, we also allow, where statistically significant, the correlation of the residuals of fathers' valuation of a characteristic as measured at the time of the baseline interview and of that same characteristic as measured again at the time of the follow-up interview.

Both the US and Polish measurement models (again, see table 7.1) meet our expectations in all respects. Those characteristics that on the basis of a priori expectation and past experience should be indicative of valuing self-direction are in all instances positively related to the underlying concept –

for fathers, for mothers, and for children. Those characteristics that should be indicative of valuing conformity to external authority are in all instances negatively related to the underlying concept – for fathers, mothers, and children. Moreover, the models for both the United States and Poland fit the data well.

The substantive information yielded by these models is the magnitude of the correlations of parents' and children's valuation of self-direction. For the United States, the father–child correlation is 0.58 and the mother–child correlation is 0.52, both considerably higher than past studies would have led one to expect. Most past studies, though, have dealt with individual characteristics, rather than with underlying dimensions of values. There is every reason to expect that parent–child agreement on so fundamental an issue as valuing self-direction or conformity would be greater than on valuation of any single characteristic. Moreover, even those past studies that did deal with dimensions of values have not been based on confirmatory factor-analytic models, which means that they have not taken measurement error into account. Our assessments of magnitude of correlation are more accurate.

What may be artifactual, though, is the somewhat higher father–child than mother–child correlation, for this may result from our having longitudinal data for fathers but not for mothers. When we re-estimate the model, using only cross-sectional (1974) data, the father–child and mother–child correlations are nearly identical: 0.46 and 0.47, respectively. Thus, if the father–child correlation is no stronger than the mother-child correlation, it is at least *as strong* as the mother–child correlation, a fact of no little importance.

For Poland, the correlation between mothers' and children's valuations of self-direction is 0.55, about the same magnitude as for the United States; the corresponding father–child correlation is 0.37, decidedly lower than the mother–child correlation. Does the lower father–child than mother–child correlation really differentiate Poland from the United States? Is this apparent cross-national difference real or artifactual?

A priori, it is possible that the cross-national difference results from two age-related features of the Polish survey: the relatively narrow age-range of the children, including adolescents but excluding young adults; the children having been one-and-a-half to two years younger when the fathers were interviewed than when the mothers were interviewed. We can learn much about the consequences of both these features of survey design by exploring the US data.

Would the father–child correlation be closer in magnitude to the mother–child correlation if we had data about fathers' values for a wider age-range of children, including not only adolescents but also young adults? We do find that in the United States the correlation of fathers' and children's values is higher for young adults than for adolescents; but so, too, is the correlation of mothers' and children's values. The difference between father–child and mother–child correlations is essentially the same for young adults as for adolescents.

Would the father–child correlation be closer in magnitude to the mother–child correlation if the Polish fathers had been interviewed at the same time as the mothers and children, instead of one-and-a-half to two years earlier? Here, too, the US data are instructive. As the first half of table 7.1 shows, the correlation between US fathers' valuation of self-direction in 1964 and children's valuation of self-direction in 1974 is as high as the correlation between fathers' valuation of self-direction in 1974 and children's valuation of self-direction at that same time. Even a ten-year gap makes no difference in the magnitude of the father–child correlation.

The US data suggest that the lower father–child than mother–child correlation that we find in Poland is not an artifact of the Polish survey design. Furthermore, the *Polish* data show that, within the age-range for which we do have data, the mother–child correlation is higher than the father–child correlation regardless of child's age. We therefore conclude that the difference in the mother–child and father–child correlations is almost undoubtedly real. In any case, even for Polish fathers the parent–child values-correlation is substantial. For Polish mothers, as for US fathers and mothers, the parent–child values-correlation is even stronger.

CLASS, STRATIFICATION, AND CHILDREN'S VALUES

Our analyses in earlier chapters show that a father's class and stratification positions decidedly affect his values for his children; and there is evidence, at least for the United States, that the same is true for mothers (Kohn, 1976b). Therefore, there is every reason to suppose that the family's class and stratification positions must affect both parents' values. Moreover, the moderate-to-high correlations between parents' and children's values in both countries suggest that there must be some "transmission" of values from parents to children. The elements are all in place for a causal chain from parents' class and stratification positions to parents' own values to children's values.

Still, inference is not empirical demonstration and other conclusions are possible: the chains from parents' positions in the social structure to children's values might attenuate along the way, so that the total effects of class and stratification on children's values become trivial (as is argued by Lueptow et al., 1979; and Gecas, 1980; but see Mortimer and Kumka,

1982). The correlations between parents' and children's valuation of self-direction might signify not value-transmission but rather that parents' and children's values are affected by similar or equivalent social processes. Perhaps the family's class and stratification positions affect children's values through some process other than the children's being influenced by their parents' values (Dalton, 1982; Nowak, 1989b; see also Rosenberg and Pearlin, 1978) – perhaps through non-family influences, such as those of neighborhood and school. It is even possible that substantial correlations between parents' and children's values could result from both parents and children being affected by shared social characteristics other than class and stratification (e.g., by race, national background, and religious background), which should be statistically controlled in causal analysis.

Several questions thus remain open: do more advantaged class position and higher stratification position result in adolescent and young-adult offspring valuing self-direction more highly? If so, what are the magnitudes of these effects? If substantial, to what extent do these result from class and stratification affecting parents' values, which in turn affect their children's values? If the processes do involve parents' values, is it mothers' values, fathers' values, or both parents' values that are involved?

Fathers' class positions and their own, their wives', and their children's values

Consider, first, the relationships of social class with parents' and children's values. For these analyses, our index of class is father's class position, since we do not have sufficient information about Polish wives' conditions of employment to develop a comprehensive model of the family's class position. The data are adequate, though, for answering two crucial questions. Are the relationships between fathers' class positions and their wives' and children's values consistent with our theoretical expectation that the wives and children of men in more advantaged class positions value self-direction more highly than do the wives and children of men in less advantaged class positions? And are the correlations (expressed in terms of *etas*) of fathers' class positions with their wives' and children's values of more than trivial magnitude?

We find (table 7.2) that, for both countries, the relationships are both meaningful and non-trivial in magnitude. The correlations (*etas*) of fathers' class positions and mothers' and children's values are of sufficient size, in both countries, to confirm that fathers' social-class positions are significantly and substantially related, not only to their own valuation of self-direction for their children, but also to their wives' and children's valuation of self-direction. Moreover, the patterns of means for wives' and children's values

Table 7.2 *Relationships of fathers' social-class positions with parents' and children's valuation of self-direction*

		Valuation of self-direction by:			
	N	Fathers 1964	Fathers 1974	Mothers 1974 Means[a]	Children 1974
A US men (fathers' class positions in 1964)					
Employers	(13)	0.59	0.70	0.33	0.41
Self-employed	(39)	0.08	0.07	0.13	0.01
Managers	(24)	0.36	0.55	0.16	0.54
First-line supervisors	(74)	0.08	−0.07	0.00	0.06
Nonmanual workers	(62)	0.19	0.31	0.39	0.15
Manual workers	(139)	−0.27	−0.28	−0.27	−0.23
Correlation (eta)[b]		0.33*	0.42*	0.35*	0.36*

	N	Fathers 1974	Mothers 1974 Means[a]	Children 1974
B US men (fathers' class positions in 1974)				
Employers	(18)	0.33	0.64	0.40
Self-employed	(43)	0.03	−0.07	−0.02
Managers	(40)	0.47	0.21	0.33
First-line supervisors	(60)	0.17	0.11	−0.04
Nonmanual workers	(54)	0.29	0.17	0.23
Manual workers	(115)	−0.39	−0.25	−0.25
Correlation (eta)[b]		0.45*	0.34*	0.35*

	N	Fathers 1978	Mothers 1979–80 Means[a]	Children 1979–80
C Polish men (fathers' class positions in 1978)				
Managers	(12)	0.22	0.41	0.39
First-line supervisors	(46)	0.29	0.07	−0.12
Nonmanual workers	(27)	0.14	0.27	0.16
Production workers	(53)	−0.23	−0.06	0.06
Nonproduction workers	(31)	−0.32	−0.35	−0.31
Self-employed	(8)	0.27	0.18	0.33
Correlation (eta)[b]		0.34*	0.30*	0.25*

[a] Expressed as standardized differences from grand mean for the particular country at the particular time.
[b] Corrected for unreliability of measurement.
* Statistically significant, $p < 0.05$.

are very similar to those for fathers.[2] For the United States, the families of employers, managers, and nonmanual workers value self-direction most highly, the families of manual workers value conformity to external authority most highly. For Poland (where our analyses are now limited to families with a child in the age-range 13–17), the families of managers, nonmanual workers, and the self-employed value self-direction most highly, the families of *nonproduction workers* value conformity to external authority most highly.[3] We find it intriguing that the families of non-production workers – the wives and children more so than the men themselves – value conformity more than do the families of production workers – perhaps a reflection of their less advantaged class position.

Social stratification and the intergenerational transmission of values

Conceptualization and measurement of family social-stratification position
In assessing the effect of social stratification on the values of adolescent and young-adult offspring, we are able to measure a family's – as distinct from an individual's – social-stratification position. Our strategy has been to develop confirmatory factor-analytic models, based on the straightforward assumption that the stratification position of the family is best inferred from the covariation of the husband's and the wife's educational levels, occupational statuses, and incomes.[4]

[2] The subsamples of fathers in these analyses are limited to men whose wives and children were interviewed. For the United States, this is not much different from the subsample of fathers used in our earlier analyses, excepting only those men whose wives and children we were unable to interview. For Poland, however, these analyses are limited to fathers of a smaller age-range of children, because the survey of wives and children was deliberately limited to families with a child in the age-range 13–17.

[3] In general, the findings for this subsample of Polish fathers are much the same as are those for the larger sample of Polish fathers, with one notable exception: for the larger sample we had found that production and nonproduction workers hold much the same values; for the subsample of fathers of older children, we now find that nonproduction workers are somewhat more likely to value conformity than are production workers. This difference between the larger sample of fathers and the smaller subsample of fathers of older children is not a function of our having used a family measurement model of parental values for the subsample. When we limit the analysis to fathers of older children, but use the fathers-only measurement model of parental values, we still find a difference between production and nonproduction workers, with nonproduction workers valuing conformity more highly.

[4] There are two principal ways to combine husband's and wife's education, occupational status, and income into a composite measure of family social-stratification position. In the one we use, a "measurement model," family stratification position is posited to be an underlying concept, with the several measures of husband's and wife's statuses treated as its "indicators." In the alternate approach, termed a "producer model," the social-stratification position of the family is based, not on the covariation of husband's and wife's statuses, but on their additive

The model for the United States (see the upper half of figure 7.1) is a third-order confirmatory factor-analytic model. The first-order factors use four measures to index husband's occupational status, and single measures to index wife's occupational status, each spouse's educational attainment, and each spouse's income.[5] The second-order factors combine occupational status and income into higher-level constructs – husband's and wife's occupational positions. The third-order factor infers the posited underlying concept, the stratification position of the family, from the covariation of husband's educational level, husband's occupational position, wife's educational level, and wife's occupational position.

The model for Poland (the lower half of figure 7.1) is similar to the US model, with two necessary exceptions: the indices of occupational status are chosen to be appropriate to Poland;[6] and because we do not have data about wives' incomes but do have data about family income, we use combined family income, husband's occupational status, husband's education, wife's occupational status, and wife's education as "indicators" of family social-stratification position.

---

contributions. Family social-stratification position is treated as a latent construct, "produced by" husband's and wife's statuses and in turn "producing" their own and their child's values. A producer model can be estimated only in context of a larger causal model. Since the latent construct, family stratification position, is an intervening variable between spouses' statuses and their own and their child's values, the contributions of husband's and wife's statuses to family stratification position will necessarily depend on the magnitudes of the correlations of the status measures with husband's, wife's, and child's values. This we regard as undesirable, for the index of family stratification position would vary, were we to examine its effects on other psychological phenomena or other aspects of family life. In any case, causal analyses based on a producer model of family stratification position yield essentially the same conclusions as do those based on a measurement model.

[5] The four indicators of US men's occupational status are the Hollingshead index of occupational status (described in Bonjean et al., 1967, pp. 441–8), Treiman's (1977, pp. 235–60) International Prestige Scale, Duncan's (1961) socioeconomic index of occupations, and the Hodge, Siegel, and Rossi (1964; Siegel, 1971) occupational status classification used by the National Opinion Research Center. For US women, we use only the Hollingshead classification, which we had routinely coded at the time the data were collected. Since our analysis of US men (in chapter 3) shows, and this model confirms, that the Hollingshead index of occupational status reflects the underlying concept nearly perfectly, it did not seem worth investing the considerable time that would have been required to recode the women's data to create the other three indices. We use data from employed wives for information about women's occupational status and income, treating such information as "missing data" for non-employed wives and employing pairwise deletion in creating the variance–covariance matrices on which the analyses are based.

[6] For both Polish men and Polish women, we use as indicators of occupational status a classification that had been prepared specifically for Poland, the Polish Prestige Scale (Slomczynski and Kacprowicz, 1979), and Treiman's (1977, pp. 235–60) International Prestige Scale.

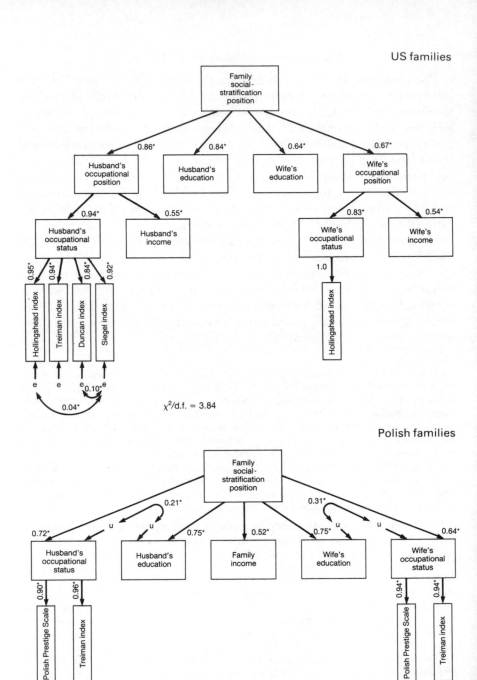

Figure 7.1 *Measurement models of family social-stratification position.* *Statistically significant, $p \le 0.05$.*

The model for the United States shows that husband's educational level and occupational position contribute more to the family's overall stratification position than do wife's educational level and occupational position, but that wife's statuses do make a substantial contribution to the family's overall position. The model for Poland shows that wife's education makes as great a contribution to the family's overall stratification position as does husband's education, and that wife's occupational status makes nearly as great a contribution as does husband's occupational status.

In both countries, then, there is very substantial covariation of husbands' and wives' statuses. Thus, not only is it meaningful to think in terms of the family's position in the social-stratification system, but it is also possible to index that position rigorously.

The effects of family social-stratification position on parents' and children's values   To assess these effects we incorporate the measurement models of family stratification position into larger causal models that permit family stratification position to affect children's values directly, as well as indirectly through fathers' and mothers' values and through children's educational level (see figure 7.2). Since we defer until later in the analysis any assessment of the reciprocal effects of husbands' and wives' values, we allow a correlation of the residuals of fathers' and mothers' values in the models for both countries. Pertinent social characteristics are allowed to affect family social-stratification position, parents' values, and children's values.

A formal difference between the US and Polish analyses results from the US sample's including both adolescent and young-adult offspring, while the Polish sample includes only adolescent offspring. For the United States, child's educational level means highest grade level for those who have left school or current grade level for those still in school; for Poland, educational level almost always means current grade level. As a result, parental stratification position can be expected to have a greater effect on children's educational level in the US than in the Polish model. Still, it is a priori possible for family stratification position to affect grade level even in the Polish model. (Although it is rare in Poland for children to be promoted ahead of their classmates or to be held back, it has under some circumstances been possible for children to begin schooling a year younger than usual when their parents have so requested.) In both countries, it also appears possible for parents' values to both affect and be affected by children's educational level; but, since we do not have adequate instrumentation to estimate such reciprocal effects, we adopt the conservative practice of simply allowing the residuals of fathers' and mothers' values to be correlated with that of children's educational level.

For the United States, the total effect of the family's stratification position

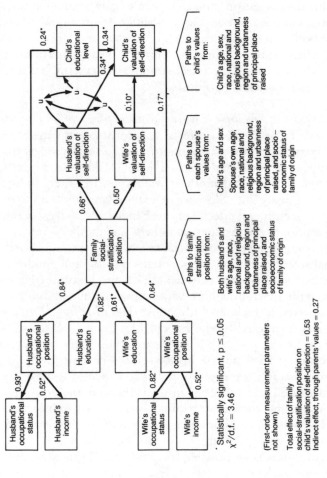

US families

Child's educational level

0.24*

Child's valuation of self-direction

0.34*   0.34*

0.34*

Husband's valuation of self-direction

u   u   u

0.10*

Wife's valuation of self-direction

0.17*

Paths to child's values from:

Child's age, sex, race, national and religious background, region and urbanness of principal place raised

0.66*   0.50*

Family social-stratification position

Paths to each spouse's values from:

Child's age and sex
Spouse's own age, race, national and religious background, region and urbanness of principal place raised, and socio-economic status of family of origin

0.84*

0.82*

0.61*

0.64*

Paths to family stratification position from:

Both husband's and wife's age, race, national and religious background, region and urbanness of principal place raised, and socioeconomic status of family of origin

Husband's occupational position

0.93*   0.52*

Husband's occupational status

Husband's income

Husband's education

Wife's education

Wife's occupational position

0.82*   0.52*

Wife's occupational status

Wife's income

* Statistically significant, p ≤ 0.05
χ^2/d.f. = 3.46

(First-order measurement parameters not shown)

Total effect of family
social-stratification position on
child's valuation of self-direction = 0.53
Indirect effect, through parents' values = 0.27

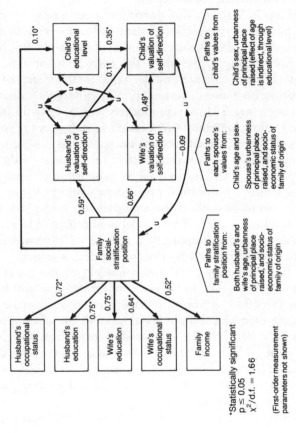

Polish families

Child's educational level

0.10*   0.35*

0.11

Child's valuation of self-direction

Husband's valuation of self-direction

Wife's valuation of self-direction

0.49*

−0.09

Family social-stratification position

0.59*

0.66*

Paths to child's values from:
Child's sex, urbanness of principal place of age raised (effect of age is indirect, through educational level)

Paths to each spouse's values from:
Child's age and sex
Spouse's urbanness of principal place raised, and socio-economic status of family of origin

Paths to family stratification position from:
Both husband's and wife's age, urbanness of principal place raised, and socio-economic status of family of origin

Husband's occupational status

0.72*

Husband's education

0.75*

Wife's education

0.75*

Wife's occupational status

0.64*

Family income

0.52*

*Statistically significant
$p \leq 0.05$
$\chi^2/\text{d.f.} = 1.66$

(First-order measurement parameters not shown)

Total effect of family social-stratification position on child's valuation of self-direction = 0.43
Indirect effect through parents' values = 0.39

Figure 7.2   *The effects of family social-stratification position on parents' and child's valuation of self-direction.*

on children's valuation of self-direction is a very substantial 0.53. A little over half of this effect (52 percent) is indirect through parents' values, mainly through fathers' values. Another portion (15 percent) of the effect is indirect, through family stratification position affecting children's educational level, and educational level in turn affecting children's valuation of self-direction. The remainder, shown in the model as a direct path of 0.17, represents the sum total of all the ways other than through parents' values or through children's educational level that family stratification position affects children's valuation of self-direction.[7]

Have these findings been in any way distorted by our having longitudinal data for fathers but only cross-sectional data for mothers? When we re-estimate the US model, increasing the correlation of mothers' and children's values to 0.59, just slightly higher than the correlation of fathers' and children's values, in the modified model, the total effects of family stratification position on fathers', mothers', and children's valuations of self-direction are unchanged. However, mothers' values have an increased effect on children's values (a path of 0.26, nearly as strong as the path from fathers' to children's values, which remains unchanged at 0.34) and family stratification position has a weaker direct effect on children's valuation of self-direction (a path of 0.11). Hence, a larger proportion (66 per cent) of the total effect of family stratification position on children's valuation of self-direction is shown to be indirect through parental values, the increase entirely through mothers' values. This model confirms, nevertheless, that fathers' values play at least as important a role as do mothers' values in explaining the effect of social stratification on children's values.

In contrast to the US findings, the Polish model (see the lower half of figure 7.2) shows mothers' values to be more important than fathers' values in accounting for the effect of family social-stratification position on the values of adolescent offspring. This is exactly as we should expect from knowing that for Poland the mother–child value-correlation is higher than the father–child value-correlation. Still, for Poland as for the United States, social stratification has a sizeable impact – a total effect of 0.43 – on the values of adolescent offspring and this results in substantial part from stratification affecting parental values.

Our estimate for Poland of the total effect of family stratification position

---

[7] Our method of modelling may cause us to underestimate the importance of parents' values on their offsprings' values, for it does not permit parents' values to directly affect their children's educational attainment. But, even if we were to allow unidirectional effects of parental values on the child's educational attainment, our interpretation would be little changed: the total effect of family social-stratification position on the child's valuation of self-direction would remain unchanged, with the proportion of that effect shown as indirect through parents' values increasing from 52 percent to 58 percent.

on children's values must be regarded as a minimum estimate, very likely an underestimate, because a model that allows a direct path from family stratification position to children's values estimates that path, anomalously, as negative, albeit statistically nonsignificant. Since this negative path is highly problematic as well as statistically nonsignificant, we fix the path at zero and instead allow a correlation of the residuals of family stratification position and children's values. This means that we are unable to estimate any effect of family stratification position on children's values above and beyond those resulting from stratification's effects on parental values and on children's grade level. Still, the total effect of family stratification position on children's values, thus estimated, is considerable.

The US model shows fathers' values as having considerable importance in the process by which family social stratification position affects offspring's values, while the Polish model shows mothers' values as having predominant importance. For both the United States and Poland, though, family stratification position has an impressive bearing on the values of adolescent and young-adult children, mainly through parental values.

Perceptions of values   How do parents' values affect children's values? Is it necessary that children's perceptions of their parents' values be accurate? (Furstenberg, 1971; Kerckhoff and Huff, 1974; and Smith, 1982, so argue; but see Clausen et al., 1981.) We operationalize this question by asking, are the effects of parents' values on children's values direct, or indirect through children's *perceptions* of parents' values? If the latter, we infer that, for parents' values to influence children's values, children must accurately perceive their parents' values. If accurate perception is not required, then parents' values must be influencing children's values through some other mechanisms, for example, by parents serving as role-models or by their structuring the children's environments to be conducive to the children's developing the values that the parents would have them develop (Morgan et al., 1979).

The US survey asked the children how they thought each of their parents would rank the set of thirteen generally valued characteristics listed in chapter 4 (p. 57). Using this information, we extend the measurement model of parents' and children's valuations of self-direction to include two additional dimensions, children's perceptions of mothers' and of fathers' valuations. We then modify the causal model to include these perceptions. The resultant model indicates that fathers' valuation of self-direction has a sizeable effect on children's perceptions of fathers' valuation, and mothers' valuation has a sizeable effect on children's perceptions of mothers' valuation – as we should certainly expect. Moreover, children's valuation of self-direction both affects and is affected by their perceptions of parents' valuations – again, as expected. The model is, then, valid on its face.

We learn from this model that the effect of mothers' values on children's values is entirely indirect, through children's perceptions of mothers' values. (This is true whether or not we increase the magnitude of the mother–child value-correlation to be slightly higher than the father–child value-correlation.) Fathers' valuation of self-direction, though, affects children's valuation only in part through the children's accurately perceiving fathers' values; a larger part of the effect of fathers' valuation on children's valuation does not depend on the children's accurately perceiving their fathers' values. Apparently, the transmission of values from mother to child requires that children accurately perceive their mothers' values. But the transmission of paternal values can occur even when children misperceive what values their fathers really hold, presumably because fathers influence their children in other ways. There might be a hint here as to why US fathers' values affect their children's values more than do Polish fathers' values.

SOCIAL STRUCTURE, OCCUPATIONAL SELF-DIRECTION, AND VALUES

Whatever the intra-family processes by which parents' values affect their children's values, our analyses have clearly shown that much of the effect of social structure on children's values is through parents' values. We next explore the processes by which social class and social stratification affect parents' and children's values. This part of the analysis is necessarily much more tentative than what has gone before, because the models require more assumptions.

To explicate process, and to make the analysis equally applicable to understanding the effects of social class and of social stratification on offspring's values, we base our models of process not on class or stratification per se, but on what our analyses in prior chapters have shown to be the crucial intervening link from social stratification to values, i.e., occupational self-direction.[8]

Our analyses in chapter 6 showed the relationships between occupational

[8] Our analyses of occupational self-direction have thus far been limited to men. We now find that analyses of US women are fully consonant with those of US and Polish men in showing that the effects of social class and social stratification upon parental values are primarily attributable to occupational self-direction. Unfortunately, our data for Polish women are not sufficiently detailed to develop separate indices of occupational position and occupational self-direction.

self-direction and men's values for their children to be reciprocal – occupational self-direction not only affects but also is affected by values. We now find this to be true for US and Polish women as well. Thus, a model of process must take into account that both men's and women's conditions of work not only affect but may also be affected by their values. Furthermore, a model of process must consider the possibilities of husbands' values affecting wives' values and of wives' values affecting husbands' values. And, perhaps crucial, a model of process should not simply assume that parents' values have unidirectional effects on children's values, but must allow for the possibility that children's values affect their parents' values as well (Bell, 1968).

In figure 7.3, we present a heuristic figure that attempts to portray a comprehensive model of process. In this model, as in all other reciprocal-effects models that we have assessed, the number of parameters to be estimated would be greater than the amount of information provided by the intercorrelations of the variables, unless some restrictions are imposed on the model. The solution that we once again employ here is to allow some effects to be only indirect, setting to zero the paths that represent the disallowed direct effects – that is, we use them as instruments to provide identification for assessing the reciprocally related paths. In the heuristic figure, the paths being estimated are shown as solid black arrows and paths that have been fixed at zero (to provide instrumentation) are shown as dashed arrows. To make the instrumentation clear, we have numbered all twelve of the paths involved in the six pairs of reciprocal relationships, and have correspondingly numbered the principal a priori instruments that make possible the estimation of these twelve paths.

Thus, for example, the path from husband's occupational self-direction to his valuation of self-direction, number 1 in figure 7.3, is identified by the corresponding instrument number 1, a disallowed path from husband's previous occupational self-direction to his current values. Our discussion of instrumentation and the corresponding figure deal only with the critical instruments that we employ to ensure adequate identification; in so complex a model, there is much additional instrumentation, some deliberate, some inadvertent. All indications are that the model is well identified throughout, with only the one exception that will be noted later.

Since the model is complex, we discuss its instrumentation and what the model teaches us in parts, beginning with the reciprocal effects of parents' occupational self-direction and values. The actual results of models for the United States and Poland corresponding to the heuristic figure 7.3 are summarized in table 7.3.

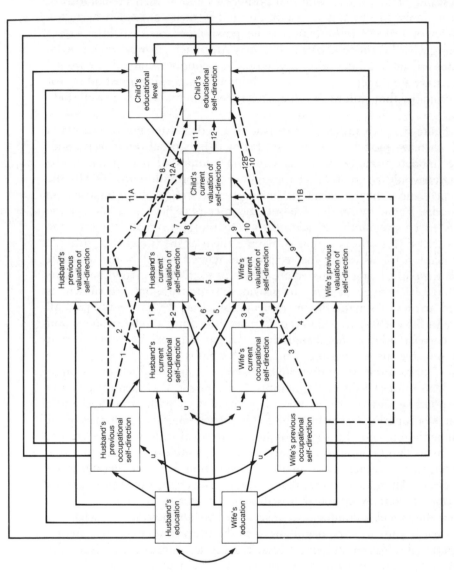

Figure 7.3 The reciprocal effects of occupational / educational self-direction, parents', and children's valuation of self-direction: heuristic model, dashed arrows representing instruments. (Paths from social characteristics to endogenous variables not shown; not all correlations of residuals shown.)

Table 7.3   *Reciprocal effects of occupational / educational self-direction, parents',*
and children's valuation of self-direction

		US model	Polish model
A	*Reciprocally related paths*		
	1 Husband's occupational self-direction to his values	0.36*	0.22*
	2 Husband's values to his occupational self-direction	0.14*	0.19*
	3 Wife's occupational self-direction to her values	0.39*	0.17*
	4 Wife's values to her occupational self-direction	0.14	0.30*
	5 Husband's values to wife's values	−0.09	0.08
	6 Wife's values to husband's values	0.16*	0.10
	7 Husband's values to child's values	0.29*	0.02
	8 Child's values to husband's values	−0.09*	0.12
	9 Wife's values to child's values	0.05*	0.37*
	10 Child's values to wife's values	0.15*	0.16
	11 Child's educational self-direction to own values	0.82*	—
	12 Child's values to educational self-direction	0.12	—
B	*Other theoretically important paths*		
	13 Child's educational level to educational self-direction	0.42*	—
	14 Child's educational level to own values	0.02*	0.39*
	15 Husband's educational level to own values	0.25*	0.00
	16 Husband's educational level to child's values	0.00	0.00
	17 Husband's educational level to child's educational self-direction	0.25*	—
	18 Wife's educational level to own values	0.00	0.00
	19 Wife's educational level to child's values	0.00	0.00
	20 Wife's educational level to child's educational self-direction	0.12*	—
	χ^2/d.f. =	1.53	2.02

* Statistically significant, $p \le 0.05$.

Occupational self-direction and parental valuation
of self-direction

Identifying the reciprocal effects of occupational self-direction and parental valuation of self-direction requires measures of both concepts at two or more times. But we have longitudinal data only for US men. Fortunately, we do have detailed job history data for Polish men, from which we can construct an accurate, albeit only quasi-longitudinal, measurement model of occupational self-direction.[9] We also have approximate job history information for US women, from which we can construct a serviceable quasi-longitudinal measurement model of occupational self-direction.[10] For Polish women, though, we have only approximate information about even current occupational self-direction and no information at all about occupational self-direction in past jobs.[11] And for no group other than US men do we have the requisite information about the values held at the time of the previous job. Thus, we are forced to simulate a measure of Polish women's "earlier" occupational self-direction, as well as measures of US women's, Polish men's, and Polish women's "earlier" values.

To introduce the hypothetical constructs, "earlier parental valuation of self-direction" by US women, Polish men, and Polish women, we have to estimate the correlations of these concepts with all other exogenous variables. We do this by extrapolating from the correlations of those same exogenous variables with their *current* values, adjusting those correlations to take account of over-time changes as inferred from longitudinal data for

[9] Our measurement models of occupational self-direction for US and Polish men are closely based on those discussed in chapter 5 (figures 5.1 and 5.2).

[10] The model for US women (based on a cross-sectional model developed in J. Miller, Schooler, Kohn, and K. Miller, 1979) is quite similar to that for US men, but extended to be quasi-longitudinal, using retrospective job-history information. We have detailed information about the substantive complexity, closeness of supervision, and routinization of the current (i.e. 1974) job; for the job preceding the current job, we have only approximate, retrospective information about the complexity of work with things, with data, and with people, plus estimates of the number of hours per week worked with things, with data, and with people, and a single indicator of closeness of supervision.

[11] For Polish women, we do not have information about actual job conditions. We do, however, have ratings on a very detailed classification of occupations, from which it is possible to assess, albeit only at an occupational level, the complexity of work with data, with things, and with people. Using these indicators, we construct a confirmatory factor-analytic measurement model, which is quite serviceable. Lacking information about the closeness of supervision or routinization of the job, we use the substantive complexity of the work as a proxy for occupational self-direction, not an unreasonable procedure, since our analyses of US and Polish men and of US women all show that substantive complexity closely reflects occupational self-direction.

US men.[12] We initially fix the "stability" of values (i.e., the path from earlier values to current values) to be the same as we find it to be for US men. We use the same procedures for Polish women's hypothetical earlier occupational self-direction, initially fixing the stability to be the same as that found for Polish men.

Using these procedures, we allow each spouse's occupational self-direction in a specified previous job to affect that person's self-direction in the current job, and that person's earlier values to affect the values currently held.[13] Cross-lagged effects, i.e., of earlier occupational self-direction on current values and of earlier values on current occupational self-direction, are fixed at zero – we use them as instruments, which is possible because it is not essential that we be able to distinguish "lagged" from "contemporaneous" effects. Thus, our models permit us to estimate the total effects of parents' occupational self-direction on their values and of their values on their occupational self-direction, but we can say nothing about whether the effects are ongoing and continuous or occur only more gradually over time.

Education is treated as having unidirectional effects on both occupational self-direction and values. Other social characteristics that might affect current values are permitted to have such effects and a subset of these characteristics, those (such as age, race, religious and national backgrounds) that might be seen by an employer as credentials for a job, are also allowed to affect current occupational self-direction. Allowing non-credentialling social characteristics to directly affect current values but not current occupational self-direction provides additional instrumentation for the paths from values to occupational self-direction.

[12] For example, to estimate the correlation of Polish women's education with their hypothetical earlier values, we multiply the correlation of Polish women's education with their current values by the ratio of the correlations of US men's education with their 1964 and 1974 values. The rationale is essentially the same for estimating the correlation of one spouse's earlier values with the other spouse's or with the child's social characteristics. The procedure becomes more complex for estimating the correlation of two hypothetical constructs (e.g., Polish husbands' earlier values with Polish wives' earlier values), but again the rationale remains the same: we base the estimated correlations for the earlier time on actual correlations for the current time, using the longitudinal data for US men only for the purpose of modifying those correlations to take account of over-time change. Since the analyses are based on a variance–covariance matrix, all these correlations are converted to covariances. It is a limitation of this procedure that we have to extrapolate from a ten-year time span for US men to an indefinite time span from "the immediately prior job" to the current job held by US women and Polish men and women.

[13] The data for US men being longitudinal, we use the job held at the time of the original survey (1964) as the "previous" job and the job held at the time of the follow-up survey (1974) as the "current" job. Having only cross-sectional data for US women and Polish men and women, and being reluctant to trust respondents' memories of the jobs they held precisely ten years before the interviews, we use information about "the job you held immediately preceding your present job."

The resultant findings are entirely consistent for US men, US women, Polish men, and Polish women (see table 7.3): occupational self-direction significantly and substantially affects valuation of self-direction, even with the effects of spouse's and child's values and pertinent social characteristics statistically controlled. The estimates of magnitude vary, but – given the differences in modelling and in the amount of hard information we have – this is not a matter of any great import. What does matter is the consistency of the positive effects. We also find that valuation of self-direction consistently affects occupational self-direction – significantly so for US men, Polish men, and Polish women, albeit not quite significantly for US women.

The reciprocal effects of husbands' and wives' values

In figure 7.2, we sidestepped the possible effects of husbands' values on wives' values and of wives' values on husbands' values by allowing the residuals of husbands' and wives' values to covary. But what, in reality, is the relationship between husbands' and wives' values? Now, with our quasi-longitudinal models, we can make a provisional assessment.

We achieve instrumentation for modelling the reciprocal effects of husbands' and wives' values (figure 7.3) by not allowing either spouse's occupational self-direction to directly affect the other spouse's values and also (not shown in the heuristic figure) by not allowing either spouse's "earlier" values (real in the case of US husbands, hypothetical in the case of US wives and Polish husbands and wives) to affect the other spouse's current values.[14] In neither country do husbands' values significantly affect their wives' values, independently of the wives' own occupational self-direction (and of their children's values). In the United States, wives' values significantly affect husbands' values; in Poland, that possible effect falls short of being statistically significant. The importance of these findings becomes apparent when we next consider the reciprocal effects of parents' and children's values.

The reciprocal effects of parents' and children's values

In figure 7.2, we assumed that parents' values affect children's values unidirectionally. But what is the actual relationship between parents' values and children's values? Is it realistic to assume that all effects are unidirectional from parents' values to children's values, or are the effects reciprocal?

---

[14] Additional instrumentation is gained in that each partner's social characteristics are allowed to directly affect that person's own values but not his or her spouse's values.

Instrumentation for assessing the reciprocal effects of parents' and children's values is achieved somewhat differently in the US and Polish models. For the US model (figure 7.3), we introduce a new concept for those offspring still in school – educational self-direction (K. Miller, Kohn, and Schooler 1985, 1986). Educational self-direction – the use of initiative, thought, and independent judgment in schoolwork – is meant to be directly analogous to occupational self-direction. It is even measured by similar first-order concepts, the substantive complexity of schoolwork and closeness of supervision by teachers.[15]

Educational self-direction is allowed to affect and be affected by the children's own values. Thus, children's educational self-direction plays a role in the model that is exactly analogous to husbands' and wives' occupational self-direction and can provide exactly parallel instrumentation. By not allowing fathers' or mothers' occupational self-direction to directly affect children's values, and by not allowing children's educational self-direction to directly affect parents' values, we achieve identification for assessing the reciprocal effects of parents' and children's values.

The family's social-structural position could affect its children's opportunities for educational self-direction in several ways; for example, by influencing which schools children attend and children's access to books and other educational materials. We therefore permit parental education and occupational self-direction to affect not only children's educational level, but also their educational self-direction. To avoid the possibility of attributing a unidirectional effect to a relationship that might be reciprocal, we use parents' earlier occupational self-direction.

Since the model is quasi-longitudinal, we can allow paths (not shown in figure 7.3) from parents' earlier values to children's current educational

[15] The substantive complexity of schoolwork is measured by four indicators – our evaluation of the complexity of the student's coursework, the student's estimate of the amount of time it takes to do "a complete job" in doing schoolwork, our evaluation of the complexity of the student's most recent term paper or outside-of-class project, and our evaluation of the complexity of the student's most complex school-related extracurricular or athletic activity. Closeness of supervision by teachers is also measured by four indicators, all of them answers to questions about how much latitude the teachers allow and how the teachers exercise their supervisory control; these questions closely parallel those asked of employed adults and used as measures of closeness of supervision in the measurement models of occupational self-direction. (For detailed information, see K. Miller et al. 1985, 1986.) Since the second-order measurement model of educational self-direction is based on only two first-order concepts – substantive complexity of school work and closeness of supervision by teachers – it is under-identified. We use the model developed by K. Miller et al. (1985, 1986), who estimated the second-order measurement parameters in context of a larger non-causal model containing other social-structural variables pertinent to educational self-direction. In our model, we treat information about educational self-direction as "missing data" for nonstudents and employ pairwise deletion in creating the variance–covariance matrix on which the analyses are based.

level. Allowing children's educational level to directly affect their own values but not their parents' values provides additional instrumentation for assessing the effects of children's values on parents' values.

To assess the reciprocal effects of children's educational self-direction and their own values requires identification for those paths. We cannot achieve this in a way exactly analogous to the procedure used for assessing the reciprocal effects of parents' occupational self-direction and values, for we do not have information about children's "earlier" educational self-direction and "earlier" values. Nor is it theoretically useful to create a hypothetical construct for "earlier" values.[16] Instead, we achieve identification for the path from children's values to children's educational self-direction by allowing parents' values to affect children's educational self-direction only indirectly, primarily by affecting children's values. This assumption may be questionable, for in principle parents' values could affect the choice of school and hence children's opportunities for educational self-direction. (We do, however, allow parents' educational levels and other pertinent social characteristics to directly affect children's educational self-direction.) Identification for the path from children's educational self-direction to children's values is achieved by allowing parents' earlier occupational self-direction to directly affect children's educational self-direction but not children's values.

Using these assumptions, we find for the United States that fathers' values do significantly affect children's values; we are unable to determine whether children's values also affect their fathers' values.[17] The relationship of mothers' and children's values, though, is reciprocal: mothers' values have a modest but statistically significant effect on children's values; children's values have a substantial effect on mothers' values. Although mothers' values have only a very modest direct effect on children's values, mothers' values, as we have seen, also affect their husbands' values, hence mothers' values also have an indirect effect on children's values. As a

---

[16] In assessing the effect of, say, fathers' occupational self-direction on their own values, we want to statistically control fathers' earlier values, thus in essence measuring the effect of occupational self-direction on *change* in fathers' values. But, in assessing the effects of parents' values on children's values, we wish to assess, not change in the children's values, but the *total* effect of parents' values on children's values. It would thus be inappropriate to statistically control children's earlier values.

[17] The effect of children's values on fathers' values is significantly negative, at −0.09, a finding that is so contrary to expectation that it would be compelling only if the instrumentation were very powerful. We therefore treat it as problematic. Given this negative path, though, it is possible that the magnitude of the reciprocal path, from fathers' to children's values, is exaggerated. We therefore re-estimate the entire model, fixing the path from children's to fathers' values at zero. The path from fathers' to children's values is undiminished, at +0.29.

result, the total effect of mothers' values on children's values is twice the direct effect – albeit still less than the effect of fathers' values on children's values.

Because we have only cross-sectional data for mothers but longitudinal data for fathers, these estimates may be biased. To assess this possibility, we re-estimate the pertinent parts of the model, substituting larger correlations between mothers' and children's values, and between mothers' and fathers' values, as inferred from a comparison of the cross-sectional and longitudinal measurement models. As we should expect, the direct effect of mothers' values on children's values increases – from 0.05 to 0.14 – but it is still not as strong as the direct effect of fathers' values on children's values, which remains 0.29. The total effect of mothers' on children's values increases to 0.22; the total effect of fathers' on children's values is 0.27. Thus, the modified model suggests that mothers may play nearly as strong a role as do fathers in the intergenerational transmission of values. It is clear, in any case, that both parents play an important role.

One other thing should be noted in the US model – the powerful effect of educational self-direction on children's valuation of self-direction. This, of course, is entirely consonant with our general interpretation that the experience of self-direction – in paid employment or in schoolwork – is important for valuing self-direction. A disaggregation of educational self-direction shows that both the substantive complexity of schoolwork and closeness of supervision by teachers contribute to the overall effect, the path from substantive complexity to values being 0.79 and that from closeness of supervision to values being −0.10, both statistically significant. What we cannot know for certain is whether the children's values also affect their educational self-direction. The path (of 0.12) falls short of being statistically significant; but this is the one path whose identification is questionable.

For the Polish model, lacking information about the substantive complexity of children's schoolwork, we cannot develop an index of educational self-direction. We therefore use children's educational level as an instrument to identify the paths from children's values to parents' values, allowing children's educational level to directly affect their own values but not those of their parents. Our confidence in this approach is heightened by the finding that a similar procedure applied to the US data yields results roughly similar to those achieved in the model employing educational self-direction as the principal instrument.

The Polish model shows that the heart of the action is the strong influence of mothers' values on children's values, with fathers' values neither significantly nor substantially affecting children's values. Polish men's values are affected by their social-structural positions and occupational experiences just as are Polish women's and US men's and women's values;

but, for Polish men, the process seems to stop at that point. Their values do not significantly affect either their wives' or their children's values.

As noted above, both the US and Polish models are based in part on hypothetical stabilities, e.g., the paths from mothers' hypothetical earlier values to their actual current values. To investigate the sensitivity of the models to changes in these hypothetical stabilities, we have systematically increased and decreased each of them by from 10 to 25 per cent. Doing so has only modest effects on the other parameters of the models, changing none of our conclusions. In this sense, the models are robust. We have also varied the correlations between the hypothetical constructs and other exogenous variables.[18] Doing so results in different estimates of magnitudes of effects, but does not change any of our conclusions. No statistically significant effect becomes nonsignificant, no nonsignificant effect becomes significant. In this sense, too, the models are robust.

CONCLUSION

Our analyses provide evidence, for both the United States and Poland, not only of a close relationship between parents' and children's values, but of an actual influence of parents' values on children's values. Most past studies have underestimated the magnitudes of the correlations between parents' and children's values, because they have not taken measurement error into account and, more fundamentally, because they have not dealt with so important a dimension of values as valuation of self-direction versus conformity to external authority. And, by and large, past studies stopped with correlations. The crux of the matter, however, is not the magnitudes of the correlations but the part played by parental values in the actual process of intergenerational value-transmission (Kohn, 1983). Our models demonstrate that parental values have a considerable effect on offspring's values, even with many other pertinent aspects of social structure taken into account. A fundamental but contested tenet of socialization theory – almost all socialization theory – has hereby been confirmed.

The present analyses do not, however, tell us what intra-family processes are responsible for parents' values affecting children's values (Mortimer and Kumka, 1982). Our analyses do show (at least for the United States) that

[18] Given the large amount of information provided by the actual variance–covariance matrix in the US model, the MILS program is able to estimate the correlations between the hypothetical constructs and all other exogenous variables. Some of the estimates diverge greatly from those achieved by the methods described above. Nevertheless, the estimates of the crucial causal parameters are not greatly changed. (We do not have sufficient information to perform a similar re-analysis of the Polish model.)

accurate perception of fathers' values is not essential for children to be influenced by those values. Presumably other processes are operating; perhaps, as suggested earlier, fathers somehow structure their children's environments to be conducive to the children's valuing self-direction.

We have further found that, in both the United States and Poland, the class and stratification positions of the parental family have a considerable effect on the values of its adolescent and (for the United States) young-adult offspring. This effect results primarily from the social-structural position of the family affecting parents' values and parents' values, in turn, affecting offspring's values. Moreover, these analyses show that all the links in the causal chain are strong: social-structural position affects parental occupational self-direction; occupational self-direction affects parental values; parental values affect children's values.

In both countries, parents' occupational self-direction substantially affects (and is affected by) their values. Moreover (on this we have data only for the United States), adolescents' and young adults' educational self-direction affects their values, just as parental occupational self-direction affects parental values. We see in this finding a confirmation of the larger thesis that the experience of self-direction in one's work, whether in paid employment or in schoolwork, has a major effect on one's values. This is as true for adolescents and early adults as it is for older adults. These findings lend support to the further argument (Kohn, 1969, pp. 135–7) that people's own experiences become more and more important for their values, with their own social-structural positions and attendant experience eventually overshadowing the influences of their parental families.

The findings also have implications for the place of socialization in the reproduction of social structure. They provide an intergenerational extension of our interpretive model for adult workers of social structure, job conditions, and personality. In that model, social-structural position affects occupational self-direction, which is reciprocally related to personality, which in turn affects job conditions and one's place in the class structure and stratification order. We can now add that social structure affects not only adults' own values but also their children's values and their children's opportunities for educational self-direction. Parental position thus affects children's values not only through the transmission of values from parents to children, but also through its effect on children's opportunities for educational self-direction.

8

Interpreting the Cross-national Differences

In this chapter, we review and assess the cross-national differences that we have discovered. Cross-nationally inconsistent findings are potentially valuable for enlarging our understanding of how history and social structure intersect. Moreover, such findings may raise questions about our interpretation of the relationship of social structure to personality – an interpretation meant to apply to industrialized societies generally – thereby providing hints for how we might modify, refine, delimit, or even enlarge that interpretation. We review these findings in more or less the same order that they appeared in the foregoing chapters, reserving until last, however, the most important of the cross-national differences, to which we shall devote the lion's share of our attention, the relationships of class and stratification to distress.

THE MAGNITUDE OF CORRELATION BETWEEN SOCIAL CLASS AND SOCIAL STRATIFICATION

The first cross-national difference that we encountered is in some respects the most surprising of all, because it goes counter to what had been expected by many students of socialist society, not only Eastern European but also Western scholars. The common expectation was that the correlation between social class and social stratification would be smaller for socialist Poland than for the capitalist United States. This expectation was based on the belief that, in a socialist economy, where ownership of the means of production has been separated from control over the means of production and the labor power of others, such control would be more diffuse than in capitalist societies. As a consequence, social class would be less strongly related to social stratification.

We find, however, that the magnitude of the correlation (*eta*) between social class and social stratification is not smaller for socialist Poland than for the capitalist United States, but even (albeit only slightly) larger (see table 3.1).[1] This finding belies the common expectation and the assumption on which it is based – that control over the means of production and over the labor power of others is more diffuse in a (highly centralized) socialist economy than in a capitalist economy. Moreover, social class is as strongly related to occupational self-direction (see table 5.1), hence to crucial aspects of psychological functioning (table 4.4), for Poland as for the United States. The social and psychological significance of social class does not diminish under socialism.

But note that the stronger relationship between class and stratification for Poland than for the United States does have one important consequence for our analyses: social class has a smaller effect, independent of that of social stratification, on psychological functioning for Poland than for the United States (table 4.6). Hence, there is less empirical gain in distinguishing between class and stratification for socialist than for capitalist society. This is not because ownership is more diffuse or because control is less concentrated, but simply because there is greater overlap in socialist society between the primary bases of classification of class and stratification. In socialist Poland, education has been the royal road to both managerial position and to higher stratification position.

In any case, the cross-national difference in the magnitudes of the correlations between social class and social stratification, although certainly pertinent to our understanding of social structure, in no way calls into question the generality of our interpretation of social structure and personality.

CONTINUITY OF EDUCATION INTO THE OCCUPATIONAL CAREER

Our data show that many Polish men have continued their formal educations well into their occupational careers; few US men have done so. This difference results in part from a particular historical period in the aftermath of the Second World War, when the re-industrialization of

---

[1] The cross-national difference is especially pronounced for the relationship between social class and one crucial dimension of social stratification – education, attesting to education's greater importance in the allocation of jobs, hence also of class position, for Poland. In the planned and centralized economy of Poland, education is a normative criterion for allocating persons to jobs. Indeed, in post-war Poland education became the legitimate basis for conferring occupational rewards. For this systemic reason, educational attainment is more closely related to occupational placement in Poland than in the United States (Slomczynski, 1989, pp. 71–2).

Poland created a need that far exceeded the supply of educated men who could assume technical and managerial positions. In those circumstances, in the 1950s and even in the 1960s, many men were hired into positions for which they lacked educational credentials, which they later attained. For political reasons as well, during those years some people were assigned jobs that required more education (or higher educational credentials) than they had attained. For this segment of the labor force, the continuity of formal education into the occupational career was a necessary step toward stabilizing their occupational positions. Further formal education was useful both for achieving upward occupational mobility and for preventing downward mobility (Slomczynski, 1978; Zagorski, 1976).

Whether formal education ended with the onset of their occupational careers – as it did for most US men – or extended on – as it did for many Polish men – seems to have had little consequence for the relationships between the level of education eventually attained and psychological functioning. Educational attainment, whenever achieved, has had similarly potent effects on psychological functioning for both countries (see table 4.5). Moreover, for both countries, this effect is exerted both directly and indirectly, through education's strong effect on occupational self-direction.

Here, again, a cross-national difference, although pertinent to our understanding of the dynamics of attaining social-structural position, does not affect the generality of our interpretation of social structure and personality.

THE RELATIVE IMPORTANCE OF THE SUBSTANTIVE COMPLEXITY OF WORK AND CLOSENESS OF SUPERVISION

We have repeatedly found that occupational self-direction plays much the same role in explaining the effects of social structure on values, intellectual flexibility, and self-directedness of orientation for Poland and for the United States. Moreover, both the substantive complexity of work and how closely it is supervised contribute to these psychological effects. Within this general picture of cross-national similarity, though, we have repeatedly found evidence of one notable cross-national difference: for the United States, the substantive complexity of work is generally more important for explaining the impact of social structure on these facets of psychological functioning than is closeness of supervision; for Poland, closeness of supervision is relatively more important (see tables 5.4 and 5.6).

Why the cross-national difference? It is *not* a matter of the substantive complexity of work being a more important component of occupational self-direction for the United States than for Poland, nor of closeness of supervision being a more important component of occupational self-direction for Poland than for the United States (compare figures 5.1 and 5.2). That being the case, the cross-national difference in the relative importance of the substantive complexity of work and closeness of supervision for explaining the psychological impact of social structure must result from these components of occupational self-direction being differentially related either to psychological functioning or to class and stratification or possibly to both.

In fact (see table 8.1), part of the explanation is that the substantive complexity of work is somewhat more highly correlated with critical facets of psychological functioning – namely, parental valuation of self-direction, intellectual flexibility, and self-directedness of orientation and many of its component dimensions – for the United States than for Poland. Another part of the explanation is that closeness of supervision is somewhat more highly correlated with class and stratification for Poland than for the United States.

Are these findings somehow an artifact of methodological differences between the two studies? We thought it possible that the higher US than Polish correlations between the substantive complexity of work and psychological functioning might have resulted from our measurement models for the United States being based on longitudinal data and those for Poland on cross-sectional data; but that does not appear to be the explanation.[2] The difference, such as it is, is real, not a methodological artifact. But we have no explanation for why it exists.

We also thought it possible that the higher Polish than US correlations of closeness of supervision with class and stratification might have resulted from our having asked rather subjective questions about supervision – certainly more subjective than those we asked about the complexity of work. Did Polish and US workers have different standards of comparison in mind when asked questions about how closely they were supervised? If that were the case, we should expect closeness of supervision to be differentially related, not only to class and stratification, but even more so to psychological functioning. We find, instead, only one noteworthy cross-national difference in the correlations of closeness of supervision with these

---

[2] Analyses similar to those of table 8.1 but with the US measurement models based only on the cross-sectional data of the 1964 survey (and using the entire sample of 3,101 men in that survey) yield the same conclusion: the US correlations of the substantive complexity of work with these facets of psychological functioning are consistently, albeit not greatly, larger than are the corresponding correlations for Poland. Moreover, cross-sectional analyses of the US data corroborate table 8.1 in showing that the US correlations of closeness of supervision with these facets of psychological functioning are not consistently lower (or higher) than are those for Poland – the major exception being that the correlation between closeness of supervision and authoritarian conservatism is higher for Poland than for the United States.

Table 8.1 Correlations of the substantive complexity of work and closeness of supervision with other variables

	Substantive complexity of work			Closeness of supervision		
Zero-order correlations with:	US (1964)	US (1974)	Poland	US (1964)	US (1974)	Poland
A Psychological functioning						
Parental valuation of self-direction	0.48	0.58	0.40	−0.30	−0.41	−0.41
Intellectual flexibility	0.76	0.79	0.65	−0.50	−0.52	−0.54
Self-directedness of orientation	0.60	0.64	0.48	−0.42	−0.43	−0.47
Distress	−0.12	−0.24	0.17	0.05	0.19	−0.14
Authoritarian conservatism	−0.57	−0.56	−0.46	0.38	0.37	0.45
Standards of morality	0.38	0.47	0.40	−0.30	−0.34	−0.37
Trustfulness	0.42	0.45	0.38	−0.33	−0.35	−0.34
Idea-conformity	−0.30	−0.19	−0.14	0.20	0.25	0.14
Self-confidence	0.26	0.22	−0.12	−0.23	−0.11	0.04
Self-deprecation	−0.24	−0.44	−0.09	0.10	0.25	0.10
Anxiety	−0.15	−0.24	0.07	0.08	0.24	−0.07
B Social structure						
Social class (etas)	0.76	0.74	0.78	0.51	0.41	0.57
Social stratification	0.93	0.95	0.89	−0.59	−0.52	−0.64

facets of psychological functioning — a higher correlation for Poland than for the United States with authoritarian conservatism.

That we find this one difference, rather than a pattern of differences, suggests a substantive rather than a methodological interpretation. We see the higher Polish than US correlation of closeness of supervision with authoritarian conservatism as reflecting the greater saliency of authority in Polish than in American society at the time of our surveys. It was in the self-interest of both the state bureaucracy and the church to support those elements of traditional Polish culture that encourage people to obey all forms of authority; the work setting was no exception. In the United States, by contrast, it was in the self-interest of those who had institutionalized economic and political power to de-emphasize, even to deny, the existence of authority structures. The relative importance of closeness of supervision for authoritarian beliefs may have been greater for Polish than for US workers because Poles had a keener awareness of hierarchical structure.

That closeness of supervision is somewhat more highly correlated with positions in the class structure and in the stratification order for Poland than for the United States adds to our conviction that the cross-national difference in the relative importance of closeness of supervision for psychological functioning is no mere methodological artifact. We think, instead, that there were, at the times of our surveys, characteristic differences between the United States and Poland in the structure of authority in the work place — the organization of work being much more centralized in Poland and the authority of supervisors extending beyond the work place and the work day.

This explanation can only be tentative. What is more certain, and for our purposes more important, is the cross-nationally consistent finding that for both countries occupational self-direction plays a primary role in explaining the psychological effects of both class and stratification. The cross-national difference with respect to which component of occupational self-direction is more important in accounting for these effects does not challenge our interpretation of the relationship between social structure and personality.

THE RELATIVE ROLES OF FATHERS AND MOTHERS IN THE INTERGENERATIONAL TRANSMISSION OF VALUES

In our analyses of the transmission of values in the family (in chapter 7), we found that the family plays an equally important role in value-transmission in the United States and in Poland: the family's position in the class and stratification structures of the society greatly affects its offspring's values; half or more of this effect is through parents' values; and there is a strong reciprocal relationship between both fathers' and mothers' occupational self-direction and their values. The processes are built into the structures of industrial societies, both capitalist and socialist.

There is, however, a cross-national difference in the relative roles of fathers and mothers in the intergenerational transmission of values. In the United States, fathers play at least as important a role as do mothers; in Poland, mothers play the predominant role. This finding does not seem to be a methodological artifact of our having longitudinal data for US fathers but only cross-sectional data for Polish fathers. Nor do we have any reason to believe that this cross-national discrepancy results from the differing economic and political systems of the two countries. Rather, we think it is a historically rooted cultural contrast: Polish fathers play a more traditional role than do US fathers in the division of labor within the family and in the socialization of children.[3]

The Polish pattern, originally characteristic of the peasantry and diffused to all segments of the society through rural-to-urban migration, is supported by the influential Catholic church (Markowska, 1975), and paradoxically also by the state. Both church and state see mothers as more responsible than fathers for the socialization process. The traditional Polish pattern, where mothers have primary responsibility for child-rearing and fathers' roles in the socialization of children focus on control and punishment, still obtains in many families. In such families, children feel more attached to their mothers than to their fathers (Tyszka, 1985, pp. 96–8). This pattern of emotional attachment may give mothers the predominant role in the transmission of values.

We see the cross-national difference in fathers' roles in the socialization of children as having considerable importance for our understanding of family dynamics, but as variation on theme rather than as a challenge to our interpretation of social structure and personality.

THE RELATIONSHIPS OF CLASS AND STRATIFICATION
WITH DISTRESS

Although each of the cross-national differences that we have thus far reviewed is of some importance in its own right, none seems to raise any fundamental question about our overall interpretation. The cross-national differences in the relationships of social class and social stratification with men's sense of distress or of well-being, however, are much more troubling

[3] It may be pertinent to remember that US fathers' values affect their children's values not only through the children's accurate perception of the fathers' values, but also through other processes – presumably the result of fathers' playing an active role in their children's lives.

– and also potentially of much greater value for modifying or amplifying the interpretation – than any of the others.

Distress has all along been the exception to an otherwise consistent pattern. Quite in contrast to our cross-nationally consistent findings about the relationships of social class and of social stratification to other facets of personality, we have found a decided inconsistency in the relationships of social structure to a principal underlying dimension of orientations to self and society – namely, a sense of well-being versus distress. For the United States, employers, managers, and first-line supervisors have a greater sense of well-being than do other social classes, particularly manual workers (see table 4.4). For Poland, nearly the opposite: managers are the second most distressed social class and manual workers have a greater sense of well-being than do members of any other employee class. Similarly for social stratification: for the United States, higher stratification position *decreases* feelings of distress; for Poland, higher stratification position *increases* feelings of distress (see table 4.5). The magnitudes of these correlations are only modest for both countries, but the cross-national difference in direction of relationships is none the less striking. Why these cross-national differences – the most interesting and potentially the most important of any that we have found?

Methodological explanations

Prudence dictates that the first hypothesis one entertain in trying to explain cross-national differences is that the inconsistent findings are somehow a methodological artifact. As Bernard Finifter noted,

There is a curious inconsistency in the way researchers interpret results from attempted replications when discrepancies crop up. Failure to reproduce a finding in the *same* culture usually leads the investigator to question the reliability, validity, and comparability of the research procedures used in the two studies for possible method artifacts. But failure to corroborate the same finding in a *different* culture often leads to claims of having discovered "cultural" differences, and substantive interpretations are promptly devised to account for the apparent differences. (1977, p. 155)

Above and beyond systematically checking for possible errors in our coding procedures, measurement models, construction of factor scores, and the like – which sounds simple but in fact is a difficult and time-consuming task – the search for methodological explanations of cross-national differences requires a careful assessment of the cross-national comparability of conceptualization and measurement.

It is most unlikely that the source of the cross-national differences in the relationship of social structure and distress could lie in the conceptualization and measurement of either social class or social stratification, for their relationships with other facets of psychological functioning are cross-nationally consistent. Might it be, then, that our measurement of either distress or of the first-order dimensions of orientation on which distress is based lack cross-national comparability? We doubt that this can be the case.

For one thing, the confirmatory factor-analytic models for the first-order dimensions of orientation that reflect distress – namely, anxiety, self-deprecation, (lack of) self-confidence, (non)conformity in one's ideas, and (dis)trust – meet our standards for cross-national comparability as well as do the models for the first-order dimensions of orientation that reflect self-directedness of orientation (see chapter 4).

Moreover, despite the correlations between self-directedness of orientation and distress being negative for the United States and positive for Poland (see figure 4.3), there is every reason to believe that our second-order measurement models of distress are cross-nationally comparable. In particular, the relationships between distress and the first-order dimensions of orientation on which it is based are markedly similar for the United States and Poland.

Finally, the cross-national differences in the relationships between social structure and distress are found, not only in analyses using the higher-order concept, distress, but also in analyses using pivotal first-order concepts, particularly self-confidence and (to a lesser extent) anxiety (see tables 4.4 and 4.5). These differences are even to be found in the relationships between social structure and the indicators of self-confidence and of anxiety. The explanation for the cross-national difference in the relationships between position in the social structure and one's sense of well-being or of distress must be substantive, not methodological.

Delimiting the meaning of "distress"

A first step in interpreting the cross-national differences in the relationships of class and stratification with men's sense of distress is to specify precisely what we mean by "distress." Can we learn anything about how broad or narrow our interpretation should be from examining closely related but differentiable concepts? Anything we can learn from such an endeavor will help us in clarifying what it is that we need to explain.

Obviously, our index of distress focuses on the realm of the affective: for both Poland and the United States, the first-order dimensions of orientation most strongly related to distress are anxiety and self-deprecation, with anxiety of somewhat greater importance for the United States, self-deprecation for Poland. Of lesser but still considerable importance, for both countries, are lack of self-confidence, distrust of others, and believing that one's ideas differ from those of one's friends, one's relatives, one's co-religionists, and the society generally. Our reason for calling this underlying dimension of orientation a sense of "well-being" versus "distress" is evident in the very recital of the first-order dimensions on which it is based.

The actual questions (see table 4.3) of which these first-order dimensions are constituted – the indicators on which our measurement models of these dimensions are based – give an even more poignant sense of what it means to score high on this dimension: to be at the extreme on our index of distress is to be overwhelmed by a sense of dismay with oneself and estrangement from others. To be at the other extreme of this dimension is to be emotionally at peace with oneself and the world. In sharp contrast to whether one's orientation is self-directed or conformist, we are dealing here with the affective component of orientation to self and others, not with its intellectual or volitional components.

What may not be so evident is the distinction that we make between "distress" and "stress." By stress, we (and many others) mean subjective reactions to particular conditions of life, as when we talk of one or another job condition being stressful. *Dis*tress, on the other hand, is a much more general and pervasive phenomenon, by no means limited to reactions to particular conditions of life. In our usage, certainly, distress refers not to the affective tone of particular events or conditions or interpersonal relations, but to a much more pervasive sense of unhappiness with self and society.

Perhaps the most precise way to delineate what we mean by distress is to differentiate distress from alienation. Roberts (1987) has used many of the same items on which our measurement models of self-directedness of orientation and distress are based, to construct second-order measurement models of alienation for both the United States and Poland. The first-order dimensions (following Kohn's [1976a] re-interpretation of Seeman [1959]) are self-estrangement, powerlessness, normlessness, cultural estrangement, and meaninglessness.[4] The second-order dimension, alienation, partakes of

---

[4] For a detailed description of the questions used to index the first-order dimensions of alienation, see Roberts, 1987, or Kohn and Schooler, 1983, pp. 86 and 333. Essentially, "self-estrangement" measures not only a negative evaluation of one's own worth, but also a sense of being detached from self, of being adrift, purposeless, bored with everything, merely responding to what life has to offer, rather than setting one's own course; "powerlessness" measures a sense of lacking personal efficacy; "normlessness" is simply our familiar "standards of morality" looked at from the opposite perspective; "cultural estrangement" is similarly "idea-conformity" in reverse; and "meaninglessness" is a single item asking whether the respondent sees the world as understandable.

all five of the first-order dimensions, most notably of self-estrangement and powerlessness.[5]

Distress and alienation are of course highly correlated; how could it be otherwise when they are conceptually similar and share many of the same indicators? But they are not perfectly correlated (the correlations being 0.75 for the United States and 0.58 for Poland). Moreover, and far more important, the relationships of both class and stratification with alienation are cross-nationally *consistent*: for both countries managers are the least alienated social class (for the United States, employers, too), and manual workers are the most alienated (for Poland, production workers and nonproduction workers are the two most alienated classes). For both countries, the higher men's social-stratification position, the less alienated they tend to be.[6] The cross-national difference that we found for the relationships between social structure and distress is not to be found in the relationships between social structure and alienation.

We are thus able to define the cross-national difference in the relationships of social structure and distress more precisely than before: it has to do specifically with the purely affective realm, not even with so affectively charged an interpretation of external reality as alienation. We seek to explain why position in the social structure has different effects on US and Polish men's pervasive sense of well-being or distress, but only on this purely affective sense, not on their beliefs about the society in which they live, nor on their values, nor on how self-directed or conformist is their general orientation to self and society, nor even on such affectively toned beliefs about social reality as those implied in alienation.

Alternative interpretations of the cross-national differences in the relationships between social structure and distress

Why, then, is it that advantageous positions in the class structures and stratification systems have cross-nationally inconsistent effects on men's sense of distress?

[5] In the model for the United States, the paths from the second-order concept, alienation, to self-estrangement are 0.88 and 0.90 for 1964 and 1974 respectively; the paths to powerlessness are 0.83 in both years; and the paths to the other first-order concepts are much smaller – in the 0.30s to low 0.50s. In the model for Poland, the paths from the second-order concept, alienation, are 0.98 for self-estrangement, 0.76 for powerlessness, 0.40 for meaninglessness, 0.25 for cultural estrangement, and 0.24 for normlessness.

[6] The correlations of social stratification with alienation are only modest: -0.31 for the United States at the time of the baseline interviews and -0.41 at the time of the follow-up interviews; for Poland, -0.21, smaller than for the United States, but consistent in direction and non-trivial in magnitude. What is impressive is not the magnitudes of these relationships but their consistency.

On one level, the question is readily answered: our analyses of chapters 5 and 6 show that class and stratification matter for values, for intellectual flexibility, and for self-directedness of orientation in large part because people of more advantaged position have greater opportunity to be self-directed in their work. Our analyses of the reciprocal effects of occupational self-direction and these facets of psychological functioning demonstrate, moreover, that occupational self-direction is not only correlated with, but actually affects, all these facets of psychological functioning (see table 6.2). The same analyses show that, although occupational self-direction has a statistically significant effect (negative, of course) on the sense of distress for the United States, it has no effect at all for Poland. It is pertinent to note here that similar analyses for Japan (Kohn et al., 1990) show that occupational self-direction has a significantly negative effect on distress for that country.[7]

Why does occupational self-direction ameliorate distress for the United States (and also for Japan) but fail to do so for Poland? We simply do not know. Nor are we ready to concede that, in actuality, occupational self-direction does not ameliorate distress for Poland. More about this possibility anon.

There is a closely related and perhaps even more important issue to face: for neither country – certainly not for Poland, but also not for the United States, nor for that matter for Japan – does occupational self-direction provide as effective an explanation of the relationships of class and stratification with distress as it does for their relationships with other facets of personality.

Given the magnitude of the effect of occupational self-direction on distress for the United States (see table 6.2), we might well expect a somewhat higher correlation of social stratification with distress than the -0.18 that we actually find. We should expect the absence of *any* relationship, not a positive relationship, for Poland. And we should expect a negative correlation of social stratification with distress for Japan, instead of the near-zero correlation (of -0.01) that we actually do find (Kohn et al., 1990).

Similarly for social class: if occupational self-direction completely explained the class–distress relationship, we should expect to find that

<hr/>

[7] We must be cautious in interpreting the Japanese model, for there is also a statistically significant *positive* effect of education on distress. When two variables that are positively related to each other (in this case, occupational self-direction and education) have statistically significant but opposite-signed effects on a third variable (distress), there is the distinct possibility of the finding being artifactual, the result of collinearity. Since, however, the model gives every sign of being well conditioned, we are inclined to treat the finding as real: occupational self-direction probably does decrease distress for Japan, as it does for the United States but does not for Poland.

members of the social classes who enjoy the greatest opportunity for occupational self-direction would be the least distressed. This is certainly the case for the United States, albeit to a lesser degree than we should expect. It is certainly not the case for Poland. And Japan adds further evidence that occupational self-direction does not provide a sufficient explanation of the class–distress relationship (Kohn et al., 1990): in Japan, it is not the manual workers, whose opportunities for occupational self-direction are minimal, but *non*manual workers who are most distressed. Evidently, more than occupational self-direction is involved in explaining the relationships of stratification and class to distress.

We face an issue of fundamental importance for our interpretation. That interpretation implies that occupational self-direction – and therefore also class and stratification – should have a cross-nationally consistent effect on feelings of distress, as it has on values, self-directedness of orientation, and cognitive functioning. Obviously, our interpretation must be revised. From the evidence at hand, though, it is not at all certain whether the interpretation requires minor revision or extensive overhaul.

The fundamental principle we must follow in modifying our interpretation is that any modifications must take account not only of what we have found to be cross-nationally different but also of what we have found to be cross-nationally similar. To be valid, any interpretation has to explain why we find cross-national differences in the relationships of class and stratification with the sense of distress, but not in their relationships with parental valuation of self-direction, self-directedness of orientation, and cognitive functioning. Explanations so broadly framed as to lead one to expect Polish men of more advantaged position to value conformity for their children, to have a conformist orientation to self and society, or not to be intellectually flexible, could not be valid. Nor would it make any sense to explain the findings in terms of a weaker linkage of social stratification or of social class to occupational self-direction for Poland than for the United States, for that is not the case; or in terms of occupational self-direction being any less important for Polish men than for US men.

There are at least four ways that the interpretive model might be modified to account for the cross-national difference *vis-à-vis* distress in a manner consistent with our findings of cross-national similarity *vis-à-vis* other facets of psychological functioning. These modifications represent enlargements of the interpretive model beyond occupational self-direction, or learning-generalization, or the historical present, or the occupational realm. None of these possible modifications is incompatible with any of the others. They can, in fact, be regarded as successively greater enlargements of the interpretive model, the question then becoming how greatly we need enlarge the model to encompass the cross-national differences that we have found.

The modification that would require the smallest change in our interpretive model would be to enlarge the range of job conditions to take cognizance that job conditions *other than* those involved in occupational self-direction may exert effects on distress countervailing to those of occupational self-direction. A further, or alternative, modification of the interpretation would be to include psychological processes other than learning-generalization, in the belief that the processes by which position in the social structure affects distress may be different from those by which position in the social structure affects parental valuation of self-direction, intellectual flexibility, and self-directedness of orientation. A third possible modification of the interpretive model would be to take account not only of currently experienced job conditions but also of the processes by which people attain their positions and the meaning that these positions have for them. Finally, the interpretation could be even further expanded, to take account of non-job conditions of life. We shall examine each of these possibilities in turn, bringing to bear whatever available empirical materials shed light on their validity.

Countervailing effects of occupational self-direction and other job conditions
The smallest change of interpretive model would be to expand the range of pertinent job conditions beyond those directly involved in occupational self-direction, while retaining the rest of the model intact. In such an enlargement of the model, we would still expect the primary process by which social structure affects psychological functioning – even distress – to be one of learning from the job and generalizing those lessons to life outside the work place.

There is nothing about a learning-generalization model that says that one can learn only from the experience of occupational self-direction. Moreover, although our US data demonstrate that occupational self-direction is of key importance for values, intellectual flexibility, and self-directedness of orientation, those same data show that *other* job conditions may be of equal or greater importance for distress (Kohn and Schooler, 1983, chapter 6). Some of these job conditions are related to stratification and class, and hence might explain the effects – or lack of effects – of stratification and class on distress. Particularly intriguing is the possibility that some job conditions associated with an advantaged position might exacerbate distress, while other job conditions also associated with an advantaged position might ameliorate distress.

We have some pertinent, albeit limited, evidence that lends credibility to this possibility. What makes this evidence especially interesting is that it is directly pertinent to our understanding differences in the relative situations of managers and manual workers in the United States and Poland, and hence the cross-national differences in the relationships of both class and stratification to distress.

For the United States, job protections (such as seniority provisions in union contracts) ameliorate distress.[8] There is a striking relationship, for all employee classes, between number of job protections and degree of distress (see part B of table 8.2), with the greatest distress evidenced by those who had fewest job protections. It is noteworthy that, for manual workers, those who have substantial job protections are no more distressed than is the average employed man. It is also striking that union members are much more likely to have substantial job protections than are other manual workers.[9]

None the less, the very social class that, at the time of our interviews, enjoyed the greatest job protections – manual workers – was also the most distressed (see part A of table 8.2). Manual workers were distressed *because* they lacked opportunities for occupational self-direction and *despite* the job protections that many of them – particularly union members – enjoyed (see part C of table 8.2). Were it not for these job protections, manual workers would have been even more distressed than they were. Correspondingly, managers – who enjoyed substantial opportunity for occupational self-direction, hence had a relatively strong sense of well-being – would have had an even greater sense of well-being if they had greater job protections. Occupational self-direction and job protections thus have countervailing effects – which accounts for the relatively modest relationship of social class with distress, even for the United States.

The countervailing effects of occupational self-direction and job protections are illustrated anew – this time from a social stratification rather than a social class perspective – in figure 8.1, which models the reciprocal relationships of occupational position with both occupational self-direction and job protections, and of occupational self-direction and job protections with distress.[10] Both occupational self-direction and job protections have

---

[8] Our index of job protections is a simple additive index of the number of questions answered affirmatively from the following battery of questions. (1) Do you have any job protection – like seniority rights, contract guarantees, union support, Civil Service, or any other form of job protection? (2) Is there a formal grievance procedure that you can use if you feel you are treated unfairly? (3) Does your job provide for your being paid while sick?

[9] We cannot make such a comparison for nonmanual workers because only thirteen of the 106 nonmanual workers in our (1974) sample belonged to a union. It is evident in the numbers of cases, though, that nonmanual workers enjoyed fewer job protections than did unionized manual workers.

[10] In this model, cross-lagged effects are used as instruments. Further instrumentation for modelling the reciprocal effects of job conditions and distress is achieved by allowing non-credentialling social characteristics to directly affect distress but to affect current job conditions only indirectly, mainly through earlier job conditions.

statistically significant *negative* effects on distress – which is to say, both ameliorate distress. But higher occupational position *increases* occupational self-direction and *decreases* job protections. Hence, occupational position has contradictory effects on distress: higher occupational position ameliorates distress insofar as it leads to greater occupational self-direction, but also exacerbates distress insofar as it limits job protections.[11] Correspondingly, lower occupational position is conducive to distress insofar as it restricts opportunities for occupational self-direction but ameliorates distress insofar as it affords greater job protections.

In Poland at the time of our survey, *all* employees of the nationalized sector of the economy – production workers, nonproduction workers, nonmanual workers, first-line supervisors, and managers alike – by law enjoyed employment security, sick leave, guaranteed vacations, and other job protections akin to those of unionized workers in the United States. Since manual workers enjoyed the same job protections as all other employees of the nationalized sector of the economy, their having such protections does not in itself explain why production and nonproduction workers were the least distressed of all employee classes. Their having such protections, though, represented a substantial, if gradual, improvement over their past situation, for it was only during the late 1960s and early 1970s that Polish labor law had been changed to give them the job protections that previously had been enjoyed only by nonmanual workers. The full implementation of those laws took place in the early 1970s, approximately five years before our survey. Thus, at the time of our survey, Polish manual

---

[11] In this model, occupational position is allowed to affect distress only indirectly, through occupational self-direction and job protections. Were we to allow a direct effect of occupational position on distress, that path would be a statistically nonsignificant $+0.29$. Not only is such a path opposite in sign to the zero-order correlation of occupational position and distress, but a path of this magnitude that is statistically nonsignificant is itself a sign of weak identification. Moreover, allowing such a path would increase the magnitude of the path from occupational self-direction to distress, from -0.14 as shown in figure 8.1, to -0.42, which we believe to be exaggeratedly large, the result of collinearity between occupational position and occupational self-direction.

The solution to this problem of collinearity that we employed in figure 5.5 and table 5.4, of having occupational position and occupational self-direction affect distress through the first-order concepts that serve as their indicators, does not solve the problem in this more complex model that also includes job protections. But, since the model for distress summarized in tables 5.4 and 5.5 clearly demonstrates that the effect of occupational position on distress is entirely attributable to occupational self-direction, it seems reasonable, in this more complex model, to posit that the effects of occupational position are entirely indirect, through occupational self-direction and job protections. The question to which this model is addressed is not whether the effects of occupational position on distress are direct or indirect – we already know that they are indirect – but whether the indirect effects of occupational position through job protections countervail those through occupational self-direction.

Table 8.2 *Social class, occupational self-direction, and distress: US men (1974)*

A Distress, occupational self-direction, and job protections by social class

Mean[a] level of:	Employers (N = 32)	Self-employed (N = 82)	Managers (N = 65)	First-line supervisors (N = 122)	Nonmanual workers (N = 106)	Manual workers (N = 219)	(eta[b])
Distress	−0.20	−0.08	−0.16	−0.16	0.04	0.18	0.18*
Occupational self-direction	0.41	−0.01	0.91	0.34	0.56	−0.79	0.74*
Job protections	—	—	−0.06	−0.20	−0.12	0.19	0.19*

B Distress by social class, union membership, and job protections[c]

				Manual Workers	
Job protections	Managers (N = 60)	First-line supervisors (N = 113)	Nonmanual workers (N = 103)	Union members (N = 121)	Nonunion members (N = 88)
0 (None)	— (0)	0.32 (10)	— (8)	— (3)	0.59 (28)
1	−0.06 (27)	−0.30 (48)	0.10 (43)	— (0)	0.47 (26)
2	−0.11 (15)	−0.13 (21)	−0.32 (15)	0.18 (21)	0.23 (18)
3 (Many)	−0.33 (18)	−0.16 (34)	0.02 (37)	0.02 (97)	−0.10 (16)

C Distress by social class, job protections, and occupational self-direction[c]

	Managers		First-line supervisors		Nonmanual workers		Manual workers	
Occupational self-direction	Low job protections[d] (N = 27)	High job protections (N = 33)	Low job protections[d] (N = 58)	High job protections (N = 55)	Low job protections[d] (N = 51)	High job protections (N = 52)	Low job protections[d] (N = 57)	High job protections (N = 152)
Low[e]	— (1)	— (3)	0.25 (16)	−0.08 (21)	0.52 (10)	0.27 (12)	0.58 (47)	0.06 (124)
High	−0.01 (26)	−0.19 (30)	−0.36 (42)	−0.18 (34)	−0.02 (41)	−0.18 (40)	−0.02 (10)	−0.12 (28)

[a] Expressed as standardized differences from the grand mean for the entire population.
[b] Corrected for unreliability of measurement.
[c] All entries are mean[a] levels of distress, followed (in parentheses) by numbers of cases on which the means are calculated.
[d] Job protections dichotomized: none or one versus two or three types of job protection.
[e] Occupational self-direction dichotomized: above versus below the mean for employees.
* Statistically significant, p<0.05.

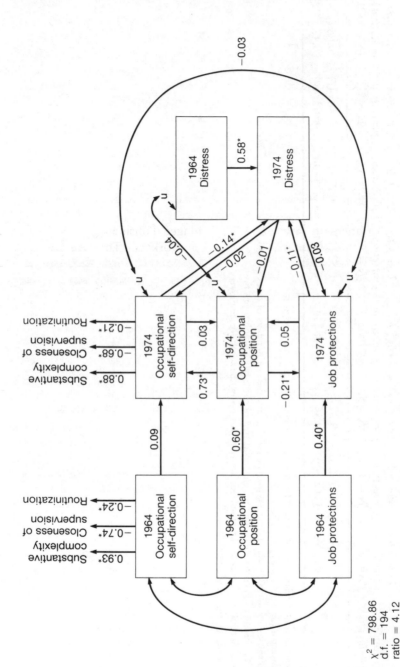

$\chi^2 = 798.86$
d.f. = 194
ratio = 4.12

Statistically significant, p ≤ 0.05; other parameters are nonsignificant.

Figure 8.1 *The reciprocal relationships of occupational position, occupational self-direction, job protections, and distress: US men. (Paths from exogenous variables and some correlations of residuals not shown.)*

workers enjoyed a degree and range of job protections and job benefits that constituted a decided improvement over those that they had had in the past. We believe that this helps explain why production workers and nonproduction workers were the least distressed of employee social classes.[12]

Moreover, manual workers, particularly production workers, enjoyed the further job security attendant on a labor market in which they were in especially great demand. And both production and nonproduction workers enjoyed other protections and benefits by virtue of their class positions in the Polish socialist society – such as preferential access to housing, the provision of health care through their place of employment, and preferential access to higher education for their children. These, too, may have contributed to manual workers' being the least distressed of all employee classes.

The same changes in law that so advantaged Polish manual workers correspondingly disadvantaged nonmanual workers. They suffered a relative loss, and some suffered an absolute loss, of their formerly privileged situation in terms of job security, length of vacations, and sick leave. These losses may well have contributed to nonmanual workers' being the most distressed of all employee classes.

As for the Polish managers, whom we have seen to be more distressed than members of any other social class except nonmanual workers, quite in contrast to the situation of managers in the United States and Japan, we have one fascinating piece of information that may help explain what it is about the conditions of life experienced by Polish managers that made them so distressed. One segment of the Polish managerial class was particularly distressed – namely, those Polish managers who were not members of the Polish United Workers (Communist) Party (see table 8.3). Although there are too few non-party managers for this finding to be definitive, it is none the less impressive that the non-party managers had decidedly higher levels of distress, compared not only to managers who were members of the party, but compared to members of any other social class, party members or not. Moreover, party membership *per se* is not related to distress; it is only the non-party managers who were particularly distressed. There is also some indication here that the non-party managers, although no less intellectually flexible than the party managers, may have been less self-directed in their orientations.

---

[12] There is no way to test this interpretation with the data in hand. Even if we had data about our Polish respondents' job protections, it might not be possible to test our hypothesis, because individual-level tests require some variation among people in the same class category. If *all* Polish employee classes enjoyed much the same job protections, there would be no way to statistically test whether class differences in job protections accounted for class differences in levels of distress.

Table 8.3   *Class position, membership of the Polish United Workers Party, and psychological functioning*

Class	Members PUWP (N)	Non-members (N)	Distress		Self-directedness of orientation		Intellectual flexibility	
			Members PUWP (Mean)[a]	Non-members (Mean)[a]	Members PUWP (Mean)[a]	Non-members (Mean)[a]	Members PUWP (Mean)[a]	Non-members (Mean)[a]
Managers	(49)	(13)	0.00	+0.45	+0.87	+0.40	+0.93	+0.86
First-line supervisors	(138)	(164)	+0.02	+0.08	+0.42	+0.20	+0.49	+0.34
Nonmanual workers	(88)	(178)	+0.13	+0.21	+0.48	+0.51	+0.63	+0.53
Production workers	(87)	(435)	+0.06	−0.12	−0.31	−0.28	−0.32	−0.37
Nonproduction workers	(44)	(283)	−0.11	−0.03	−0.72	−0.29	−0.53	−0.39
Self-employed	(4)	(69)	—	−0.17	—	−0.16	—	−0.04
All social classes	(410)	(1,142)	+0.03	−0.01	+0.21	−0.07	+0.28	−0.10

[a] Means are expressed as standardized deviation from grand mean for the entire population.

The implications of these findings, we think, are that being a non-party manager in the Polish system of centralized planning (circa 1978, the time of our survey) entailed uncertainties, risks, and insecurities – greater than those experienced by managers who were members of the party, and greater than those experienced by managers in the less centralized systems of capitalist countries. The Polish system may have held these managers responsible for accomplishments they had neither the leeway nor the resources to achieve.

Our evidence, admittedly incomplete, thus suggests that not only does occupational self-direction fail to have the cross-nationally consistent effect on distress that it has on other facets of psychological functioning, but also that other job conditions – job uncertainties and insecurities, and protections from those uncertainties and insecurities – may have counter-vailing effects. It is these countervailing effects that seem to explain, at least in part, the striking cross-national difference in the relationships of social structure and distress.[13] To adequately explain the relationships of social structure to job conditions and to distress, we must enlarge the range of job conditions beyond those directly involved in occupational self-direction. A model that appears to be sufficient for other aspects of psychological functioning does not adequately account for distress.

These findings may even provide an explanation of the failure of our analyses to show any distress-alleviating effects of occupational self-direction for Poland. If, as we continue to hypothesize, occupational self-direction actually does alleviate distress for Poland, our analyses may fail to detect such an effect because the distress-ameliorating effects of occupational self-direction are suppressed by the distress-producing consequences of the

[13] There is modest support for such an interpretation in our data for Japan, too. Kohn et al. (1990) found that two job conditions positively related to occupational self-direction – namely, believing that one works under considerable pressure of time, and believing that people in one's occupation may be held responsible for things outside of their control – are also positively related to distress. Although these findings may merely reflect a propensity for distressed people to overestimate the pressures and uncertainties of their jobs, it is at least plausible that these job conditions do increase distress, thus counteracting the ameliorative effects of occupational self-direction.

Moreover, a model of the reciprocal effects of occupational self-direction and distress for Japan shows a positive effect of education on distress, suggesting as well that either education itself, or job conditions related to education, increases distress. The countervailing effects of occupational self-direction, which decreases distress, and of education or other job conditions, which increase distress, may help explain not only why the overall relationship of class to distress is modest, but also why nonmanual workers are more distressed than are manual workers in Japan. This may explain as well the apparent anomaly that, for Japan, there is a near-zero correlation between social stratification and distress: occupational self-direction does decrease distress in Japan, but something else about social stratification (perhaps education, perhaps some other variable related to social stratification) has a countervailing effect.

uncertainties and risks attendant on many occupationally self-directed jobs.[14] In models that explicitly include no job conditions other than occupational self-direction, the countervailing effects of occupational self-direction and other correlated job conditions may appear only as a net effect of zero. We are therefore unwilling to abandon the hypothesis that, for Poland as for the United States, occupational self-direction actually does ameliorate distress. Hence our use of the expression, "the countervailing effects of occupational self-direction and other job conditions," for Poland as well as for the United States. This terminology, of course, is nothing more than a hope, which can be tested only with more extensive occupational data than those presently available.

Different psychological mechanisms   A further possible modification – or enlargement – of our interpretive model would question our effort to apply a learning-generalization model to the processes by which job conditions affect distress. The reformulation would posit, instead, that the psychological mechanisms by which job conditions affect distress may be different from those by which job conditions affect cognitive functioning, values, and self-directedness of orientation. Positing different mechanisms for different facets of personality would be, at best, inelegant, but there are worse sins in social science than inelegant interpretations.

Our model of the processes by which job affects personality is simple and straightforward: people learn from their job experiences and apply those lessons to non-occupational realms of life. Admittedly, we stretch the ordinary meanings of "learning" and "generalization" when we apply these concepts to the processes by which job conditions may lead to distress. The crux of the matter, though, is our belief that job conditions have *straightforward* psychological effects, not only on values, intellectual flexibility, and self-directedness of orientation, but even on distress. Is this hypothesis reasonable when applied to distress? Perhaps one should instead employ some other model of psychological process for dealing with distress – one that posits some *indirect* process by which job conditions affect

---

[14] Our causal model of the reciprocal effects of occupational self-direction and distress (table 6.2) shows a zero effect of occupational self-direction, and a positive effect of educational attainment, on distress. We have interpreted the positive effect of education as meaning either that education itself, or that some correlate of education not explicitly included in the model, exacerbates distress. One might similarly interpret the zero effect of occupational self-direction as meaning either that occupational self-direction has no effect on distress or that occupational self-direction actually does ameliorate distress but that *other* job conditions correlated with occupational self-direction exacerbate distress. If we were able to include both occupational self-direction and these other job conditions in the same model (much as we did for the United States in figure 8.1), these would show as countervailing effects.

psychological functioning. Two such possibilities have been extensively discussed in the research literature: job (dis)satisfaction and stress.

The rationale for believing that job satisfaction may be an intervening link between job conditions and off-the-job distress is that some job conditions may lead to dissatisfaction with those particular job conditions or even with the entire job; dissatisfaction with the job, in turn, may lead to a more generalized sense of distress. The hypothesis posits a sort of two-stage learning-generalization process, the "learning" stage centered on the processes by which job conditions lead to job dissatisfaction, the "generalization" stage centered on the processes by which dissatisfaction with the job is generalized to a pervasive sense of dismay, by no means limited to feelings about the job itself.

That such processes might be particularly applicable to distress, less so to cognitive functioning, values, and self-directedness of orientation, is certainly plausible. For job satisfaction to play an important intervening role in the relationship of job conditions to distress, though, would require job satisfaction to be strongly correlated both with job conditions and with distress. The empirical evidence, to the contrary, is that job satisfaction is only moderately correlated with job conditions (Kahn, 1972; Kohn and Schooler, 1973; J. Miller, 1980). Moreover, our US data refute the assumption of a close connection between job satisfaction and distress.[15] There is no reason to accord to job satisfaction the role of intermediary; job satisfaction (or dissatisfaction) is simply one of many psychological consequences of work, and not the key to understanding the effects of job conditions on distress or, for that matter, on any other facet of off-the-job psychological functioning.

Another and more appealing candidate for the role of intervening link in the processes by which job affects a sense of *distress* is *stress*. The hypothesis is that some job conditions are experienced as stressful; these experiences of job-related stress, in turn, are generalized far beyond the job itself to a pervasive sense of *distress*.[16] The hypothesis does not merely assert that

---

[15] The correlations of job satisfaction with distress are −0.35 for 1964 and −0.45 for 1974. Although these correlations are moderately large, they are not large enough for job satisfaction to be a crucial intervening link between job conditions and distress. Moreover, a full assessment would have to take account that the relationship between job satisfaction and distress might not be unidirectional.

[16] In many social-psychological studies, stress is explicitly or implicitly defined as negative *feelings* about particular job conditions, and is measured by asking respondents whether they consciously experience their job conditions as stressful or unpleasant. In many medical studies, though, stress is defined not in terms of feelings about job conditions but in terms of some physiological or biochemical response to those conditions, and is assessed not by asking respondents how they feel about their job conditions but by measuring pulse or blood pressure or hormone level. To attempt to encompass both formulations, we use the term, "experienced

some job conditions result in workers' experiencing stress. Nor is the hypothesis limited to the assertion that experienced stress is one of the psychological consequences of work. The hypothesis asserts much more: that job stress is a necessary intervening variable between job conditions and at least some facets of off-the-job psychological functioning, notably distress. Were it not that job conditions produce the experience of on-the-job stress, they would not result in a pervasive feeling of off-the-job distress. A weaker version of the hypothesis would say that, absent stress, job conditions would have substantially smaller or less pervasive effects on off-the-job psychological functioning.

Stress is a plausible link from job conditions to distress. Moreover, as we have seen, some job conditions that are generally thought to be stressful, and others that are generally thought to be stress-alleviating, do seem to affect distress. But the evidence for a "stress" model, even when applied only to distress, is less than compelling.

We know of no research, with the partial exception of that by House (1980), that adequately tests the stress hypothesis, for no study includes measures of all the necessary elements: objective job conditions, experienced job stress, and pertinent aspects of off-the-job psychological functioning. Most studies addressed to the stress hypothesis fail to measure actual job conditions. In the absence of information about actual job conditions, though, it is impossible to say whether what appear to be the psychological consequences of stress actually result from stress or from the job conditions themselves.

Studies that do measure job conditions, on the other hand, typically do not measure whether these job conditions are experienced as stressful, hence can only infer that some job conditions must be stressful, and that stress plays the role of intervening link between these particular job conditions and off-the-job psychological functioning. The list of putatively stressful job conditions is endless, including even the lack of opportunity for occupational self-direction. When stress is imputed to job conditions, without directly measuring whether these conditions are actually experienced as stressful, the argument is tautological. Nor is the evidence improved by what purports to be a validation, namely, that job conditions deemed by the investigator to be stressful correlate with such psychological phenomena as anxiety and depression. Such evidence constitutes a validation if and only if

---

as stressful," and do not distinguish between "consciously experienced" and "physiologically experienced." For our purposes the distinction between the two conceptualizations of stress is less important than what they have in common: both posit an *indirect* process, with job conditions affecting psychological functioning (or health or some other outcome) through some consciously felt or biologically experienced reaction to those job conditions.

one has already accepted the stress hypothesis as the only possible explanation of why job conditions might result in anxiety and depression.

Kohn and Schooler's findings (1982; 1983, chapter 6) cast further doubt on stress interpretations, for they indicate that purportedly stressful job conditions do not have uniformly deleterious psychological consequences – as would be implied by most stress interpretations (but see LaRocco et al., 1980; Karasek, 1979). Still, there is evidence in this research that some job conditions generally thought to be stressful – close supervision, dirty work, a lack of job protections – do lead to feelings of distress. Thus, the stress hypothesis, though irrelevant to explaining the effects of job conditions on intellectual flexibility, valuation of self-direction, or self-directedness of orientation, may be pertinent for explaining the effects of job conditions on distress – hence to interpreting our cross-nationally inconsistent findings *vis-à-vis* distress. The question nevertheless remains: is it necessary to posit such an indirect process? Perhaps we are making too fine a distinction, but we are reluctant to complicate an interpretation that says that job conditions have straightforward psychological consequences by positing a more complex indirect process (see Spenner, 1988b). We are reluctant to do so, that is, until we see further evidence that the psychological process really is this complex.

The processes by which people attain their positions and the meanings these positions have to them   A further enlargement of the interpretation would incorporate not only a wider range of possibly pertinent current job conditions, and perhaps also indirect psychological processes, but would take greater account of the processes by which people attain their occupational positions and of the meaning these positions have to them. In our first published report on the US–Polish comparative analyses (Slomczynski et al., 1981), we speculated at length about the implications of historical developments after the Second World War that resulted in differences between the United States and Poland in structural mobility, job-selection processes, and the symbolic importance attached to class position – differences that might explain why social stratification bears a different relationship to distress for the two countries:

[In] the aftermath of World War II and the rapid reindustrialization of Poland, many people of working-class and peasant backgrounds who might not otherwise have had the opportunity for higher education and responsible jobs did get these opportunities. This resulted from several historical processes: the Nazis' systematic massacre of the Polish intelligentsia, the rapid increase in industrialization and bureaucratization from pre-war levels, and the deliberate policy of socialist governments to make educational opportunities available to the children of workers and peasants. Whatever the reasons, it is possible that rapid social mobility has resulted in some feelings of self-doubt among people who occupy higher positions. Alternatively, during the transitional stages to a new economic and political system, higher positions may be more precarious than lower positions. As a consequence, people in higher positions may wonder whether they really are sufficiently competent to carry out the responsibilities of their jobs. Another possible explanation focuses on the widespread belief, in part a derivative of the aristocratic culture of pre-war Poland, that status is not so much a result of superior job performance as of fate or the intervention of well-placed friends. Hence, finding oneself in a high position would provide little assurance of one's ability to meet the demands of the position.

These explanations focus on the reasons why Polish men of higher educational and occupational position may not have as favorable self-conceptions as one might have expected. It is equally pertinent to ask why Polish men of lower educational and occupational position may be more self-confident and less anxious than one might have expected. Although, as individuals, these men may not have experienced much social mobility, certainly the segment of the society to which they belong – the working class – has benefited from post-war changes in socialist Poland. Their economic situation has improved and they are now held in higher social regard; there is every reason for them to feel more confident. Post-war changes in Polish social structure have enhanced the circumstances of the working class to a much greater extent than those of white-collar workers and professionals. (p. 742)

These speculations still seem plausible, not as the basic explanation of the cross-national difference in the relationships of position in the social structure and distress, but as supplementary to enlarging the range of job conditions.

Non-job conditions of life   Finally, one could broaden the scope of the interpretation even more, by taking account of conditions of life other than those involved in job and career. It might be, for example, that cross-national differences in family structure, or in religious belief, or in whether the urban population is primarily rural in origin, or in "national culture," bear on the sense of distress. The pivotal questions, though, are not whether family, religion, rural origins, or culture result in differences in Polish and American men's sense of distress, but whether such non-occupational conditions help explain why social class and social stratification bear different relationships to the sense of distress for Poland and the United States. Perhaps they do; but we have no way of testing these possibilities with the data in hand.

CONCLUSION

In this chapter, we have reviewed the cross-national differences discovered in our analyses. Although all of these differences are of some importance in their own right, with one major exception they raise no serious questions about the validity of our interpretation of the relationships between social structure and psychological functioning in industrialized societies.

Thus, the somewhat stronger correlation (*eta*) between class and stratification for Poland than for the United States, even though contrary to many theorists' expectations, is entirely compatible with our interpretation; it does, however, mean that class and stratification are less empirically differentiable for Poland than for the United States.

Our finding that formal education continues further into Polish men's than American men's occupational careers may or may not have been a historically limited phenomenon; but in any case it has little import for our understanding of the psychological effects of either education or occupational self-direction.

The relatively greater importance of closeness of supervision for explaining the impact of social-structural positions on the psychological functioning of Polish than of US men (and, correspondingly, the relatively greater importance of the substantive complexity of work for US than for Polish men), while itself calling out for a more thoroughgoing interpretation, is but a variant on the main theme: for both countries, occupational self-direction plays a pivotal role in explaining the psychological effects of class and stratification.

Similarly, the relatively greater role of US than of Polish fathers in the intergenerational transmission of values points to an important cross-national difference in family dynamics. But this difference, too, is a variant on what for our interpretation are the principal findings: in both the United States and Poland, parents' positions in the larger social structure of their society have a decided bearing on their adolescent and early-adult offspring's values; this comes about through the parents' social-structural positions affecting their opportunities for occupational self-direction; the experience of occupational self-direction in turn decidedly affects parents' values; and parents' values decidedly affect their offspring's values. This chain of effects is remarkably similar for the two countries, except for the relative importance of mothers' and fathers' values in this process.

The one cross-national difference that does raise a serious question for our interpretation is the effect of social-structural position on men's sense of well-being or distress. Our evidence belies the possibility of this cross-national difference being merely a methodological artifact. We could simply call the difference an "exception" to an otherwise consistent pattern of cross-national similarities, limiting our generalizations to the effects of social structure on values, cognitive functioning, and self-directedness of orientation, while excluding from that generalization the effects of social structure on the realm of the affective. Even if we were to call the difference an exception to what is otherwise a consistent set of findings, however, we could do so only as a temporary stopgap, until such time as we are able to encompass the cross-national difference in an enlarged interpretation that accounts both for the cross-national similarities and for this one cross-national difference.

Even though we do not have the data in hand to fully develop and test any such enlarged interpretation, we have examined four possible ways of modifying the interpretive model to incorporate the cross-national difference while still accounting for all the cross-national similarities. All are compatible with existing data.

We considered the possibility that we may have unduly restricted the range of job conditions in our interpretation: that although the job conditions directly involved in occupational self-direction may be of prime importance for explaining the effects of social-structural position on values, cognitive functioning, and self-directedness of orientation, *other* job conditions – in particular, job uncertainties and insecurities, and protections from those uncertainties and insecurities – are important, perhaps even more important, for understanding the relationships between position in the social structure and the sense of distress.

Our US data do indeed confirm countervailing effects of occupational self-direction and some other job conditions, notably job protections, associated with social-structural position. These countervailing effects result in class and stratification having a smaller effect on distress than one would expect from knowing only the ameliorative effect of occupational self-direction.

But the crucial case in this instance is Poland, not the United States, for it is in Poland that occupational self-direction, contrary to our expectation, fails to ameliorate distress. The Polish data are consistent with a countervailing-effects interpretation. In particular, our finding that Polish manual workers, both production and nonproduction workers, are the least distressed of all Polish employee classes, is consistent with the great improvement, in the years shortly before our survey, in their job protections and even in privileges attendant on their class positions. And the high levels of distress found among Polish managers can be pinpointed as resulting from the exceptionally high level of distress of those few Polish managers who were not members of the Polish United Workers (Communist) Party. We see this as suggesting that *these* managers were especially subject to uncertainty and risk – thus as lending credence to our belief that job conditions other than those directly involved in occupational self-direction may indeed contribute to distress.

We then considered (with somewhat jaundiced eyes) the possibility that we have unduly limited our interpretation by seeing the direct process of learning from the job and generalizing what has been learned to other realms of life as the dominant process by which job conditions affect off-the-job psychological functioning – even distress. Although we are reluctant to posit different modes of psychological process for different facets of psychological functioning, and even though we are not convinced that it is necessary to posit that job conditions affect distress indirectly, by first affecting job satisfaction or dissatisfaction or by first inducing experienced job stress, we cannot dismiss these possibilities, particularly the latter.

Finally, we considered briefly two other modifications that we see as potentially fruitful extensions of our interpretation, but which we do not have adequate data to explore: that our interpretation should not only take account of current job conditions but also of the processes by which people attain those positions and the meaning that those positions have to them; and that it should take differences in non-job conditions of life more fully into account.

In any case, on the basis of presently available evidence, we still do not have an adequate explanation of why occupational self-direction ameliorates distress for the United States but not for Poland; and we have only a partially formulated explanation of the countervailing effects of occupational self-direction and other job conditions. The most we can claim is a partial explanation, only partially tested, of why social class and social stratification have cross-nationally inconsistent effects on the sense of distress. Unsatisfactory though we find this to be, we value the cross-national evidence for making clear wherein the interpretation with which we began our inquiry applies and wherein it does not, thus defining what is at issue. Were it not for the cross-national evidence, there would have been little reason to doubt that the original formulation, as tested on US data, applies (albeit not quite as well) to the sense of distress just as it does to values, to cognitive functioning, and to self-directedness of orientation.

9

A Re-evaluation of the Thesis and its Implications for Understanding the Relationship between Social Structure and Personality

In this chapter we reassess our interpretation. We recapitulate the principal thesis and the evidence that we have brought to bear in its support. We assess the implications for our interpretation of the principal limitations of our data and analyses. We review pertinent evidence from other studies, particularly studies done in other countries. Finally, we reflect on the implications of our analyses for the more general theoretical problem of interpreting the relationships of social structure and personality in cross-national perspective.

RECAPITULATION OF THE THESIS AND OF RELEVANT EVIDENCE

Since we have developed a rather complex thesis, brought many strands of data-analysis to bear on this thesis, considered many alternative interpretations, and given considerable attention to departures from our expectations, it might be well to recapitulate the principal thesis and the evidence that bears on it.

Class and stratification

We see social class and social stratification as alternative conceptualizations of essentially the same social-structural phenomena, both conceptualizations theoretically useful, albeit not necessarily for answering the same questions. We regard class as the more fundamental organizing principle of socioeconomic structure, with stratification providing a basis for a more fine-grained analysis of social structure and personality.

The first element of our thesis is that it is conceptually meaningful and empirically possible to develop indices of social class and social stratification, not only for capitalist but also for socialist society. We have in fact developed indices of class and stratification that are broadly comparable for the capitalist United States and socialist Poland, yet each was developed with due attention to the particular historical, cultural, and political circumstances of that country. We find that social class and social stratification are not only conceptually but also empirically distinct – sufficiently so that it is meaningful to use both concepts in analyses of social structure and personality.

Class, stratification, and psychological functioning

We hypothesized that members of more "advantaged" social classes would be more intellectually flexible, would value self-direction more highly for their children, and would have more self-directed orientations to self and society than would members of less advantaged social classes. By "advantaged," we do *not* mean higher in social-stratification position, but rather advantaged in terms of the very definition of social class: having greater control over the means of production and greater control over the labor power of others.

Hence, we expected managers and (in the United States) employers, who have greatest control over the means of production and the labor power of others, to value self-direction most highly, to be the most intellectually flexible, and to have the most self-directed orientations of all the social classes. We expected manual workers, who have least control over the means of production and the labor power of others, to be at the other extreme. These expectations were strikingly confirmed.[1]

---

[1] Since our analyses have been based on data for men, our conclusions must also be limited to men. We do find, though, that for the United States the relationships between wives' psychological functioning and their husbands' class positions are very much the same as the relationships between husbands' psychological functioning and their own class positions. We do not have as extensive information about Polish wives' psychological functioning, but those data that we do have – for parental valuation of self-direction, intellectual flexibility, authoritarian conservatism, trustfulness, and self-confidence – consistently show that Polish wives' psychological functioning is likewise related to their husbands' class positions much as is Polish husbands'. Extrapolating from our samples of wives to women generally, and generalizing from the partial information that we have about Polish wives' psychological functioning, it seems highly probable that, for both countries, the relationships between social class and psychological functioning are much the same for women as for men.

We similarly expected men of higher social-stratification position to value self-direction more highly for their children, to be more intellectually flexible, and to have more self-directed orientations to self and society than do men of lower social-stratification position. These expectations, too, were strikingly confirmed.[2] Moreover, we found that class and stratification each have at least some significant effect on psychological functioning, independent of one another.

Occupational self-direction as a key intervening link

Why do men's positions in the social structure affect their psychological functioning? Our basic premise is that what is psychologically crucial to social-structural position is control over the conditions of one's life. We therefore advanced the same hypothesis for both class and stratification: that position in the social structure – whether the class structure or the stratification order – affects psychological functioning in large part because such position greatly affects one's opportunities to be self-directed in one's work. Thus, men who are more advantageously located in the class structure or have a higher position in the stratification order have greater opportunity to be self-directed in their work; the experience of occupational self-direction, in turn, profoundly affects their values, orientations, and cognitive functioning.

As we have noted, this is a very strong hypothesis. We defined social class in terms of control over the means of production and the labor power of others; but we hypothesize that the reason why social class affects values, intellectual flexibility, and self-directedness of orientation is because class position greatly affects how much control one has over the conditions of one's own work. We defined social stratification in terms of a hierarchy of power, privilege, and prestige, and we measured social-stratification position in terms of occupational status, educational attainment, and job income; but we hypothesize that stratification position affects psychological functioning not because of the status the job confers, or the income that it affords, but because higher stratification position affords greater opportunities for occupational self-direction. Even the education component of social stratification matters only in part because the educational process

---

[2] Here again our conclusions are based on analyses of men. We do find, though, that the relationships between *family* social-stratification position and wives' psychological functioning are much the same as those between family stratification position and husbands' psychological functioning. Again extrapolating from wives to women, and generalizing from the partial information that we have about Polish wives' psychological functioning, it seems entirely probable that, for both the United States and Poland, the relationships between social stratification and psychological functioning are much the same for women as for men.

itself affects psychological functioning; education matters, too, because educational attainment greatly affects the substantive complexity of one's job.

We have found, in fact, that the relationships of both social class and social stratification with occupational self-direction are very strong in both countries. More advantageous positions in the class structure and higher positions in the stratification order markedly increase men's opportunities to be self-directed in their work. Moreover, and crucially, the exercise of occupational self-direction plays a major part in explaining the psychological effects of class and stratification. For both the United States and Poland, the effects of class and stratification position on parental valuation of self-direction, intellectual flexibility, and self-directedness of orientation are attributable in very substantial degree to occupational self-direction.

Directions of effects in the relationships of social structure and personality

Our entire thesis rests on the premises that social-structural position not only is correlated with, but actually affects, men's opportunities to exercise self-direction in their work; and that doing self-directed work is not only correlated with, but actually affects, off-the-job psychological functioning.

Our analyses demonstrate that men's class and stratification positions do affect their exercise of occupational self-direction. These analyses further demonstrate that occupational self-direction decidedly affects men's values, intellectual flexibility, and self-directedness of orientation. There is solid evidence that self-direction in work leads one to value self-direction more highly, to be more intellectually flexible, and to have a more open, flexible orientation to society. Lack of opportunity for self-direction in work leads one to value conformity to external authority, to be less intellectually flexible, and to have a generally conformist orientation to self and society.

The analyses further indicate that, over time, personality also affects class placement and status attainment. The relationships are quintessentially reciprocal.

Occupational self-direction plays a pivotal role in explaining both the effects of social structure on personality and the effects of personality on position in the social structure. Men's positions in the class structure and in the stratification order affect their values, intellectual flexibility, and self-directedness of orientation primarily because class and stratification affect occupational self-direction, which in turn affects these facets of personality.[3]

[3] It may seem a reasonable extrapolation from our research to hypothesize that deliberately instituted change in the job conditions that facilitate or restrict opportunities for occupational self-direction would affect people's values, orientations, and intellectual functioning. We

These facets of personality affect men's attained positions in the class structure and the stratification order mainly because personality affects occupational self-direction.

Intergenerational processes

We next hypothesized that the effects of social structure on job conditions, and of job conditions on *parental* values, would extend intergenerationally to *offspring's* values.

We found that, for both the United States and Poland, the class and stratification positions of the parental family have a considerable effect on the values of adolescent and young-adult offspring. The process is primarily one of family social-structural position affecting parents' opportunities for occupational self-direction, parents' experience of occupational self-direction affecting their values, and parents' values affecting their children's values.

Just as occupational self-direction affects their parents' values, so too does *educational* self-direction affect the values of adolescents and young adults. We see in this finding a confirmation of the larger thesis that the experience of self-direction in one's work, whether in paid employment or in schoolwork, has a major impact on values at every stage of life.

Cross-nationally inconsistent findings and their implications for our interpretation

Our detailed review of cross-nationally inconsistent findings led us to conclude that only one requires any substantial revision of our interpretation

---

should not necessarily expect dramatic changes in job conditions to bring about equally dramatic changes in the personalities of the workers; but our findings do suggest that even small changes in the pivotal job conditions may have modest but enduring – and therefore, in the long run, important – psychological consequences. When one looks for actual experimental evidence, though, one finds surprisingly little that is pertinent (see Kohn, 1990). An even more critical issue is whether the pertinent job conditions can be substantially modified, not just as an experiment but as a regular practice. If so, can this be done within the structure of capitalist enterprise or does it require worker ownership of the enterprise or even worker control over the means of production generally? For that matter, is substantial modification of job conditions possible even under conditions of worker ownership? Despite considerable research and much discussion of the issues, the answers to these questions are largely unknown. The evidence about worker-owned companies within capitalist economies is equivocal, the most general finding being that no real effort has been made in most such companies to appreciably alter job structure. As for the socialist countries, their modal form of industrial organization seems to have offered their workers no greater, and quite possibly less, opportunity for occupational self-direction than have most firms and organizations in capitalist countries. Perhaps the only conclusion warranted at this time is that job conditions are so integral to social structure that substantial modification of job conditions may very well require substantial modification of the class structure and of the system of social stratification.

of the relationships between social structure and personality. This one, of course, is the effect of social-structural position on the sense of well-being or distress.

We could, of course, deal with this cross-national difference by simply limiting our generalizations to the effects of social structure on values, cognitive functioning, and self-directedness of orientation. Rather than constricting our interpretation, though, we have explored the possibilities of enlarging the interpretation to encompass both the cross-national similarities and the cross-national difference.

One possible enlargement of our interpretation is to expand the range of job conditions. Although those job conditions that facilitate or restrict the exercise of occupational self-direction may be of prime importance in explaining the effects of social-structural position on values, cognitive functioning, and self-directedness of orientation, *other* job conditions may be important, perhaps even more important, for distress. What makes such a possibility particularly attractive is that we do have (admittedly, incomplete) evidence that certain other job conditions – notably, those associated with job uncertainties, insecurities, and protections from such uncertainties and insecurities – countervail the ameliorating effects of occupational self-direction. This evidence seems to explain the dramatically different levels of distress of managers and manual workers in the United States and Poland.

A further possible enlargement of our interpretation would be to incorporate psychological processes other than learning-generalization. Perhaps job conditions affect distress through some more indirect process, such as engendering dissatisfaction with the job or with some aspects of the job, and that dissatisfaction with the job is generalized to dissatisfaction with other realms of life. Or perhaps some job conditions engender experienced job stress, and job stress is generalized to off-the-job distress. The evidence in support of such indirect processes is less than fully convincing; moreover, we are loath to posit different psychological mechanisms explaining the effects of job conditions on different facets of personality. Still, we cannot dismiss these possibilities.

There are two other potentially fruitful extensions of our interpretation: to take account not only of current job conditions, but also of the processes by which people attain those positions and the meaning that those positions have to them; and to take non-job conditions of life more fully into account. Would that we were able to do so!

We are left in the unsatisfactory position of knowing that our original formulation does not explain the relationship of social structure and distress, yet not being certain how greatly we must enlarge that interpretation to encompass what for now must still be counted as a cross-national inconsistency. To make our interpretation applicable to distress certainly requires us to expand the range of pertinent job conditions. It is not at all certain, though, whether it is necessary to enlarge the interpretation even further. It may yet prove necessary to make more fundamental modifications.

LIMITATIONS OF DATA AND ANALYSIS, AND THEIR IMPLICATIONS FOR OUR INTERPRETATION

To assess the evidentiary basis of our interpretation, we need to assess the limitations of data and analysis that might bear on the solidity of the evidence on which that interpretation relies. We shall not in this discussion attempt to encompass methodological issues of general relevance to empirical inquiry in the social sciences, nor even methodological issues pertinent to any research based on sample surveys of the population, of which there are all too many for serious attention here. We shall not even discuss the limitations of survey research for studying the relationship of job conditions to personality (on this, see Kohn, 1990; see also Spenner, 1988b), or our failure to include in our surveys many types of information that, in principle, one can secure in sample surveys. Our purpose, instead, is to assess the data that we do have and the methods that we have used, to evaluate the evidentiary value of our empirical analyses.

The datedness of the surveys

The original US survey was conducted in 1964, twenty-six years before this book went to press. Even the follow-up survey was carried out sixteen years ago, and the Polish study more than a decade ago – before the dramatic events of *Solidarnosc*, martial law, and *rapprochement*. Are the data of these studies outmoded? Or are the data of the US and Polish studies noncomparable because the data were collected at different times? We think not, for both theoretical and empirical reasons; but any full resolution of the issues requires new studies to see whether our conclusions apply to new times and new circumstances.

The theoretical reason for doubting that the passage of time since these surveys were conducted, or differences in when the US and Polish surveys were carried out, impairs our conclusions is that *relationships* between social structure and personality should, in principle, be time-invariant. This is by no means to assert that the past quarter-century has seen no changes in social structure, or job conditions, or values, or orientations, or even cognitive functioning, or that such changes are not continuing today. The dramatic changes in the political and social structures of Poland since the time of our survey, and the considerable evidence of changes in the substantive complexity of the work performed by various segments of the US labor force (see, for example, Spenner, 1983; Form, 1987) would be enough to challenge so naive a belief. Our argument, instead, is that changes in any of these domains are likely to occur in conjunction with changes in the other domains.

Social change does not mean that social structures disappear or that they cease to have psychological impact. It does mean that the analyst has to ask, not simply whether change is occurring, but whether these changes affect the relationships between social structure and personality. We see no theoretical reason to believe that whatever changes have occurred over the years since our first survey, or are occurring today, greatly modify these relationships; nor are we aware of any empirical evidence of change in these relationships.[4]

An analysis of US and Polish age-cohorts by J. Miller, Slomczynski, and Kohn (1985) adds empirical support to our belief that the relationships of social structure and personality are relatively invariant over time. One can think of both the US and Polish samples not simply as cross-sections of employed men, but also as each comprised of distinct cohorts of men born at different times and having been subject to distinctly different sets of historically conditioned experiences. If one divides the 1964 US and 1978 Polish samples into three age groups – 30 years of age or younger at the time of the survey, 31 through 45, and 46 or older – one not only delineates subsamples of relatively equal size, but also defines meaningful cohorts.

From a historical perspective, the three Polish cohorts have had unique generational experiences. The majority of men in the oldest age-group completed their elementary educations before the Second World War and entered the labor force before the rapid industrialization of the 1950s had begun. A critical experience for this generation was the Nazi occupation and, later, the Stalinist era, terminated by the national upheaval of the "Polish October" in 1956. Men in the intermediate age-group were just entering their adult lives in the mid-1950s. At the early stages of their occupational careers, they experienced the post-October economic and political stabilization, which ended with the students' protests in 1968 and the workers' revolt in 1970. The youngest group came of age under the

---

[4] As a case in point: Alwin has argued (e.g., in 1989a) that there has been a significant increase in parental valuation of self-direction in the United States over the past twenty or more years. Although his evidence is equivocal, it is certainly possible that this has occurred. It is also possible, as he argues (1986), that certain religious and ethnic groups have come to value self-direction more highly as their socioeconomic position has improved. There is no evidence, though, of a change in the relationship between social stratification and valuation of self-direction versus conformity to external authority.

relative prosperity of the Gierek regime, which started showing visible cracks in 1976 during the workers' riots.

Although both the middle and the youngest age-groups were educated in the common-school system introduced under the socialist regime, they differ with respect to their vocational preparation. The transition from more general to more specialized education experienced by these two age-groups paralleled the economic development of the country. Forced industrialization of the 1950s – when the majority of the middle age-group started to work – provided many new job opportunities for persons without specialized education. In contrast, the youngest group entered a more competitive labor market created by a declining number of new industrial positions and a structural shift from the industrial to the service sector.

Since the US men were interviewed fourteen years before the Polish men, the experiences of all three US age-groups are of rather different historical eras from those of their Polish counterparts. The oldest group (who were born in 1918 or before) had experienced the Great Depression as children or young adults and the Second World War as adults. The middle age-group (born between 1919 and 1933) includes both those for whom the Second World War was a childhood experience and those whose young adult lives were disrupted by wartime experience. The youngest men (born between 1934 and 1948) are essentially a post-war generation. As in Poland, educational requirements for many jobs increased from cohort to cohort.

It is apparent that in distinguishing the "same" three age-groups for Poland and the United States, we are actually comparing age-cohorts from markedly dissimilar historical periods. This means that any evidence of similar relationships between job conditions and personality across the three Polish and three US age-cohorts lends substantial support to the belief that, even if considerable change has been occurring in either or both countries, the relationships of social structure and personality are invariant. Correspondingly, evidence of dissimilar relationships between job conditions and personality would cast doubt on the invariance of the relationships between social structure and personality.

Miller, Slomczynski, and Kohn actually found remarkable *invariance* among the age-cohorts in the relationships of occupational self-direction and intellective process. These analyses show that, for both countries, the effects of occupational self-direction on intellective process are of roughly equal magnitude for all three cohorts of men. Since a "cohort" reflects both age and historical experience, these analyses speak not only to changes associated with the men's own biological aging, stage of life-course, and stage of career, but also to historical changes in the relationship of job conditions and personality. The relatively invariant effects across cohorts argue in favor both of the conclusion that occupational self-direction similarly affects older and younger men and of the conclusion that the relationships of job conditions and intellective process remain much the same for men who have had decidedly different life experiences.

Objectivity of our indices of job conditions

Although our approach to work and personality deliberately focuses on objective job conditions, we have not succeeded in measuring job conditions as objectively as we should like. Our concern here is that subjectivity in job reports may exaggerate the correlations between job conditions and personality (Steinkamp, 1983).

Our measures are based on interview reports, not on observations by trained analysts.[5] Still, we have made strenuous efforts to validate interview-based indices with other sources of information.

Using the cross-sectional US data, Kohn and Schooler (1973) assessed the job condition central to all our analyses, the substantive complexity of work. They compared their index of the substantive complexity of work, which was based on workers' descriptions of their own work with data, with people, and with things – thus precisely tailored to the specifics of the worker's own job – to the classifications made in the *Dictionary of Occupational Titles* (United States Department of Labor, 1965) for every occupation in the US economy. Notwithstanding that the *Dictionary's* ratings are averages for entire occupations, thereby lacking the specificity of indices based on descriptions of particular jobs, and that they are imperfect in important respects (Cain and Treiman, 1981), they are based on observations by trained occupational analysts and can thereby serve as a source of external validation.

The multiple correlation between Kohn and Schooler's index of the substantive complexity of work (a forerunner of the index we use in this book) and the independently coded *Dictionary*-based ratings of complexity of work with data, with things, and with people is 0.78 – sufficiently high to give assurance that interview-based appraisals of substantive complexity accurately reflect the realities of the respondents' work.[6] If the correlation

[5] Consider, by contrast, the rigorous attempts by German occupational psychologists to obtain truly objective measures of job conditions: see, for example, Hacker, 1981; Volpert et al., 1983; Oesterreich, 1984; Resch et al. 1983. Their methods are designed for intensive observational studies of particular work settings. Unfortunately, such methods are not readily transferred to cross-sectional studies of the employed population.

[6] The index of substantive complexity of work that Kohn and Schooler used at that time was based on an exploratory factor analysis. Hence, correlations with other variables – in this case, a multiple correlation with the *Dictionary* ratings of complexity of work with things, data, and people – could not be corrected for measurement error. The 0.78 correlation is therefore an underestimate of the true correlation.

A Re-evaluation of the Thesis

were much higher, we would wonder whether it is necessary to go to the trouble and expense of securing job-specific information about the substantive complexity of work, rather than settling for the crude approximation provided by occupational-level data.[7]

Using the Polish data and Polish materials on occupational classifications, scales, and descriptions (Collective Work, 1970, 1973; Slomczynski and Kacprowicz, 1979), Janicka, Kacprowicz, and Slomczynski (1983) did a similar analysis, with similar results – a multiple correlation of 0.81. They then further assessed the validity of the index of substantive complexity used in both the original US study and the Polish replication. On the rationale that relatively brief descriptions of what a respondent does in his work with data, with things, and with people may be subject to an unknown amount of subjective distortion, they re-interviewed subsamples of their sample of employed Polish men in two industrial cities, Lodz and Wroclaw, securing much more detailed descriptive information about job content than would be possible in any broader survey. Using confirmatory factor-analytic measurement models, each based on the complexity of the respondent's work with things, with data, and with people, they found the correlation between the substantive complexity of work, as measured in the original interviews, and the substantive complexity of work, as measured in the Lodz–Wroclaw re-interviews, to be 0.91. (For further information, in Polish, see Slomczynski and Kohn, 1988, p. 230.)[8]

---

[7] Few studies have had the requisite descriptive data for a job-level index of substantive complexity. To fill the gap, several approximate measures of substantive complexity have been developed, beginning with one that Kohn and Schooler (1973) developed to measure the substantive complexity of past jobs; including also Temme's (1975), now used by the National Opinion Research Center in the codes it provides for its General Social Surveys; Spenner's (1977, 1980); and Cain and Treiman's (1981). All these indices extrapolate from *Dictionary of Occupational Titles'* classifications of entire occupations to the substantive complexity of particular jobs. Used cautiously, such indices do provide serviceable approximations for use in studies that lack precise data about the substantive complexity of particular jobs. It must be kept in mind, though, that such approximate indices seriously underestimate the magnitudes of the relationships of the substantive complexity of work with other variables.

[8] There is also limited but highly reassuring evidence from a study of skilled metal workers conducted in West Berlin by Lempert, Hoff, and Lappe (for a description of the study, see Hoff et al., 1982, 1983). Theirs is an intensive study of twenty-one young apprenticed workers, whom they followed into their occupational careers. They observed the men at work, using precisely calibrated methods of observation, supplemented by interviews with the men's supervisors. Their collaborator, Manfred Moldaschl, coded this information according to Kohn and Schooler's scheme for rating the overall complexity of work (Kohn and Schooler, 1983, appendix B). He then independently rated this same dimension of complexity, this time using only such information as had been secured from interviews with the men themselves – interviews focused not on job conditions but on psychological functioning. The correlation between the observation-based and interview-based ratings of complexity is 0.75. Considering that we are dealing with an extremely narrow range of jobs, that the interviews were not

However reassuring the evidence for the objectivity of our index of the substantive complexity of work, we must wonder about our much more subjective indices of closeness of supervision and of routinization. We think it unlikely that the subjectivity of our index of closeness of supervision accounts for the cross-national differences that we do find in the relative importance of closeness of supervision and the substantive complexity of work for explaining the psychological impact of social structure; but we cannot be certain. As for our index of routinization, we can hardly have exaggerated its importance; more likely, we have simply failed to measure it well enough to capture the psychological importance that the concept may well have. In short, we have considerable confidence in the objectivity of our index of the substantive complexity of work, less confidence in the objectivity of our index of closeness of supervision, and little confidence in the objectivity (or efficacy) of our index of routinization.

Assumptions made in identifying causal models and in simulating longitudinal data

Our interpretation is based on the premise that position in the social structure not only is correlated with, but actually affects, occupational self-direction; and, more crucial still, that occupational self-direction not only is correlated with, but actually affects, personality. The evidence in support of this basic premise comes largely from our linear structural-equation models. Such models are necessarily dependent on the assumptions one makes to identify them.

In estimating our models, we have extensively explored alternative specifications. We have also examined all of our models for cautionary signs: any indication that the model as a whole or any of its open parameters may not be well conditioned;[9] any indication that standard errors may be unduly high; any instances of positively correlated variables having opposite-signed effects on the dependent variable of some equation or of negatively correlated variables having same-signed effects; any

---

designed to secure systematic information about job conditions, and that the reliability of a single indicator of substantive complexity must inevitably fall considerably short of the reliability of a multi-indicator measurement model, a correlation of 0.75 is indeed encouraging. It implies that a correlation based on a representative sample of workers, systematic data, and multiple indicators would be much higher.

[9] Even though a model may be logically correct in all its specifications, the model or one or more of its constituent parameters may not be adequately identified – if, for example, the correlations between instruments and the variables that they are not permitted to directly affect are not strong enough to provide adequate identification for the paths that they are intended to identify. The MILS program provides invaluable information for assessing how well conditioned is the model as a whole and how well identified is each of its open parameters.

instances where one member of a pair of reciprocally related variables has a positive effect on its partner but is in turn negatively affected by that partner.[10] Our models pass all these tests and pass them well.

Still, as any experienced analyst knows, linear structural-equations models can be sensitive to small changes in the rationale of the model, particularly in specifying whether to allow or not to allow the residuals of particular pairs of variables to be correlated. Complex reciprocal-effects models – the final model in our analysis of the intergenerational transmission of values having six interrelated pairs of reciprocal effects – are especially delicate contrivances, requiring replication before they are fully convincing. One ought also to be cautious in drawing conclusions from models that disaggregate such extremely high correlations as that between occupational position and occupational self-direction.

Moreover, in dealing with issues of causal directionality, there is no fully satisfactory substitute for longitudinal data. We have tried to overcome the serious limitation of having only cross-sectional data for Polish men, US women, and Polish women by carrying out quasi-longitudinal analyses, based on explicitly stated assumptions. Even though the assumptions seem justified, and even though sensitivity analyses show the models to be robust, nothing can substitute for actual longitudinal data. Thus, all analyses other than those of US men must be taken as providing only prima facie evidence in support of our interpretation. That the results for Polish men, US women, and Polish women accord so well with those for US men lends considerable credence to this evidence, but still it is far from being definitive.

The actual processes of learning and generalization

Whether or not learning-generalization applies to the affective realm, it certainly does apply to the processes by which job conditions affect values, cognitive functioning, and self-directedness of orientation. Nowhere in our data is there evidence, for example, that men turn their occupational frustrations loose on the non-occupational world or try to find compensation in non-occupational realities for occupational lacks and grievances. Nowhere – save perhaps *vis-à-vis* distress – is there any need to posit the necessity of indirect processes. Instead, the simple explanation that accounts

---

[10] In principle, opposite-signed reciprocal effects could occur, but this would lead to a very unstable relationship. To take such a finding seriously, one would have to have very powerful a priori reasons to expect such opposite-signed effects; and one would have to have very well justified and very powerful instruments. In practice, such a finding usually results from inadequate instrumentation and therefore should be interpreted as in all probability being artifactual.

for virtually all of our findings is that the process is direct, i.e., learning from the job and extending the lessons to the non-occupational realm.

But *how* does this occur? We must acknowledge that our analyses have not shed much light on the actual processes by which learning and generalization take place. As Spenner (1988a) comments:

An additional line of critique centers on the meaning of "learning generalization" in microsituations. The survey designs in this area of research typically cover months, years, or a decade or more. At the survey design level of reality, the process of learning generalization is not directly observed, specified, or tested. Telescope down to the shorter intervals of time in which a structural feature of a job actually makes a change in a worker's personality or intellectual functioning. Is the learning part of the process as straightforward as the textbook images in reinforcement or cognitive psychology? What are the microdynamics of learning generalization? (pp. 272–3)

Perhaps the answers to these questions will require other types of data and other types of analysis, for example, extended observational studies or even experimental studies. Or perhaps they will require, not a different method of inquiry, but instead much more detailed information than we have collected, and re-interviews at shorter intervals. We see no way of pursuing the issues further with the data that we have. In any case, we do think our analyses point to the right psychological processes, even if they do not tell us very much about the particulars of those processes. In short, on this crucial issue, we see our analyses as decidedly incomplete, but certainly not invalid.

Time as a parameter in the effects of job on personality

Our longitudinal models of the reciprocal effects of occupational self-direction and personality are based on information from two interviews, secured ten years apart.[11] Ten years is an arbitrary interval, selected happenstantially on the basis of when we were able to design a follow-up study and when it was possible to secure funds. Might our findings somehow be a function of our having selected this particular time-interval – rather than some shorter or longer period of time – as the interval between the baseline and follow-up interviews?

[11] We focus this part of the discussion on the length of time between interviews. It is also worth noting that having interviews at only two times poses additional difficulties. Identifying the models would be simpler and more certain with measurements at three times. Moreover, having measurements at three (or more) times would make possible the differential assessment of contemporaneous and lagged effects, which would contribute greatly to our understanding of the timing of effects. To appraise the actual timing of effects, we should ideally have measurements at several times (for this purpose, three is probably not enough). Only then would we be able to sharply differentiate contemporaneous from lagged effects.

From information based on a research design that measures change only once, after an interval of ten years, we can properly infer that job conditions do affect personality, but we cannot say when these processes begin, whether they are continuous or discontinuous, or whether they taper off after some time or cumulate indefinitely (see Frese, 1983). Yet, timing is a crucial parameter of the work–personality relationship and should be explicitly built into our formulations. It may be that some effects of job on personality occur even before the individual actually experiences new working conditions, in anticipation of conditions that will be encountered or of what a new job will signify. For example, a promotion might lead to an increase (or decrease) in self-confidence even before, or perhaps especially before, the individual actually begins a new job. Other job conditions might have their effects early on, diminishing as the individual grows accustomed to the conditions of work. It is possible, for example, that tasks that seem at first to be challenging will in time become old hat. The opposite might also happen; some job conditions – one thinks of routinized conditions of work – might become more onerous as one endures them longer.

There are other obvious possibilities, all of them requiring that we regard present findings as representing the net outcome of many processes, some of which may have run their course long before the follow-up interviews, others of which may still be ongoing, and still others barely having gotten under way. Distinguishing the many strands of the actual process requires a much more fine-grained analysis than we have done, using data collected at closer intervals.

What implications would it have for our conclusions if the psychological effects of occupational self-direction were not relatively constant, but instead increased or decreased over time? In all probability, our estimates of magnitudes of effects would thereby be affected: if the effects of occupational self-direction on personality actually decrease over time, we probably have underestimated the magnitudes of those effects; if the effects of occupational self-direction actually increase over time, we probably have overestimated the magnitudes of those effects. It is improbable, though, that the degree of exaggeration or underestimation of those effects can have been very great.

In any case, we deal here only with issues of magnitude, not of causal directionality. Occupational self-direction certainly does have substantial effects on values, intellectual flexibility, and self-directedness of orientation. What is not certain is whether we have measured the magnitudes of these effects at their maximum, at their average, or at some point after their maximum, when they were in decline.

We should also note that both occupational self-direction and psychological functioning are generated by dynamic processes; but our models are structural, not dynamic. As Spenner (1988a) points out:

A central feature of the design . . . involves snapshots of job conditions at two points in time taken 10 years apart. . . . This type of design assumes a work–personality system in equilibrium, a static versus mathematically dynamic state-of-affairs. Time and change are not explicitly modeled features of reality and hence timing effects, threshold effects, time paths of change, oscillations, and rates of change are not available. Dynamic models applied to event histories of jobs and personality afford a more direct "motion picture" view of adult development. (p. 272; see also Spenner, 1988b)

Although Spenner does not tell us how we might secure the needed event histories of jobs and personality or how we might assess the reciprocal effects of jobs and personality were we to secure such information, he is undoubtedly right. Fortunately, Schoenberg (1977) has demonstrated that a static model of what in reality is an underlying dynamic process will underestimate the magnitudes of the parameters but will not otherwise be misleading. Thus, here again, it is hardly likely that our models are grossly inaccurate; but they only summarize total effects, rather than specifying the dynamics of the process.

The interaction of occupational self-direction with other social and psychological phenomena

Our analyses have been based on the assumption that occupational self-direction has generally similar effects on the personalities of all workers – in statistical terms, that the effects of occupational self-direction on personality, and of personality on occupational self-direction, are "main effects." Alternative formulations would have it that what we see as main effects are in reality "interaction effects" – that occupational self-direction affects workers differentially, depending on their social circumstances or on their personalities.

One theoretically appealing possibility is that occupational self-direction may affect personality differentially, depending on the organizational structure, or the location in the economy, of the firm or enterprise in which these conditions are experienced. It might well be that occupational self-direction has different effects in bureaucratized and non-bureaucratized firms and organizations. It might also be that occupational self-direction has a greater effect on the personalities of workers employed in the primary sector of the economy, where they are better paid and more secure, while job risks and job uncertainties are of greater consequence for the personalities of workers employed in the secondary sector. Alternatively, occupational self-direction might have differential psychological impact depending on the presence or absence of *other* job conditions (Karasek, 1979; House, 1980; Karasek et al., 1981).

Occupational self-direction might also affect personality differentially, depending on the needs, abilities, or values of the worker – the so-called "fit" hypothesis (see Locke 1976; Lofquist and Dawis, 1969; Hackman and Lawler, 1971; Coburn, 1975; but see Mortimer, 1979; O'Brien and Dowling, 1980). Substantively complex work, for example, might be stimulating to most workers, yet be more burden than challenge to those workers who value extrinsic over intrinsic qualities of work.

These (and other) interaction hypotheses are appealing, in part because – at a sufficiently detailed level of analysis – they must be true. It is almost inconceivable that all workers react to occupational self-direction in precisely the same ways. For our interpretation, though, where the issues are not those of individual-differences psychology but of social structure and personality, the question is, what are the relative magnitudes of the main effects and the interaction effects?

If main effects are substantial and interaction effects insubstantial, then our formulations have been sensible, our statistical models appropriate, and our conclusions justified. Any of the interaction-based hypotheses might well be true, but for purposes of interpreting the relationships between social structure and personality, each would be only variation on the principal theme.

If, however, interactions are substantial, then our formulations have been erroneous, our statistical analyses inappropriate, and our conclusions suspect. In that case, the proper tests of the relationships between occupational self-direction and personality would not be models of the reciprocal effects of occupational self-direction and one or another facet of personality, but models in which personality at the current time is posited to be some function of the interaction of occupational self-direction and other job conditions, or of occupational self-direction and other social phenomena, or of occupational self-direction and that same facet of personality as measured at some earlier time. What we have interpreted to be effects of social structure on personality might better be interpreted as the resultant of much more complex processes.

The analytic problem is that it is exceedingly difficult to deal with reciprocal effects and statistical interactions in the same analyses. In ordinary multiple-regression analyses – which assume unidirectionality of effects – one can test interactions by using as an independent variable a term representing the product of two independent variables – for example, the product of the substantive complexity of work and the size of the organization in which the work is performed. This would test whether the substantive complexity of work has a differential effect depending on the size of the organization. (Even then, one tests only the linear interaction and it can be difficult to interpret the meaning of a significant interaction, but at least it is feasible to test the statistical significance of the interaction term.) In reciprocal-effects modelling, where each endogenous variable is both an independent variable in at least one equation and a dependent variable in another, it is not yet feasible to test interactions.[12]

In any case, a full assessment of interactions requires separate analyses of delineated subgroups – for example, separate analyses of the reciprocal relationships of occupational self-direction and personality for workers in larger and smaller organizations, or for workers who value the intrinsic qualities of their work and for those who value its extrinsic rewards. Such analyses are exceedingly difficult and time-consuming to do: a full-fledged analysis of subgroups requires re-estimating the measurement models for each of the pertinent subgroups, recalculating the correlations among variables for each of those subgroups, adjusting those correlations for unreliability, and re-estimating the causal model for each subgroup – a formidable undertaking. Worse yet, since such analyses are done separately for each subgroup, they require large sample sizes, the finer-grained the analysis the more cases required.

Unless one has infinite time and computer resources to spend on such analyses, much larger bodies of data than we have, and strong theoretical guidance to direct the research, one has to gamble on whether it is more important to deal with reciprocal effects or with interactions. Our choice has been to give primacy to assessing reciprocal effects, since we think that to do otherwise would be to prejudge the central issues of our research. Moreover, we see little evidence that the interactions really are sizeable. There is scant evidence, for example, that occupational self-direction has differential effects, depending on the individual's needs, values, and abilities (Kohn and Schooler, 1973; Kohn, 1976a). Our analyses suggest, instead,

---

[12] Schoenberg has worked out a method in principle but not yet in practice. In a model of the reciprocal effects of occupational self-direction and intellectual flexibility, he would create an exogenous variable for the interaction of occupational self-direction and, say, size of organization. This interaction term would directly affect intellectual flexibility but would not directly affect occupational self-direction. He would similarly create another exogenous variable for the interaction of intellectual flexibility and size of organization, which would directly affect occupational self-direction but not intellectual flexibility. In principle, this would test the significance of the interactions, although the necessity of treating the interaction terms as exogenous does pose interpretive problems. In any case, he has not yet figured out how to calculate standard errors for the interaction terms. Since the whole point of the exercise is to determine whether the interactions are statistically significant, this poses a formidable stumbling block.

that occupational self-direction is related to such basic needs and values as to be important to all workers, at least under the conditions of working life generally experienced in the United States.

The analyses, however, have been far from definitive. Interactions may yet be shown to play a part in the process, if not as the main theme, at least as a secondary theme. It is hardly likely, though, that our failure to analyze interactions extensively raises any serious doubt about the cross-nationally consistent findings that we do have, or about our interpretation of those findings.

Considerations of life-course and career

Conspicuously lacking in our analyses is any systematic attention to issues of life-course and career. We have implicitly treated all sequences of jobs as if they were equally continuous or discontinuous along some meaningful career line. A more realistic conceptualization would have to take into account that some job changes represent logical progressions in a meaningful sequence, while others represent shifts out of one career sequence, perhaps into another. We know of no really satisfactory way of dealing with this issue, despite early efforts by Wilensky (1961) and several more recent efforts by others (e.g., Spilerman, 1977) at classifying career patterns. Nor have we considered the possibility that the relationships of social-structural position to job conditions, and of job conditions to personality, change over the life-course.[13] Instead, we have assumed that the psychological effects of job conditions are relatively invariant over the work lifespan and that processes of learning and generalization do not much differ at different stages of life-course and career.

In fact, recent work in developmental and social psychology does suggest that learning, particularly as represented in "crystallized" (or synthesized) intelligence, continues throughout the lifespan.[14] In principle, since "transfer of learning" is "an essential characteristic of the learning process" (Gagne, 1968, p. 68), not only initial learning but also the generalization of what has been learned should continue as workers grow older.

It is nevertheless possible that learning-generalization does not occur at the same rate or to the same extent at all ages and at all stages of life-course or career. The process may be especially pronounced in younger workers, at early stages of their occupational careers, before they are preoccupied with family responsibilities, but may diminish as workers grow older, advance in

[13] For pertinent discussions of "life-course," see Elder, 1974; Elder and Rockwell, 1979; Baltes, 1983; Riley, 1979; and Spenner, 1988a.

[14] For reviews and assessments of this literature, see Baltes and Labouvie, 1973; Horn and Donaldson, 1980, pp. 468–76; Baltes et al., 1984; Klarkowski, 1981.

their careers, and have changing family responsibilities. It is also possible that either learning or generalization diminishes as workers grow older, simply because of biological decrements (Jarvik and Cohen, 1973, pp. 227–34; Horn and Donaldson, 1980, pp. 476–81, but see Labouvie-Vief and Chandler, 1978; Riley and Bond, 1983). On the other hand, as Spenner (1988a) imaginatively argues, the very processes by which occupational self-direction and personality reciprocally affect one another may result in *increased* effects of job on personality at later stages of life-course and career.

To see whether learning and the generalization of learning continue unabated throughout adult life requires analyses of how job conditions affect the psychological functioning of workers at different ages, or different stages of career, or different stages of life-course. As we have seen, J. Miller, Slomczynski, and Kohn (1985) have done one such analysis, designed to see whether occupational self-direction has as great an effect on intellective process for older workers as for younger and middle-aged workers. Their analysis unequivocally shows as great an effect of occupational self-direction, particularly of the substantive complexity of work, on intellectual flexibility and on authoritarian conservatism for the oldest segment of both the US and Polish work forces as for the youngest and middle segments. These findings argue strongly for the continuity of the learning-generalization process, regardless of the age of the worker and – by extrapolation – regardless of stage of career and stage of life-course. Still, one analysis, even when done comparatively for the United States and Poland, is hardly definitive, particularly when it cannot differentiate age-groups from cohorts defined on the basis of stage of career or of life-course.

All of the limitations of data and analysis that we have discussed are real; all are important. They call for replication, finer-grained analysis, better indices, and any number of improvements in method. Certainly, these limitations imply that our findings are inexact, our assessments only approximate. Yet, do these limitations, individually and taken all together, cast serious doubt on our findings and interpretation? We think not.

EVIDENCE FROM OTHER STUDIES AND ITS IMPLICATIONS FOR OUR INTERPRETATION

For a full evaluation of our interpretation, it is essential not only to appraise the solidity of our own findings, but also to take account of the findings of other pertinent studies, particularly of studies carried out in countries other than the United States and Poland.

With one conspicuous exception – Naoi and Schooler's Japanese study that we have already noted in our discussion of distress, and about which we shall have much more to say shortly – these studies provide mainly piecemeal evidence: one or another study in one or another country replicates (or attempts to replicate) some portion of our analysis, or tests some portion of our interpretation, or provides evidence that bears on our interpretation. What is impressive about the evidence is not that any of the studies (other than the Japanese study) in and of itself provides crucial evidence, but that in the aggregate the evidence is almost entirely consistent with our findings and interpretation.[15]

First of all, there is a great deal of evidence affirming the descriptive generalization that social stratification is correlated with parental valuation of self-direction – this evidence from studies conducted in Italy, Taiwan, the Federal Republic of Germany, France, Great Britain, and Ireland, as well as from studies other than our own conducted in the United States and Poland.[16] All of these studies use measures of parental values modelled more or less closely on our own and thus provide evidence reasonably comparable to our own.

For evidence about the relationship of social stratification to self-directedness of orientation and to cognitive functioning we have to rely on studies using quite different measures from those we have used (studies, for example, of perceptions of internal versus external locus of control; or of "intelligence" as measured by standard intelligence tests). With only minor and partial exceptions, these studies – conducted in many countries – affirm the descriptive generalization that social stratification is correlated with aspects of psychological functioning similar to what we are terming self-directedness of orientation and intellectual flexibility. There cannot be much doubt about the generality of the relationships of social stratification with those aspects of psychological functioning that concern us – distress, of course, aside – at least for industrialized countries.

[15] The evidence to 1983 is discussed in greater detail in Kohn, 1981 and in chapter 12 of Kohn and Schooler, 1983. Here we summarize the evidence without describing individual studies in detail.

[16] The evidence for Italy comes from a study of Turin by Pearlin (see Pearlin and Kohn, 1966 or Pearlin, 1971 or Kohn, 1969, chapter 3); for Taiwan, from a study of Taipei by Olsen (1971); for France, by Perron (1971); for Great Britain, by Platt (unpublished); for Ireland, by Hynes (1979); for the Federal Republic of Germany, by Bertram (unpublished; for a general description of the study see Bertram, 1976a,b) and by Hoff and Grüneisen (1978). Evidence from other studies done in the United States is to be found in Franklin and Scott, 1970; Clausen, 1974; Campbell, 1978; Morgan et al., 1979; and Alwin, 1989b. The most extensive US evidence is based on the NORC General Social Surveys (see Kohn, 1976b; Kohn and Schoenbach, 1980). In addition to the Polish study that forms the basis of this book, further evidence is provided by a study of Warsaw mothers conducted by Sokolowska and Firkowska-Mankiewicz (see Sokolowska et al., 1978 or Firkowska et al., 1978).

Evidence about the generality of the relationships we have found between social class and values, intellectual flexibility, and self-directedness of orientation is provided by only one study – the Japanese study. More on that shortly.

There is considerable evidence affirming the relationships of occupational self-direction – or, what is more usually the case, some analogue to or approximate measure of occupational self-direction – with personality. Much of this evidence comes from studies conducted in the United States;[17] there is evidence as well from studies conducted in the Federal Republic of Germany, Canada, and Norway.[18] There is, in addition, some evidence (J. Miller, 1980; Mortimer, 1979) – including evidence from Poland (Sarapata, 1977; Kuczynski and Sanyal, 1985) and from the Soviet Union (Zdravomyslov and Yadov, 1967; Byakhman and Shkaratan, 1977) – that work complexity affects job satisfaction and attitudes to work. In the main, though, the evidence about the psychological effects of occupational self-direction is based on cross-sectional data, with only the studies by Mortimer and her colleagues (Mortimer, Lorence, and Kumka, 1986) relying on fully longitudinal data.

There is only fragmentary evidence from studies of other industrialized countries on the crucial issue of the role of occupational self-direction in explaining the psychological effects of social stratification. Studies of Italy, Canada, and Ireland do lend support to our hypothesis that occupational self-direction plays an important part in explaining the psychological effects of social stratification.[19] But none of these studies uses longitudinal data. And there is no evidence at all on the issue of whether occupational self-

[17] The most important US evidence – because based on longitudinal analysis – comes from the studies of University of Michigan graduates conducted by Mortimer and her associates (Mortimer and Lorence, 1979a,b; Mortimer et al., 1986). In reciprocal-effects models similar to our own, they have found that "work autonomy" (which they see as an approximation to our occupational self-direction) affects values and self-conceptions in ways quite similar to what we have found. Also valuable are: Spade's finding (1983) that, in dual-career families, each spouse's occupational self-direction affects his or her values; Spenner and Otto's finding (1985) that, for young men and women a decade or so into their occupational careers, work complexity affects self-concept; and Joanne Miller and her associates' finding (in analyses based on data provided by the wives of the men in our US sample) that women's job conditions – notably including occupational self-direction – affect their off-the-job psychological functioning very much as do men's (J. Miller et al., 1979).

[18] For the Federal Republic of Germany, see Hoff and Grüneisen, 1978, or Grüneisen and Hoff, 1977; for Canada, see Coburn and Edwards, 1976, and Grabb, 1981a; for Norway, see Dalgard, 1981.

[19] The Italian study is reported in Pearlin and Kohn, 1966, in Pearlin, 1971, and in Kohn, 1969; the Canadian study in Grabb, 1981b; and the Irish study in Hynes, 1979. Pertinent too is Alwin's study of Detroit (1989b).

direction plays an important part in explaining the psychological effects of social class – research on Japan again being the conspicuous exception.

Although we do not claim that our interpretation applies to non-industrialized or to partially industrialized nations, it is pertinent to note that studies of Taiwan and Peru cast doubt on whether occupational self-direction explains the relationships of social stratification to personality in those countries.[20] It is unclear, though, whether these negative findings are real or merely reflect methodological imperfections of the particular studies (see the discussion in Kohn and Schooler, 1983, chapter 12).

There is, then, considerable cross-national evidence affirming the relationships of stratification and of occupational self-direction with personality, but rather less that bears directly on the crucial issue of whether occupational self-direction actually does affect personality, and even less as to whether occupational self-direction provides a key to interpreting the relationships of class and stratification with personality. The paucity of evidence on these key issues makes the Japanese study all the more important.

The Japanese study, planned by Atsushi Naoi and Carmi Schooler and conducted in 1979 by Naoi and his associates, was based on a random probability sample of 629 men, 26–65 years old, employed in civilian occupations in the Kanto plain of Japan. This area, which includes Tokyo and six other prefectures in north-central Japan, is a mix of urban, suburban, and rural locales. The study was carefully designed to replicate our US and Polish studies and extensively pretested to ensure the meaningfulness and appropriateness of the questions.

Using these data, Naoi and Schooler (1985) have demonstrated that occupational self-direction affects parental valuation of self-direction, intellectual flexibility, and self-directedness of orientation in Japan very much as it does in the United States and Poland. They have further demonstrated (Schooler and Naoi, 1988) that occupational self-direction continues to affect these facets of psychological functioning, even when traditionality of job settings and economic centrality of industry are statistically controlled. Thus, they provide confirmatory evidence on a crucial element of our interpretation: that occupational self-direction is not only correlated with, but has an actual causal effect on, psychological functioning. This evidence extends the generality of our findings and of this part of the interpretation to a non-Western capitalist country.

Further analyses, directly comparable to the analyses of the relationships of social class and social stratification with psychological functioning reported in this book, confirm the generalizability to Japan of other essential

[20] The Taiwanese study is reported in Olsen, 1971, the Peruvian study in Scurrah and Montalvo, 1975.

elements of our interpretation (Kohn et al., 1990). These analyses demonstrate: that it is possible to conceptualize and to index both social class and social stratification for Japan in ways that take into account the distinctive historical and cultural traditions of that country yet are entirely comparable to what we have done for the United States and Poland; that class and stratification are related to parental valuation of self-direction, to intellectual flexibility, and to self-directedness of orientation for Japan very much as they are for the United States and Poland; and that occupational self-direction plays precisely the same role in explaining the relationships of social class and of social stratification with personality for Japan as it does for the United States and Poland.[21] In all these respects, the Japanese study provides crucial evidence of the generality of our findings and interpretation as they apply to a particularly strategic third country, a non-Western country.

In sum, the evidence from studies done in industrialized societies is entirely consistent with what we have found for the United States and Poland. Aside from the Japanese study, most of the other studies provide only limited data, but what they do provide consistently lends support to our interpretation. The Japanese study, by far the most comparable to ours in design and execution and by far the most pertinent in terms of dealing with crucial interpretive issues, provides the most compelling evidence; and that evidence is entirely consistent with what we have found for the United States and Poland.

IMPLICATIONS OF OUR THESIS FOR INTERPRETING THE RELATIONSHIPS OF SOCIAL STRUCTURE AND PERSONALITY IN CROSS-NATIONAL PERSPECTIVE

We believe that the distinctively sociological contribution to social psychology lies in systematically linking two levels of analytic discourse – the large-scale social and the individual. Our way of drawing these linkages is to ask, how does position in the larger social structure affect the immediately impinging conditions of people's lives, and how do people's conditions of life affect their values, their orientations, and their thinking processes?

---

[21] No one has yet attempted to develop a causal model of the relationship of social stratification to occupational self-direction for Japan nor to extend such a model to the assessment of the role of occupational self-direction in explaining the psychological impact of social stratification. Nor has anyone yet assessed the intergenerational transmission of values; data for such an assessment are only now being readied for analysis.

Admittedly, there is a considerable gap – not in substance but in scope – between our delimited analyses and our more ambitious aim of drawing systematic linkages between social structure and personality. Our analyses have focused on the role of occupational self-direction in explaining the psychological effects of social class and social stratification. Our goal is to explain how immediately impinging conditions of life – not restricted to occupational self-direction nor even to job conditions – mediate the psychological effects of social structure – not limited to social class and to social stratification, however central they may be to social structure.

How far can we extrapolate from the evidence of our own research to the larger issues we should like to address? We approach this question in two steps, first asking whether it is reasonable to extrapolate from occupational self-direction to the exercise of self-direction in other realms of life, later asking about the more general implications of our analyses for the understanding of social structure and personality.

The exercise of self-direction in other realms of life

In principle, the exercise of self-direction in other realms of life should have precisely the same psychological consequences as in the occupational realm, albeit not necessarily to the same degree. This belief is based on our fundamental premise – that what is psychologically crucial about position in the social structure is control over the conditions of one's life. Two of our US analyses – one of housework, the other of schooling – are directly in point and thus worth summarizing.

The exercise of self-direction in housework   We see housework as work, in many respects similar to the work that is done in paid employment, even though unpaid, carried out in a decidedly different organizational context, and subject to greater discretionary control. Some of the pivotal conditions of work experienced in paid employment are experienced as well in housework; there are exact analogues between such job conditions as the substantive complexity of work experienced in paid employment and the substantive complexity of housework.

In the follow-up interviews of 1974, Kohn and Schooler asked both husbands and wives about their household activities, attempting to map the "job conditions" of housework. From this information, Schooler, Kohn, Karen Miller, and Joanne Miller (1983) developed indices of the substantive complexity of housework, its routinization, and several other conditions of work as experienced in housework. They then assessed the reciprocal relationships between housework and psychological functioning, using models similar to those that we have employed in this book.[22]

In the main, they found that the conditions of work that *wives* experience in housework affect their psychological functioning much as do similar conditions of work as experienced in paid employment. For example, doing substantively complex work in the household, just as in paid employment, is conducive to intellectual flexibility, to having a self-directed orientation, and to a sense of well-being. Moreover, this is true both for women who are employed outside the home and for those who are not. Further (unpublished) analyses of employed women show that substantively complex housework and substantively complex work in paid employment independently (and additively) facilitate intellectual flexibility and self-directedness of orientation.

For *husbands*, the substantive complexity of housework seems to have little psychological impact; instead, heaviness of housework seems to be more important – physically heavy work facilitating intellectual flexibility, self-directedness of orientation, and a sense of well-being. This is somewhat puzzling. One possible explanation is that men's housework is likely to be solely in the realm of working with "things" (maintenance of household equipment and repairs, rather than reading recipes or books on child-rearing) and focused on delineated "projects" rather than on the everyday activities of running a household. In such circumstances, to do physically heavy work may be tantamount to having a substantial involvement in housework. Moreover, housework does not have the same demand characteristics for husbands that it has for wives. As Schooler et al. conclude:

For many women, household work has much the same demand characteristics as does the work required in paid employment; thus, housework is a structural imperative whose psychological effects are similar to those of the structural imperatives of paid employment. For most men, in contrast, housework exerts no such imperative and thus does not have psychological effects similar to those of paid employment. . . . It may only be when it is imperative that work demands be met that the conditions of work have their usual psychological effects. (1983, p. 260)

These findings tell us that doing self-directed work may have much the same psychological effects whether or not that work is performed in paid employment. The findings also caution, though, that we should not necessarily expect the exercise of self-direction to have much psychological import where the work or activity is not an imperative.

---

[22] As they point out, though, there are many methodological problems in these analyses, ranging from inadequacies in the indices of housework to uncertain identification of the models. All conclusions based on these analyses must be regarded as tentative.

Educational self-direction   In another extrapolation from occupational self-direction to the exercise of self-direction in other institutional realms, Kohn and Schooler hypothesized that students' exercise of self-direction in schoolwork would have psychological consequences quite similar to those of adults' exercise of self-direction in paid employment. To test this hypothesis, they built a battery of questions about "educational self-direction" into the interview schedule used for the children of the men in the follow-up study, most of these offspring still being students at the time they were interviewed. Karen Miller, Kohn, and Schooler (1985, 1986) used these data to develop a measurement model of educational self-direction[23] – which we have borrowed for our analysis of the transmission of values.

Using indices based on this measurement model and measurement models of personality similar to those that we have developed for adult men, they assessed the reciprocal effects of educational self-direction and personality. The data being cross-sectional, and there being no sensible way to approximate longitudinal models, these assessments could not take account of either "earlier" educational self-direction or "earlier" psychological functioning. The models could and did, however, statistically control the *parents'* psychological functioning, thus taking into account, to some substantial degree, family-experiential and genetic determinants of personality.

From their analysis of the reciprocal effects of educational self-direction and intellectual flexibility, Miller et al. concluded:

> that the exercise of self-direction by students in their schoolwork has a decided impact on their cognitive functioning and that their cognitive functioning, in turn, has a decided impact on their exercise of self-direction in schoolwork. These conclusions apply both to secondary-school and to college students. More specifically, the impact of educational self-direction on intellectual functioning results mainly from the substantive complexity of students' schoolwork – its scope, difficulty, and challenge. (1985, p. 941)

After extending their analyses to include self-directedness of orientation and distress, they further concluded that:

> educational self-direction affects *non-cognitive* aspects of personality as well. In models that examine separately each of the two major non-cognitive dimensions of personality – self-directedness versus conformity of orientation, and sense of distress versus well-being – we find that educational self-direction affects both. Greater self-direction in schoolwork – in particular, substantively more complex schoolwork –

---

[23] Educational self-direction is a second-order concept, the first-order concepts being the substantive complexity of schoolwork (as inferred from information about the complexity of coursework and of outside-of-classroom activities) and closeness of supervision by teachers.

increases the self-directedness of the student's orientation. Greater self-direction in schoolwork also *decreases* the student's sense of distress, with both substantively complex schoolwork and freedom from close supervision contributing to a greater sense of well-being. (1986, p. 388)

These findings, too, apply to both high-school and college students.

As Miller et al. conclude,

the causal relationship between the exercise of self-direction in work and personality is remarkably similar for students and adult workers. The similarity of findings suggests some fundamental linkages between work, regardless of setting, and the personality of the worker. For schooling, as for paid employment, the opportunity to exercise self-direction in one's own work appears to have impressive psychological effects. This constitutes a striking affirmation of the applicability of an interpretive model designed to explain the social psychology of work in paid employment to the social psychology of work in school. (1986, pp. 388–9)

We would now add: these findings lend further credibility to the belief that the exercise of self-direction may have similar psychological consequences in *any* realm where the work or activity is "an imperative."

These findings also help explain the importance of educational attainment for values, cognitive functioning, and self-directedness of orientation. We have repeatedly found that educational attainment decidedly affects these facets of psychological functioning, independently of occupational position, both for the United States and for Poland. We have also found that a substantial part of education's psychological impact is indirect, through educational attainment affecting job conditions (particularly the substantive complexity of the work), which, in turn, affect personality. But not all of the effect of educational attainment on personality is indirect; some is direct, a long-lasting residue of the educational experience itself. We see in the "educational self-direction" findings an explanation of this long-lasting direct effect: the core of the educational experience is educational self-direction – learning to think for oneself. Education is (or can be) doubly powerful, by itself providing experience conducive to the experience of self-direction and by providing both the credentials and the learned capacities for occupational careers that continue to afford opportunity for self-directed activity.

Self-direction and other structural imperatives of work and of life

Our thesis is not that occupational self-direction explains everything, nor even that the experience of self-direction in paid employment and in other institutional settings has profound psychological consequences, but that the explanation of the psychological effects of social structure must always lie in the proximate conditions of life attendant on social-structural position.

In our research on class and stratification, this assumption has led us to emphasize job conditions, particularly those job conditions that are conducive to or restrictive of the opportunity to exercise self-direction in one's work: the substantive complexity of that work, how closely it is supervised, and how routinized it is. We have demonstrated that occupational self-direction plays a key role in explaining the effects of social class and social stratification on values, intellectual flexibility, and self-directedness of orientation. Certainly, there are other linkages between social structure and personality as well. Occupational self-direction does not completely explain the impact of class and stratification even on these dimensions of psychological functioning. And, as we have seen, other conditions of work – job protections, for example – play an important role in the processes whereby class and stratification affect distress. Still, our analyses do demonstrate that job conditions, particularly even if not solely those job conditions facilitative of occupational self-direction, play a crucial role in the psychological impact of class and stratification.

It is entirely understandable that a principal intervening link from class and stratification to personality is to be found in the conditions of life experienced in paid employment. After all, class and stratification are closely tied to occupational roles; one might even think of occupational self-direction as the job-structure analogue of class and stratification. Even housework and schoolwork are analogous to work in paid employment: we conceptualize them as work; we hypothesize that exercising self-direction in such work will affect psychological functioning in much the same way as does exercising self-direction in paid employment; and we find this indeed to be the case.

Nevertheless, the findings for housework and for schooling suggest that what is important for valuing self-direction, for effective cognitive functioning, and for holding a self-directed orientation is not necessarily *occupational* self-direction, but the *experience* of self-direction, whether in paid employment or in other institutional realms.

But what happens when we move even further from "work," in whatever realm? Many other facets of social structure are not so closely tied to work and work-like activities as are class, stratification, and even housework and schooling. It may well be that proximate conditions of life other than those directly involved in the exercise of self-direction may better explain the psychological impact of race, gender, and other dimensions of social structure. And – we are again reminded of our findings for distress – the experience of self-direction is not necessarily central for all facets of psychological functioning. Clearly, the experience of self-direction has direct carryover to valuing self-direction, to having a self-directed orientation, and to thinking for oneself, all of which are direct psychological analogues to being self-directed. It may well be that other proximate conditions of life are more important for facets of psychological functioning that are more remote from the experience of self-direction.

We therefore would not *necessarily* expect conditions determinative of the opportunity for self-direction to play so large a role in explaining the psychological effects of other facets of social structure as they do in explaining those of class and stratification. Nor would we necessarily expect conditions determinative of the opportunity for self-direction to play so large a role in explaining the effects of social structure on other facets of psychological functioning as they do for values, cognitive functioning, and self-directedness of orientation. We would certainly want to search for *other* proximate conditions that might play a role for other facets of social structure analogues to that played by occupational self-direction for class and stratification, and to search for other proximate conditions that help explain the relationships of social structure to facets of psychological functioning other than values, cognitive functioning, and self-directedness of orientation. The challenge is to discover these proximate conditions and to demonstrate how they link social-structural position to personality.

Our findings for class, for stratification, for housework, and for schooling, though, do suggest that, in examining the psychological impact of *any* social institution or any component of social structure, one should always ask whether and how people's positions might affect their opportunities for self-direction. The place to look would not necessarily be *occupational* self-direction, but self-direction in the particular institutional realm, whether or not the activities be thought of as "work". The possibility that self-direction might provide the interpretive key should certainly be explored, no matter which institution or which facet of social structure one considers.

It is well to remember in this connection that the central component of occupational (and of educational) self-direction is neither freedom from close supervision, which is merely the absence of a condition that would limit the possibilities for exercising self-direction, nor non-routinized conditions, but the substantive complexity of the activity. It is by engaging in substantively complex activity that one learns to value self-direction, enhances one's intellectual flexibility, and develops a self-directed orientation to self and to society. Our hypothesis would be that substantively complex *activity*, whether in paid employment, in housework, in schoolwork, or in any other realm of life where such activity is sufficiently important to take on the quality of a "structural imperative" would have similar psychological consequences.[24] Paid employment is not the only realm of life that affords (or restricts) opportunities for engaging in substantively complex activities. The experience of thinking for oneself is too important to personality ever to be overlooked.

[24] For a general interpretation of the psychological effects not only of the substantive complexity of work in paid employment, housework, and education, but of complexity wherever experienced, see Schooler, 1984.

References

Adamski, Wladyslaw 1981: "Badania nad rodzina a procesy reprodukcji struktury spolecznej." [Studies on the family and the processes of social structure reproduction.] *Studia Socjologiczne* no. 1 (88): 119–34.

—— 1985: "Aspiracje – interesy – konflikt." [Aspirations – interests – conflicts.] *Studia Socjologiczne* no. 2. (97): 21–40. Subsequently published in English, *Sisyphus: Sociological Studies* 1989, V: 85–101.

Almond, Gabriel A., and Sidney Verba 1963: *The Civic Culture: Political Attitudes and Democracy in Five Nations.* Princeton, NJ: Princeton University Press.

Alwin, Duane F. 1973: "Making inferences from attitude-behavior correlations." *Sociometry* 36: 253–78.

—— 1976: "Attitude scales as congeneric tests: A re-examination of an attitude–behavior model." *Sociometry* 39: 377–83.

—— 1986: "Religion and parental child-rearing orientations: Evidence of a Catholic–Protestant convergence." *American Journal of Sociology* 92: 412–40.

—— 1989a: "Changes in qualities valued in children in the United States, 1964 to 1984." *Social Science Research* 18: 195–236.

—— 1989b: "Social stratification, conditions of work, and parental socialization values," pp. 327–46 in Nancy Eisenberg, Janusz Reykowski, and Ervin Staub (eds), *Social and Moral Values: Individual and Societal Perspectives.* Hillsdale, NJ: Lawrence Erlbaum.

Alwin, Duane F., and David J. Jackson 1982a: "The statistical analysis of Kohn's measures of parental values," pp. 197–223 in K. G. Jöreskog and H. Wold (eds), *Systems under Indirect Observation: Causality, Structure, Prediction.* Amsterdam: North Holland.

—— 1982b: "Adult values for children: An application of factor analysis to ranked preference data," pp. 311–29 in Robert M. Hauser, David Mechanic, Archibold O. Haller, and Taissa S. Hauser (eds), *Social Structure and Behavior: Essays in Honor of William Hamilton Sewell.* New York: Academic Press.

Alwin, Duane F., and Jon A. Krosnick 1985: "The measurement of values in surveys: A comparison of ratings and rankings." *Public Opinion Quarterly* 49: 535–52.

Antonovsky, Aaron 1979: *Health, Stress, and Coping.* San Francisco: Jossey–Bass.

—— 1984: "The sense of coherence as a determinant of health." *Advances, American Institute for the Advancement of Health* 1: 37–50.

—— 1987: *Unravelling the Mystery of Health: How People Manage Stress and Stay Well.* San Francisco: Jossey–Bass.

Armer, Michael 1973: "Methodological problems and possibilities in comparative research," pp. 49–79 in Michael Armer and Allen D. Grimshaw (eds), *Comparative Social Research: Methodological Problems and Strategies.* New York: Wiley. '

Bakke, Edward W. 1940: *The Unemployed Worker: A Study of the Task of Making a Living without a Job.* New Haven: Yale University Press.

Baltes, Paul B. 1983: "Life-span developmental psychology: Observations on history and theory revisited," pp. 79–111 in Richard M. Lerner (ed.), *Developmental Psychology: Historical and Philosophical Perspectives.* Hillsdale, NJ: Lawrence Erlbaum.

Baltes, Paul B., Freya Dittmann-Kohli, and Roger A. Dixon 1984: "New perspectives on the development of intelligence in adulthood: Toward a dual-process conception and a model of selective optimization with compensation," pp. 33–76 in Paul B. Baltes and Orville G. Brim (eds), *Life-Span Development and Behavior.* New York: Academic Press.

Baltes, Paul B., and Gisela V. Labouvie 1973: "Adult development of intellectual performance: Description, explanation, and modification," pp. 157–219 in Carl Eisdorfer and M. Powell Lawton (eds), *The Psychology of Adult Development and Aging.* Washington, DC: American Psychological Association.

Bell, Richard Q. 1968: "A reinterpretation of the direction of effects in studies of socialization," *Psychological Review* 75: 81–95.

Bengtson, Vern L. 1975: "Generation and family effects in value socialization." *American Sociological Review* 40: 358–71.

Bengtson, Vern L., and Mary Christine Lovejoy 1973: "Values, personality, and social structure: An intergenerational analysis." *American Behavioral Scientist* 16: 880–912.

Bernstein, Basil 1971: *Class, Codes and Control,* vol. 1. *Theoretical Studies Toward a Sociology of Language.* London: Routledge and Kegan Paul.

—— 1973: *Class, Codes and Control,* vol. 2. *Applied Studies Toward a Sociology of Language.* London: Routledge and Kegan Paul.

Bertram, Hans 1976a: "Gesellschaftliche und Familiäre Bedingungen moralischen Urteilens." Doctoral dissertation, Universität Düsseldorf.

—— 1976b: "Probleme einer sozialstrukturell orientierten Sozialisationsforschung." *Zeitschrift für Soziologie* 5: 103–17.

—— 1983: "Berufsorientierung erwerbstatiger Mutter." *Zeitschrift für Sozialisationsforschung und Erziehungssoziologie* 3: 29–40.

Bielby, William T., Robert M. Hauser, and David L. Featherman 1977: "Response errors of black and nonblack males in models of the intergenerational transmission of socioeconomic status." *American Journal of Sociology* 82: 1242–88.

Blalock, Hubert M. 1969: "Multiple indicators and the causal approach to measurement error." *American Journal of Sociology* 75: 264–72.

Blumer, Herbert 1956: "Sociological analysis and the 'variable'." *American Sociological Review* 21: 683–90.

Bonjean, Charles M., Richard J. Hill, and S. Dale McLemore 1967: *Sociological Measurement: An Inventory of Scales and Indices*. San Francisco: Chandler.

Bosker, Roel, Rolf van der Velden, and Leun Otten 1989: "Social stratification and educational career," pp. 99–120 in W. Jansen, J. Dronkers and K. Verrips (eds), *Similar or Different? Continuities in Dutch Research on Social Stratification and Social Mobility*. Amsterdam: SISWO Publication 338.

Breer, Paul E., and Edwin A. Locke 1965: *Task Experience as a Source of Attitudes*. Homewood, IL: Dorsey.

Burns, Ailsa, Ross Homel, and Jacqueline Goodnow 1984: "Conditions of life and parental values." *Australian Journal of Psychology*. 36: 219–37.

Burt, Ronald S. 1973: "Confirmatory factor-analytic structures and the theory construction process." *Sociological Methods and Research* 2: 131–90.

Byakhman, L. and O. Shkaratan 1977: *Czeloviek v Myre Truda*. [Man in the World of Work.] Moscow: Politizdat.

Cain, Pamela S., and Donald J. Treiman 1981: "The *Dictionary of Occupational Titles* as a source of occupational data." *American Sociological Review* 46: 253–78.

Campbell, John D. 1978: "The child in the sick role: Contributions of age, sex, parental status, and parental values." *Journal of Health and Social Behavior* 19: 35–51.

Carchedi, G. 1975a: "On the economic identification of the new middle class." *Economy and Society* 4: 1–86.

—— 1975b: "Reproduction of social classes at the level of production relations." *Economy and Society* 4: 361–417.

Clausen, John A. 1974: "Value transmission and personality resemblance in two generations." Paper presented to the annual convention of the American Sociological Association, Montreal.

Clausen, John A., Paul H. Mussen, and Joseph Kuypers 1981: "Involvement, warmth, and parent–child resemblances in three generations," pp. 299–319 in Dorothy H. Eichorn, John A. Clausen, Norma Haan, Marjorie P. Honzik, and Paul H. Mussen (eds), *Present and Past in Middle Life*. New York: Academic Press.

Coburn, David 1975: "Job–worker incongruence: Consequences for health." *Journal of Health and Social Behavior* 16: 198–212.

Coburn, David, and Virginia L. Edwards 1976: "Job control and child-rearing values." *Canadian Review of Sociology and Anthropology* 13: 337–44.

Collective Work 1970: *Systematyczny Slownik Zawodow*. [Systematic Dictionary of Occupations.] Warsaw: Central Statistics Office.

—— 1973: *Encyklopedyczny Przewodnik: Zawody i Specjalnosci w Szkolnictwie Zawodowym*. [Encyclopedic Guide to Occupations and Specializations in Vocational Schools.] Warsaw: Polish Scientific Publishers.

Dalgard, Odd Steffen 1981: "Occupational experience and mental health, with special reference to closeness of supervision." *Psychiatry and Social Science* 1: 29–42.

Dalton, Russell J. 1982: "The pathways of parental socialization." *American Politics Quarterly* 10: 139–57.

Danilowicz, Pawel, and Pawel Sztabinski 1977: *Pytania Metryczkowe.* [Questions Pertaining to the Basic Characteristics of Respondents.] Warsaw: Institute of Philosophy and Sociology of the Polish Academy of Sciences.

Drazkiewicz, Jerzy 1980: "Development of social structure and the concept of interest." *Polish Sociological Bulletin* no. 1(49): 23–38.

Duncan, Otis Dudley 1961: "A socioeconomic index for all occupations," and "Properties and characteristics of the socioeconomic index," pp. 109–61 in Albert J. Reiss et al. *Occupations and Social Status.* New York: Free Press.

—— 1967: "Some linear models for two-wave, two-variable panel analysis." *Psychological Bulletin* 72: 177–182.

—— 1975: *Introduction to Structural Equation Models.* New York: Academic Press.

Elder, Glen H., Jr 1974: *Children of the Great Depression: Social Change in Life Experience.* Chicago: University of Chicago Press.

Elder, Glen H., Jr, and Richard C. Rockwell 1979: "The life-course and human development: An ecological perspective." *International Journal of Behavioral Development* 2: 1–21.

Elder, Joseph W. 1976: "Comparative cross-national methodology." pp. 209–30 in Alex Inkeles (ed.), *Annual Review of Sociology,* vol. 2. Palo Alto, CA: Annual Reviews, Inc.

Eldridge, J. E. T. (ed.) 1971: *Max Weber: The Interpretation of Social Reality.* New York: Charles Scribner's Sons.

Festinger, Leon 1957: *A Theory of Cognitive Dissonance.* Evanston, IL: Row, Peterson.

Finifter, Bernard M. 1977: "The robustness of cross-cultural findings." *Annals New York Academy of Sciences* 285: 151–84.

Firkowska, Anna, Antonina Ostrowska, Magdalena Sokolowska, Zena Stein, Mervyn Susser, and Ignacy Wald 1978: "Cognitive development and social policy: The contribution of parental occupation and education to mental performance in 11-year olds in Warsaw." *Science* 200 (23 June): 1357–62.

Form, William 1987: "On the degradation of skills," pp. 29–47 in W. Richard Scott and James F. Short, Jr (eds), *Annual Review of Sociology,* vol. 13. Palo Alto, CA: Annual Reviews.

Fox, John 1980: "Effect analysis in structural equation models." *Sociological Methods and Research* 9: 3–28.

Franklin, Jack L., and Joseph E. Scott 1970: "Parental values: An inquiry into occupational setting." *Journal of Marriage and the Family* 32: 406–9.

Frese, Michael 1983: "Der Einfluss der Arbeit auf die Persönlichkeit: Zum Konzept des Handlungsstils in der beruflichen Sozialisation." *Zeitschrift für Socializationsforschung und Erziehungssoziologie* 3: 11–28.

Furstenberg, Frank F., Jr 1971: "The transmission of mobility orientation in the family." *Social Forces* 49: 595–603.

Gagliani, Giorgio 1981: "How many working classes?" *American Journal of Sociology* 87: 259–85.

Gagne, Robert M. 1968: "Learning: Transfer," pp. 168–73 in David L. Sills, (ed.), *International Encyclopedia of the Social Sciences*, vol. 9. New York: MacMillan and Free Press.

Galtung, Johan 1967: *Theory and Methods of Social Research*. Oslo: Universitetsforlaget.

Gecas, Viktor 1980: "Father's occupation and child socialization: An examination of the linkage hypothesis." Paper presented to the annual convention of the American Sociological Association, New York City.

Gewirtz, Jacob L. 1969: "Mechanisms of social learning: Some roles of stimulation and behavior in early human development," pp. 57–212 in David D. Goslin (ed.), *Handbook of Socialization Theory and Research*. Chicago: Rand McNally.

Grabb, Edward G. 1981a: "Class, conformity, and political powerlessness." *Canadian Review of Sociology and Anthropology* 18: 362–9.

—— 1981b: "The ranking of self-actualization values: The effects of class, stratification, and occupational experiences." *The Sociological Quarterly* 22: 373–83.

Grüneisen, Veronika, and Ernst-Hartmut Hoff 1977: *Familienerziehung und Lebenssituation: Der Einfluss von Lebensbedingungen und Arbeitserfahrungen auf Erziehungseinstellungen und Erziehungsverhalten von Eltern*. Weinheim, W. Germany: Beltz Verlag.

Habermas, Jürgen 1979: *Communication and the Evolution of Society*. Boston, Mass.: Beacon Press.

Hacker, Winfried 1981: "Perceptions of and reactions to work situations: Some implications of an action control approach," pp. 113–34 in David Magnusson (ed.), *Toward a Psychology of Situations: An Interactional Perspective*. Hillsdale, NJ: Lawrence Erlbaum.

Hackman, J. Richard, and Edward E. Lawler III 1971: "Employee reactions to job characteristics." *Journal of Applied Psychology Monograph* 55: 259–86.

Hauser, Robert M., and Arthur S. Goldberger 1971: "The treatment of unobservable variables in path analysis," pp. 81–117 in Herbert L. Costner (ed.), *Sociological Methodology, 1971*. San Francisco: Jossey–Bass.

Heise, David R. 1969: "Separating reliability and stability in test–retest correlation." *American Sociological Review* 34: 93–101.

—— 1970: "Causal inference from panel data," pp. 3–27 in Edgar F. Borgatta and George M. Bohrnstedt (eds), *Sociological Methodology, 1970*. San Francisco: Jossey–Bass.

—— 1975: *Causal Analysis*. New York: Wiley.

Heise, David R., and George W. Bohrnstedt 1970: "Validity, invalidity, and reliability," pp. 104–29 in Edgar F. Borgatta and George M. Bohrnstedt (eds), *Sociological Methodology, 1970*. San Francisco: Jossey–Bass.

Hill, Reuben 1962: "Cross-national family research: Attempts and prospects." *International Social Science Journal* 14: 425–51.

Hochfeld, Julian 1967: "The concept of class interest." *Polish Sociological Bulletin* no. 2(16): 5–14.

Hodge, Robert W., Paul M. Siegel, and Peter H. Rossi 1964: "Occupational prestige in the United States, 1925–63." *American Journal of Sociology* 70: 286–302.

Hoff, Ernst 1982: "Kontrollbewusstsein: Grundvorstellungen zur eigenen Person und Umwelt bei jungen Arbeitern." *Kölner Zeitschrift für Soziologie und Sozialpsychologie* 34: 316–39.

Hoff, Ernst-Hartmut, and Veronika Grüneisen 1978: "Arbeitserfahrungen, Erziehungseinstellungen und Erziehungsverhalten von Eltern," pp. 65–89 in H. Lukesch und K. Schneewind (eds), *Familiäre Sozialisation: Probleme, Ergebnisse, Perspektiven.* Stuttgart: Klett–Cotta.

Hoff, Ernst, Lothar Lappe, and Wolfgang Lempert 1982: "Sozialisationstheoretische Uberlegungen zur Analyse von Arbeit, Betrieb, und Beruf." *Soziale Welt: Zeitschrift für Sozialwissenschaftliche Forschung und Praxis* 33: 508–36.

—— 1983: *Methoden zur Untersuchung der Sozialisation Junger Facharbeiter.* Materialien aus der Bildungsforschung Nr. 24, Teil I und Teil II. Berlin: Max Planck Institut für Bildungsforschung.

Hoge, Dean R., Gregory H. Petrillo, and Ella I. Smith 1982: "Transmission of religious and social values from parents to teenage children." *Journal of Marriage and the Family* 44: 569–80.

Hollingshead, August B. and Fredrick C. Redlich 1958: *Social Class and Mental Illness: A Community Study.* New York: Wiley.

Hope, Keith 1975: "Models of status inconsistency and social mobility effects." *American Sociological Review* 40: 322–43.

Horn, John L., and Gary Donaldson 1980: "Cognitive development in adulthood," pp. 445–529 in Orville G. Brim, Jr and Jerome Kagan (eds), *Constancy and Change in Human Development.* Cambridge, Mass.: Harvard University Press.

House, James S. 1980: *Occupational Stress and the Physical and Mental Health of Factory Workers.* Report on NIMH Grant no. 1R02MH28902. Research Report Series: Institute for Social Research, University of Michigan, Ann Arbor.

—— 1981: "Social structure and personality," pp. 525–61 in Morris Rosenberg and Ralph H. Turner (eds), *Social Psychology: Sociological Perspectives.* New York: Basic Books.

Hryniewicz, Janusz 1983: "Metodologiczne aspekty analizy struktury klasowej w Polsce. Stosunki produkcji, wladza, klasy spoleczne." [Methodological aspects of the analysis of class structure in Poland. Relations of production, power, social classes.] *Studia Socjologiczne* no. 1(88): 43–73.

—— 1984: "Stosunki produkcji, klasy i ruchliwosc spoleczna w Polsce." [Economic relations, classes, and social mobility in Poland.] *Studia Socjologiczne* no. 1(92): 35–62.

Hynes, Eugene 1979: "Explaining Class Differences in Socialization Values and Behavior: An Irish Study." Unpublished PhD Dissertation, Southern Illinois University, Carbondale.

Jackson, David J., and Duane F. Alwin 1980: "The factor analysis of ipsative measures." *Sociological Methods and Research* 9: 218–38.

Jalowiecki, S. 1978: *Struktura Systemu Wartosci: Stadium Zroznicowan Miedzygeneracyjnych.* [Structure of Value System: A Study of Intergenerational Differentiation.] Warsaw: Polish Scientific Publishers.

Janicka, Krystyna, Grazyna Kacprowicz, and Kazimierz M. Slomczynski 1983: *Zlozonosc pracy jako zmienna socjologiczna: Modele pomiaru i proponowane zastosowania.* [Complexity of work as a sociological variable: Measurement models and proposed applications.] *Studia Socjologiczne* no. 3(90): 5–33.

Jarvik, Lissy F., and Donna Cohen 1973: "A biobehavioral approach to intellectual changes with aging," pp. 220–80 in Carl Eisdorfer and M. Powell Lawton (eds), *The Psychology of Adult Development and Aging.* Washington, DC: American Psychological Association.

Jasinska, Aleksandra, and Leszek Nowak 1973: "Foundations of Marx's theory of class: A reconstruction," pp. 141–69 in P. K. Crosser (ed.), *East–West Dialogues.* Amsterdam: Rodopi.

Jennings, M. Kent, and Richard G. Niemi 1968: "The transmission of political values from parent to child." *The American Political Science Review* 62: 169–84.

Jöreskog, Karl G. 1969: "A general approach to confirmatory maximum likelihood factor analysis." *Psychometrika* 34: 183–202.

—— 1970: "A general method for analysis of covariance structures." *Biometrika* 57: 239–51.

—— 1973a: "Analysis of covariance structures," pp. 263 85 in Paruchuri R. Krishnaiah (ed.), *Multivariate Analysis – III.* New York: Academic Press.

—— 1973b: "A general method for estimating a linear structural equation system," pp. 85–112 in Arthur S. Goldberger and Otis Dudley Duncan (eds), *Structural Equation Models in the Social Sciences.* New York: Seminar Press.

Jöreskog, Karl G., Gunnar T. Gruvaeus, and Marielle van Thillo 1970: *ACOVS: A General Computer Program for Analysis of Covariance Structures.* Research Bulletin 70–15. Princeton, NJ: Educational Testing Service.

Jöreskog, Karl G., and Dag Sörbom 1976a: "Statistical models and methods for analysis of longitudinal data," pp. 285–325 in Dennis J. Aigner and Arthur S. Goldberger (eds), *Latent Variables in Socioeconomic Models.* Amsterdam: North Holland.

—— 1976b: "Statistical models and methods for test–retest situations," pp. 135–50 in D. N. M. deGruijter, L. J. Th. van der Kamp, and H. F. Crombag (eds), *Advances in Psychological and Educational Measurement.* New York: Wiley.

Jöreskog, Karl G., and Marielle van Thillo 1972: *LISREL: A General Computer Program for Estimating a Linear Structural Equation System Involving Multiple Indicators of Unmeasured Variables.* Research Bulletin 72–56. Princeton, NJ: Educational Testing Service.

Kahn, Robert L 1972: "The meaning of work: interpretation and proposals for measurement," pp. 159–203 in Angus Campbell and Philip E. Converse (eds), *The Human Meaning of Social Change.* New York: Russell Sage Foundation.

Kalleberg, Arne L., and Larry J. Griffin 1980: "Class, occupation, and inequality in job rewards." *American Journal of Sociology* 85: 731–68.

Karasek, Robert A., Jr 1979: "Job demands, job decision latitude, and mental strain: implications for job redesign." *Administrative Science Quarterly* 24: 285–308.

Karasek, Robert, Dean Baker, Frank Marxer, Anders Ahlbom, and Tores Theorell 1981: "Job decision latitude, job demands, and cardiovascular disease: A prospective study of Swedish men." *American Journal of Public Health* 71: 694–705.

Kerckhoff, Alan C., Richard T. Campbell, Jerry M. Trott, and Vered Kraus 1989: "The transmission of socioeconomic status and prestige in Great Britain and the United States." *Sociological Forum* 4: 155–77.

Kerckhoff, Alan C., and Judith L. Huff 1974: "Parental influence on educational goals." *Sociometry* 37: 307–27.

Klarkowski, Andrzej 1981: "Rola zdolnosci intelektualnych w reprodukcji struktury spolecznej" [The role of intellectual abilities in the reproduction of social structure,] pp. 88–120 in Kazimierz M. Slomczynski and Wlodzimierz Wesolowski (eds), *Zroznicowanie Spoleczne w Perspektywie Porownawczej*. [Social Differentiation in Comparative Perspective.] Wroclaw: Ossolineum.

Kohlberg, Lawrence 1976: "Moral stages and moralisation: The cognitive-developmental approach," pp. 31–5 in T. Lickona (ed.), *Moral Development and Behavior*. New York: Holt, Rinehart, and Winston.

Kohlberg, Lawrence, and Carol Gilligan 1972: "The adolescent as a philosopher: The discovery of the self in a post-conventional world," pp. 144–79 in Jerome Kagan and Robert Coles (eds), *Twelve to Sixteen: Early Adolescence*. New York: Norton.

Kohn, Melvin L. 1959: "Social class and parental values." *American Journal of Sociology* 64: 337–51.

—— 1963: "Social class and parent–child relationships: An interpretation." *American Journal of Sociology* 68: 471–80.

—— 1969: *Class and Conformity: A Study in Values*. Homewood, IL: Dorsey Press. (Second edition, University of Chicago Press, 1977.)

—— 1976a: "Occupational structure and alienation." *American Journal of Sociology* 82: 111–30.

—— 1976b: "Social class and parental values: Another confirmation of the relationship." *American Sociological Review* 41: 538–45.

—— 1977: "Reassessment, 1977," pp. xxv–lx in *Class and Conformity: A Study in Values*, 2nd edn. Chicago: University of Chicago Press.

—— 1980: "Job complexity and adult personality," pp. 193–210 in Neil J. Smelser and Erik H. Erikson (eds), *Themes of Work and Love in Adulthood*. Cambridge, Mass.: Harvard University Press.

—— 1983: "On the transmission of values in the family: A preliminary formulation," pp. 3–12 in Alan C. Kerckhoff (ed.), *Research in Sociology of Education and Socialization*, vol. 4. Greenwich, CT: JAI Press.

—— 1987: "Cross-national research as an analytic strategy: American Sociological Association 1987 presidential address." *American Sociological Review* 52: 713–31.

—— 1989: "Social structure and personality: A quintessentially sociological approach to social psychology." *Social Forces* 68: 26–33.

—— 1990: "Unresolved issues in the relationship between work and personality," in Kai Erikson and Steven P. Vallas (eds), *The Nature of Work: Sociological Perspectives*. New Haven, CT: Yale University Press (in press).

Kohn, Melvin L., Atsushi Naoi, Carrie Schoenbach, Carmi Schooler, and Kazimierz M. Slomczynski 1990: "Position in the class structure and psychological functioning in the United States, Japan, and Poland." *American Journal of Sociology* 95: 964–1008.

Kohn, Melvin L., and Carrie Schoenbach 1980: "Social stratification and parental values: A multi-national assessment." Paper presented to the Japan–US Conference on Social Stratification and Mobility, Maui, Hawaii, January.

—— 1983: "Class, stratification, and psychological functioning," pp. 154–89 in Melvin L. Kohn and Carmi Schooler, *Work and Personality: An Inquiry into the Impact of Social Stratification*. Norwood, NJ: Ablex.

Kohn, Melvin L., and Carmi Schooler 1969: "Class, occupation, and orientation." *American Sociological Review* 34: 659–78.

—— 1973: "Occupational experience and psychological functioning: An assessment of reciprocal effects." *American Sociological Review* 38: 97–118.

—— 1978: "The reciprocal effects of the substantive complexity of work and intellectual flexibility: A longitudinal assessment." *American Journal of Sociology* 84: 24–52.

—— 1981: "Job conditions and intellectual flexibility: A longitudinal assessment of their reciprocal effects," pp. 281–313 in David J. Jackson and Edgar F. Borgatta (eds), *Factor Analysis and Measurement in Sociological Research: A Multi-Dimensional Perspective*. London: Sage.

—— 1982: "Job conditions and personality: A longitudinal assessment of their reciprocal effects." *American Journal of Sociology* 87: 1257–86.

—— 1983: With the collaboration of Joanne Miller, Karen A. Miller, Carrie Schoenbach, and Ronald Schoenberg. *Work and Personality: An Inquiry into the Impact of Social Stratification*. Norwood, NJ: Ablex.

Kohn, Melvin L., Kazimierz M. Slomczynski, and Carrie Schoenbach 1986: "Social stratification and the transmission of values in the family: A cross-national assessment." *Sociological Forum* 1: 73–102.

Koralewicz–Zebik, Jadwiga 1982: "Wartosci rodzicielskie a stratyfikacja spoleczna." [Parental values and social stratification.] *Studia Socjologiczne* no. 3–4(86–87): 225–38.

Kozyr-Kowalski, Stanislaw 1970: "Marx's theory of classes and social strata and 'Capital'." *Polish Sociological Bulletin*, no. 1: 17–32.

Krosnick, Jon A., and Duane F. Alwin 1988: "A test of the form-resistant correlation hypothesis: Ratings, rankings, and the measurement of values." *Public Opinion Quarterly* 52: 526–38.

Kuczynski, Jan, and Bikas C. Sanyal (eds) 1985: *Education and Work in Poland*. Warsaw: Polish Scientific Publishers.

Kuechler, Manfred 1987: "The utility of surveys for cross-national research." *Social Science Research* 16: 229–44.

Labouvie-Vief, Gisela, and Michael J. Chandler 1978: "Cognitive development and life-span developmental theory: Idealistic versus contextual perspectives," pp. 181–210 in Paul B. Baltes (ed.), *Life-Span Development and Behavior*, vol. 1. New York: Academic Press.

Ladosz, Jaroslaw 1977: "Contradictions in the development of socialist society." *Dialectics and Humanism* 4: 83–93.

Lane, David, and George Kolankiewicz 1973: *Social Groups in Polish Society*. New York: Columbia University Press.

LaRocco, James M., James S. House, and John R. P. French, Jr 1980: "Social support, occupational stress, and health." *Journal of Health and Social Behavior* 21: 202–18.

Lenski, Gerhard E. 1954: "Status crystallization: A non-vertical dimension of social status." *American Sociological Review* 19: 405–13.

Locke, Edwin A. 1976: "The nature and causes of job satisfaction," pp. 1297–1349 in Marvin D. Dunnette (ed.), *Handbook of Industrial and Organizational Psychology*. Chicago: Rand McNally.

Lockwood, David 1958: *The Blackcoated Worker: A Study in Class Consciousness*. London: Allen and Unwin.

Lofquist, Lloyd H., and Rene V. Dawis 1969: *Adjustment to Work: A Psychological View of Man's Problems in a Work-oriented Society*. New York: Appleton–Century–Crofts.

Looker, E. Dianne, and Peter C. Pineo 1983: "Social psychological variables and their relevance to the status attainment of teenagers." *American Journal of Sociology* 88: 1195–219.

Lord, F. M., and M. R. Novick 1968: *Statistical Theories of Mental Test Scores*. Reading, Mass.: Addison–Wesley.

Lueptow, Lloyd B., McKee J. McClendon, and John W. McKeon 1979: "Father's occupation and son's personality: Findings and questions for the emerging linkage hypothesis." *The Sociological Quarterly* 20: 463–75.

Mach, Bogan W., and Wlodzimierz Wesolowski 1986: *Social Mobility and Social Structure*. London: Routledge and Kegan Paul.

Markowska, Danuta 1975: *Wspolczesna rodzina w Polsce*. Warsaw: Ksiazka i Wiedza.

Marody, Maria, and Krzysztof Andrzej Nowak 1983: "Wartosci i dzialania." [Values and actions.] *Studia Socjologiczne* no. 4(92): 5–30.

Marsh, Robert M. 1967: *Comparative Sociology: A Codification of Cross-Societal Analysis*. New York: Harcourt, Brace and World.

Marshall, Gordon 1988. "Classes in Britain: Marxist and official." *European Sociological Review*. 4: 141–54.

Marx, Karl 1964: *Early Writings*. Edited and translated by T. B. Bottomore. New York: McGraw–Hill.

—— 1971. *The Grundrisse*. Edited and translated by David McLellan. New York: Harper and Row.

Mason, William M., Robert F. Hauser, Alan C. Kerckhoff, Sharon Sandomirsky Poss, and Kenneth Manton 1976: "Models of response error in student reports of parental socioeconomic characteristics," pp. 443–94 in William H. Sewell, Robert M. Hauser, and David L. Featherman (eds), *Schooling and Achievement in American Society*. New York: Academic Press.

Miller, Joanne 1980: "Individual and occupational determinants of job satisfaction: A focus on gender differences." *Sociology of Work and Occupations* 7: 337–66.

Miller, Joanne, Carmi Schooler, Melvin L. Kohn, and Karen A. Miller 1979: "Women and work: The psychological effects of occupational conditions." *American Journal of Sociology* 85: 66–94.

Miller, Joanne, Kazimierz M. Slomczynski and Melvin L. Kohn 1985: "Continuity of learning-generalization: The effect of job on men's intellective process in the United States and Poland." *American Journal of Sociology* 91: 593–615.

Miller, Joanne, Kazimierz M. Slomczynski, and Ronald J. Schoenberg 1981: "Assessing comparability of measurement in cross-national research: Authoritarian-conservatism in different sociocultural settings." *Social Psychology Quarterly* 44: 178–91.

Miller, Karen A., and Melvin L. Kohn 1983: "The reciprocal effects of job conditions and the intellectuality of leisure-time activities," pp. 217–41 in *Work and Personality: An Inquiry into the Impact of Social Stratification*, by Melvin L. Kohn and Carmi Schooler. Norwood, NJ: Ablex.

Miller, Karen A., Melvin L. Kohn, and Carmi Schooler 1985: "Educational self-direction and the cognitive functioning of students." *Social Forces* 63: 923–44.

—— 1986: "Educational self-direction and personality." *American Sociological Review* 51: 372–90.

Morgan, William R., Duane F. Alwin, and Larry J. Griffin 1979: "Social origins, parental values, and the transmission of inequality." *American Journal of Sociology* 85: 156–66.

Mortimer, Jeylan T. 1979: *Changing Attitudes toward Work*. Work in America Institute Studies in Productivity, vol. II. Scarsdale, NY.: Work in America Institute.

Mortimer, Jeylan T., and Donald Kumka 1982: "A further examination of the 'occupational linkage hypothesis'." *Sociological Quarterly* 23: 3–16.

Mortimer, Jeylan T., and Jon Lorence. 1979a: "Work experience and occupational value socialization: A longitudinal study." *American Journal of Sociology* 84: 1361–85.

—— 1979b: "Occupational experience and the self-concept: A longitudinal study." *Social Psychology Quarterly* 42: 307–23.

Mortimer, Jeylan T., Jon Lorence, and Donald S. Kumka 1986: *Work, Family, and Personality: Transition to Adulthood*. Norwood, NJ: Ablex.

Naoi, Atsushi, and Carmi Schooler 1985: "Occupational conditions and psychological functioning in Japan." *American Journal of Sociology* 90: 729–52.

Niemi, Richard G., R. Danforth Ross, and Joseph Alexander 1978: "The similarity of political values of parents and college-age youths." *Public Opinion Quarterly* 42: 503–20.

Nowak, Stefan 1976: "Meaning and measurement in comparative studies," pp. 104–32 in *Understanding and Prediction: Essays in the Methodology of Social and Behavioral Theories*. Dordrecht, Holland: D. Reidel.

—— 1977: "The strategy of cross-national survey research for the development of social theory," pp. 3–47 in Alexander Szalai and Riccardo Petrella (eds), *Cross-National Comparative Survey Research: Theory and Practice*. Oxford: Pergamon Press.

—— 1981: "Values and attitudes of the Polish people." *Scientific American* 245: 45–53.

—— 1989a: "Comparative studies and social theory," pp. 34–56 in Melvin L. Kohn (ed.), *Cross-National Research in Sociology*. Newbury Park, CA: Sage/American Sociological Association Presidential Series.

—— 1989b: *Ciaglosc i Zmiana Tradycji Kulturowej.* [Continuity and Change in Cultural Tradition.] Warsaw: Polish Scientific Publishers.

O'Brien, Gordon E., and Peter Dowling 1980: "The effects of congruency between perceived and desired job attributes upon job satisfaction." *Journal of Occupational Psychology* 53: 121–30.

Oesterreich, Rainer 1984: "Zur Analyse von Planungs- und Denkprozessen in der industriellen Produktion – Das Arbeitsanalyseinstrument VERA." *Diagnostica* (Heft 3): 216–34.

Olsen, Stephen Milton 1971: "Family, Occupation and Values in a Chinese Urban Community." PhD dissertation. Cornell University.

Ossowski, Stanislaw 1963 [1957]: *Class Structure in the Social Consciousness.* London: Routledge and Kegan Paul.

Otto, Luther B., and David L. Featherman 1975: "Social structural and psychological antecedents of self-estrangement and powerlessness." *American Sociological Review* 40: 701–19.

Parsons, Talcott, Edward A. Shils, Gordon W. Allport, Clyde Kluckhohn, Henry A. Murray, Robert R. Sears, Richard C. Sheldon, Samuel A. Stouffer, and Edward C. Tolman 1951: "Some fundamental categories of the theory of action: A general statement," pp. 3–29 in Talcott Parsons and Edward A Shils. (eds), *Toward a General Theory of Action.* Cambridge, Mass.: Harvard University Press.

Pearlin, Leonard I. 1971: *Class Context and Family Relations: A Cross-National Study.* Boston, Mass.: Little, Brown.

Pearlin, Leonard I., and Melvin L. Kohn 1966: "Social class, occupation, and parental values: A cross-national study." *American Sociological Review* 31: 466–79.

Perron, Roger 1971: *Modeles d'enfants, enfants modeles.* Paris: Presses Universitaires de France.

Piaget, Jean n.d.: *The Moral Judgment of the Child.* Glencoe, IL: Free Press.

Pohoski, Michal, and Kazimierz M. Slomczynski 1978: *Spoleczna Klasyfikacja Zawodow.* [Social Classification of Occupations.] Warsaw: Institute of Philosophy and Sociology of the Polish Academy of Sciences.

Pohoski, Michal, Kazimierz M. Slomczynski, and Wlodzimierz Wesolowski 1976: "Occupational prestige in Poland, 1958–1975." *Polish Sociological Bulletin* no. 4(36): 86–94.

Poulantzas, Nicos 1975: *Classes in Contemporary Capitalism.* London: New Left Books.

Przeworski, Adam, and Henry Teune 1970: *The Logic of Comparative Social Inquiry.* New York: Wiley–Interscience.

Ragin, Charles, and David Zaret 1983: "Theory and method in comparative research: Two strategies." *Social Forces* 61: 731–54.

Resch, M., W. Volpert, K. Leitner, and T. Krogoll 1983: "Regulation requirements and regulation barriers – Two aspects of partialized action in industrial work," pp. 29–32 in T. Martin (ed.), *Design of Work in Automated Manufacturing Systems with Special Reference to Small and Medium Size Firms.* Oxford: Pergamon Press.

Riley, Matilda White (ed.). 1979: *Aging from Birth to Death: Interdisciplinary*

Perspectives. Boulder, Colorado: Westview Press [for the American Association for the Advancement of Science].

Riley, Matilda White, and Kathleen Bond 1983: "Beyond ageism: Postponing the onset of disability," pp. 243–52 in Matilda White Riley, Beth B. Hess, and Kathleen Bond (eds), *Aging in Society: Selected Reviews of Recent Research*. Hillsdale, NJ: Lawrence Erlbaum.

Roberts, Bruce R. 1987: "A confirmatory factor-analytic model of alienation." *Social Psychology Quarterly* 50: 346–351.

Robinson, Robert V., and Jonathan Kelley 1979: "Class as conceived by Marx and Dahrendorf: Effects on income inequality and politics in the United States and Great Britain." *American Sociological Review* 44: 38–58.

Rosenberg, Morris, and Leonard I. Pearlin 1978: "Social class and self-esteem among children and adults." *American Journal of Sociology* 84: 53–77.

Rotter, Julian B. 1966: "Generalized expectancies for internal versus external control of reinforcement." *Psychological Monographs* 80(1), whole no. 609.

Rychlinski, Stanislaw 1938: "Warstwy spoleczne." [Social strata.] *Przeglad Socjologiczny* 8: 153–97.

Sarapata, Adam 1977: *O Zadowoleniu i Niezadowoleniu z Pracy.* [On job satisfaction and dissatisfaction.] Warsaw: Instytut Wydawniczy CRZZ.

—— 1985: "Researchers' habits and orientations as factors which condition international cooperation in research." *Science of Science* 5: 157–82.

Sarapata, Adam, and Wlodzimierz Wesolowski 1961: "The evaluation of occupations by Warsaw inhabitants." *American Journal of Sociology* 66: 581–91.

Scheuch, Erwin K. 1967: "Society as context in cross-cultural comparisons." *Social Science Information* 6: 7–23.

—— 1968: "The cross-cultural use of sample surveys: Problems of comparability," pp. 176–209 in Stein Rokkan (ed.), *Comparative Research across Cultures and Nations*. Paris: Mouton.

Schoenberg, Ronald 1977: "Dynamic models and cross-sectional data: The consequences of dynamic misspecification." *Social Science Research* 6: 133–44.

—— 1982: "Multiple indicator models: Estimation of unconstrained construct means and their standard errors." *Sociological Methods and Research* 10: 421–33.

Schooler, Carmi 1972: "Social antecedents of adult psychological functioning." *American Journal of Sociology* 78: 299–322.

—— 1984: "Psychological effects of complex environments during the life span: A review and theory." *Intelligence* 8: 259–81.

—— 1989: "Social structure effects and experimental situations: Mutual lessons of cognitive and social science," pp. 129–53 in K. Warner Schaie and Carmi Schooler (eds), *Social Structure and Aging: Psychological Processes*. Hillsdale, NJ: Lawrence Erlbaum.

Schooler, Carmi, Melvin L. Kohn, Karen A. Miller, and Joanne Miller 1983: "Housework as work," pp. 242–60 in Melvin L. Kohn and Carmi Schooler, *Work and Personality: An Inquiry into the Impact of Social Stratification*. Norwood, NJ: Ablex.

Schooler, Carmi, and Atsushi Naoi 1988: "The psychological effects of traditional and of economically peripheral job settings in Japan." *American Journal of Sociology* 94: 335–55.

Schooler, Carmi, and Karen C. Smith 1978: ". . . and a Japanese wife: Social structural antecedents of women's role values in Japan." *Sex Roles* 4: 23–41.

Scurrah, Martin J., and Abner Montalvo 1975: *Clase Social y Valores Sociales en Peru*. Lima, Peru: Escuela de Administracion de Negocios Para Graduados (Serie: Documento de Trabajo no. 8).

Seeman, Melvin 1959: "On the meaning of alienation." *American Sociological Review* 24: 783–91.

Siegel, Paul M. 1971: "Prestige in the American Occupational Structure." Unpublished PhD dissertation, University of Chicago.

Simon, Herbert A. 1957: "Casual ordering and identifiability," pp. 10–36 in Herbert A. Simon (ed.), *Models of Man: Social and Rational*. New York: Wiley.

Skinner, Burrhus F. 1953: *Science and Human Behavior*. New York: Macmillan.

Skocpol, Theda 1979: *States and Social Revolutions: A Comparative Analysis of France, Russia, and China*. Cambridge: Cambridge University Press.

Skvoretz, John V., and Ubol Kheoruenromne 1979: "Some evidence concerning the value hypothesis of intergenerational status transmission: A research note." *Social Science Research* 8: 172–83

Slomczynski, Kazimierz M. 1978. "The Role of Education in the Process of Intragenerational Mobility," pp. 102–21 in Kazimierz Slomczynski and Tadeusz Krauze (eds), *Class Structure and Social Mobility in Poland*. White Plains, NY: M. E. Sharpe.

—— 1986: "The attainment of occupational status: A model with multiple indicator constructs," pp. 78–104 in Kazimierz M. Slomczynski and Tadeusz K. Krauze (eds), *Social Stratification in Poland: Eight Empirical Studies*. Armonk, NY: M. E. Sharpe.

—— 1989: *Social Structure and Mobility: Poland, Japan, and the United States*. Warsaw: Institute of Philosophy and Sociology of the Polish Academy of Sciences.

Slomczynski, Kazimierz M., and Grazyna Kacprowicz 1979: *Skale Zawodow*. [Scales of Occupations.] Warsaw: Institute of Philosophy and Sociology of the Polish Academy of Sciences.

Slomczynski, Kazimierz M., and Melvin L. Kohn 1988: *Sytuacja Pracy i Jej Psychologiczne Konsekwencje: Polsko–Amerykanskie Analizy Porownawcze*. [Work Conditions and Psychological Functioning: Comparative Analyses of Poland and the United States.] Wroclaw: Ossolineum. [Publication of the Polish Academy of Sciences.]

Slomczynski, Kazimierz, and Tadeusz Krauze (eds) 1978: *Class Structure and Social Mobility in Poland*. White Plains, NY: M. E. Sharpe.

Slomczynski, Kazimierz M., Joanne Miller, and Melvin L. Kohn 1981: "Stratification, work, and values: A Polish–United States comparison." *American Sociological Review* 46: 720–44.

—— 1987: "Stratification, work, and values: A Polish–United States comparison." *Sisyphus: Sociological Studies* (Polish Academy of Sciences) IV: 59–100.

Smelser, Neil J. 1968: "The methodology of comparative analysis of economic activity," pp. 62–75 in *Essays in Sociological Explanation*. Englewood Cliffs, NJ: Prentice-Hall.

—— 1988: "Social Structure," pp. 103–29 in Neil J. Smelser (ed.), *Handbook of Sociology*. Newbury Park, CA: Sage.

Smith, Karen C., and Carmi Schooler 1978: "Women as mothers in Japan: The effects of social structure and culture on values and behavior." *Journal of Marriage and the Family* 40: 613–20.

Smith, Thomas Ewin 1982: "The case for parental transmission of educational goals: The importance of accurate offspring perceptions." *Journal of Marriage and the Family* 44: 661–74.

—— 1983: "Parental influence: A review of the evidence of influence and a theoretical model of the parental influence process," pp. 13–45 in Alan C. Kerckhoff (ed.), *Research in Sociology of Education and Socialization*, vol. 4. Greenwich, CT: JAI Press.

Sokolowska, Magdalena, Anna Firkowska-Mankiewicz, Antonina Ostrowska, and Miroslaw P. Czarkowski 1978: *Intellectual Performance of Children in the Light of Socio-cultural Factors – the Warsaw Study*. Warsaw: Polish Academy of Sciences.

Spade, Joan Z. 1983: "The Nature of the Work Activity: Its Impact on the Family." Unpublished PhD dissertation, University of New York at Buffalo.

Spaeth, Joe L. 1976: "Characteristics of the work setting and the job as determinants of income," pp. 161–76 in William H. Sewell, Robert M. Hauser, and David L. Featherman (eds), *Schooling and Achievement in American Society*. New York: Academic Press.

Spenner, Kenneth I. 1977: "From Generation to Generation: The Transmission of Occupation". Unpublished PhD dissertation, University of Wisconsin, Madison.

—— 1980: "Occupational characteristics and classification systems: New uses of the *Dictionary of Occupational Titles* in social research." *Sociological Methods and Research* 9: 239–64.

—— 1983: "Deciphering Prometheus: Temporal change in the skill level of work." *American Sociological Review* 48: 824–37.

—— 1988a: "Occupations, work settings, and the course of adult development: Tracing the implications of select historical changes." pp. 243–85 in Paul B. Baltes, David L. Featherman, and Richard M. Lerner (eds) *Life-Span Development and Behavior*, vol. 9. Hillsdale, NJ: Lawrence Erlbaum.

—— 1988b: "Social stratification, work, and personality," pp. 69–97 in W. Richard Scott and Judith Blake (eds), *Annual Review of Sociology*, vol. 14. Palo Alto, CA: Annual Reviews.

Spenner, Kenneth I. and Luther B. Otto 1985: "Work and self-concept: Selection and socialization in the early career," pp. 197–235 in Alan C. Kerckhoff (ed.), *Research in Sociology of Education and Socialization*, vol. 5. Greenwich, CT: JAI Press.

Spilerman, Seymour 1977: "Careers, labor market structure, and socioeconomic achievement." *American Journal of Sociology* 83: 551–93.

Staines, Graham L. 1980: "Spillover versus compensation: A review of the literature on the relationship between work and nonwork." *Human Relations* 33: 111–29.

Steinkamp, Günther 1983: "Auf der Suche nach den sozialstrukturellen Bedingungen sozialen Handelns: Melvin L. Kohn." *Zeitschrift für Sozialisationsforschung und Erziehungssoziologie* 3: 105–16.

Sudman, Seymour, and Jacob J. Feldman 1965: "Sample design and field procedures," pp. 482–5 of appendix 1 in John W. C. Johnstone and Ramon J. Rivera (eds), *Volunteers for Learning: A Study of the Educational Pursuits of American Adults.* Chicago: Aldine.

Sulek, Antoni 1985: "Life values of two generations: From a study of the generation gap in Poland." *Polish Sociological Bulletin* no. 1–4: (69–72): 31–42.

Szczepanski, Jan 1978: "Early stages of socialist industrialization and changes in social class structure." pp. 11–36 in Kazimierz M. Slomczynski and Tadeusz Krauze (eds), *Class Structure and Social Stratification in Poland.* White Plains, NY: M. E. Sharpe.

Tellenback, Sten 1974: "Patterns of stratification in socialist Poland." *Acta Sociologica* 17: 25–47.

Temme, Lloyd V. 1975: *Occupation: Meanings and Measures.* Washington, DC: Bureau of Social Science Research.

Titkow, Anna 1983: *Wartosc Dziecka.* [Valuing a Child.] Warsaw: Institute of Philosophy and Sociology of the Polish Academy of Sciences. [An abridged English version, *Child and Values*, was made available by the Institute in 1984.]

Treiman, Donald J. 1977: *Occupational Prestige in Comparative Perspective.* New York: Academic Press.

Troll, Lillian, and Vern Bengtson 1979: "Generations in the family," pp. 127–61 in Wesley R. Burr, Reuben Hill, F. Ivan Nye, and Ira L. Reiss (eds), *Contemporary Theories about the Family*, vol. 1, *Research-based Theories.* New York: Free Press.

Tyszka, Zbigniew (ed.) 1985: *Sociologia Rodziny.* [Sociology of the Family] Poznan: UAM.

United States Department of Labor 1965: *Dictionary of Occupational Titles.* Washington, DC: US Government Printing Office, 3rd edn.

Vallas, Steven Peter 1987: "The labor process as a source of class consciousness: A critical examination." *Sociological Forum* 2: 237–56.

Vanneman, Reeve, and Fred C. Pampel 1977: "The American perception of class and status." *American Sociological Review* 42: 422–37.

Volpert/Oesterreich/Gablenz-Kolakovic/Krogoll/Resch 1983: *Verfahren zur Ermittlung von Regulationserfordernissen in der Arbeitstätigkeit (VERA). Analyse von Planungs- und Denkprozessen in der Industriellen Produktion. Handbuch.* Köln: Verlag TUV Rheinland.

Walton, John 1984: *Reluctant Rebels: Comparative Studies of Revolution and Underdevelopment.* New York: Columbia University Press.

Wejland, Andrzej, and Pawel Danilowicz 1978: Pilotaz do baden "Wymiary sytuacji pracy i jej psychologiczne Konsekwencje." [Pilot study of the survey, "Dimensions of the work situation and their psychological consequences."] Warsaw: Institute of Philosophy and Sociology of the Polish Academy of Sciences.

Werts, Charles E., Karl G. Jöreskog, and Robert L. Linn 1973: "Identification and estimation in path analysis with unmeasured variables." *American Journal of Sociology* 78: 1469–84.

Werts, Charles E., Robert L. Linn, and Karl G. Jöreskog 1971: "Estimating the parameters of path models involving unmeasured variables." pp. 400–9 in Hubert M. Blalock (ed.), *Causal Models in the Social Sciences*. Chicago: Aldine–Atherton.

Wesolowski, Wlodzimierz 1969a: "The notions of strata and class in socialist society," pp. 122–45 in Andre Beteille (ed.), *Social Inequality: Selected Readings*. Harmondsworth, England: Penguin Books.

—— 1969b: "Strata and strata interests in socialist society. Toward a new theoretical approach," pp. 465–77 in Celia S. Heller (ed.), *Structured Social Inequality: A Reader in Comparative Social Stratification*. New York: Macmillan.

—— 1975: *Teoria, Badania, Praktyka. Z Problematyki Struktury Klasowej*. Warszawa: Ksiazka i Wiedza.

—— 1979: *Classes, Strata and Power*. London: Routledge and Kegan Paul.

—— 1988: "Does Socialist Stratification Exist?" *The Fifth Fuller Bequest Lecture*. Department of Sociology, University of Essex.

Wesolowski, Wlodzimierz, and Kazimierz M. Slomczynski 1977: *Investigations on Class Structure and Social Stratification in Poland, 1945–1975*. Warsaw: The Institute of Philosophy and Sociology of the Polish Academy of Sciences.

Wheaton, Blair, Bengt Muthen, Duane F. Alwin, and Gene F. Sommers 1977: "Assessing reliability and stability in panel models," pp. 84–136 in David R. Heise (ed.), *Sociological Methodology, 1977*. San Francisco: Jossey–Bass.

Widerszpil, Stanislaw 1978: "Problems in the theory of the development of a socialist society." *Polish Sociological Bulletin* no. 2 (42): 23–36.

Wilensky, Harold L. 1961: "Orderly careers and social participation: The impact of work history on social integration in the middle mass." *American Sociological Review* 26: 521–39.

Williams, Robin M., Jr 1960: *American Society: A Sociological Interpretation*. New York: Alfred A. Knopf, 2nd edn.

—— 1968: "The concept of values," pp. 283–7 in David L. Sills (ed.), *International Encyclopedia of the Social Sciences*, vol. 16. New York: Macmillan and Free Press.

—— 1970: *American Society: A Sociological Interpretation*. New York: Alfred A. Knopf, 3rd edn.

Witkin, H. A., R. B. Dyk, H. F. Faterson, D. R. Goodenough, and S. A. Karp 1962: *Psychological Differentiation: Studies of Development*. New York: Wiley.

Wright, Erik Olin 1976: "Class boundaries in advanced capitalist societies." *New Left Review* 98: 3–41.

—— 1978: *Class, Crisis and the State*. London: New Left Books.

—— 1985: *Classes*. London: New Left Books.

Wright, Erik Olin, and Luca Perrone 1977: "Marxist class categories and income inequality." *American Sociological Review* 42: 32–55.

Zagorski, Krzysztof 1976: *Zmiany Struktury i Ruchliwosc Spoleczno-Zawodowa w Polsce*. [Changes of Structure and Occupational Mobility in Poland.] Warsaw: Central Statistical Office.

Zdravomyslov, A. G. and V. A. Yadov 1967: *Chelovek i Ero Rabota*. Moscow: Mysl. An English-language version was subsequently published as: Zdravomyslov, A. G., V. P. Rozhin, and V. A. Iadov (eds) 1970: *Man and his Work*. White Plains, NY: International Arts and Sciences Press, Inc.

Index